EGALIA'S
DAUGHTERS

D0376279

*E*GALIA'S
DAUGHTERS
A SATIRE OF THE SEXES
by Gerd Brantenberg

Translated from Norwegian by Louis Mackay
in cooperation with Gerd Brantenberg

The Seal Press

Originally published in Norwegian as *Egalias døtre*, 1977.
This U.S. edition first published in 1985 by The Seal Press, 312 S.
Washington, Seattle, Washington 98104. Published by arrangement
with the Journeyman Press, Ltd., London, England.

Library of Congress Cataloging-in-Publication Data

Brantenberg, Gerd, 1941-
   Egalia's daughters.
   Translation of: Egalias døtre.
   I. Title.
PT8951.12.R34E313   1985   839.8'2374   85-22191
ISBN 0-931188-35-0
ISBN 0-931188-34-2 (pbk.)

Cover illustration and design by Deborah Brown.

Contents

PART ONE

Bram, the director, and her family

'After all, it is *menwim* who beget children,' said Bram, throwing her son a reproving glance over the top of the *Egalsund Post*. It was evident that she was finding it difficult to control her temper. 'Anyway, I'm reading the paper.' Looking irritated, she continued reading from the point at which she had been interrupted.

'But I want to be a seawom! I'll just take the baby with me,' said Petronius ingeniously.

'And what do you think the child's mother would say? Oh no. There are some things in life you have to put up with. In time you'll learn to appreciate them. Even in a democratic society like ours, everyone can't be completely identical. Besides, it would be tremendously boring. Dreary and depressing.'

'It's more dreary and depressing not being able to be what one wants!'

'Who said you can't be what you want? All I'm saying is, you must be realistic. You can't have your cake and eat it. If you have children, you have children. Listen, Petronius, when I was young I had a lot of grandiose dreams too, about what I was going to be. The romance of the sea, that's what you're suffering from. You'll have to stop reading all those adventure stories about the exploits of seawim and stick to books for boys instead. Then your dreams will be more realistic. No real menwim want to go to sea.'

'But most of the seawim I know of have children!'

'That's another matter altogether. A mother can never be like a father to a child, Petronius.'

His sister laughed derisively. She was a year and a half younger and she teased him constantly. 'Ha, ha! And a manwom can't be a seawom either, a mafele seawom! Ho ho! Or perhaps you're going to be a cabin *boy* or a sea*manwom*, or a helms*manwom*? I'll die laughing, I will. The only menwim who go to sea are either whores or Pallurians.'

'Pallurians?'

'Exactly. Pallurians. And in every harbour the whores stand in line with open arms, waiting for the seawim.' She tugged his hair.

'Dad! Ba's pulling my hair!'

'Lady God! Is there never any peace and quiet in this house?' Msass Bram, the director's housebound, came rushing out of the bathroom with his beard full of curlers. 'Calm down you kids! Ba, remember Petronius has soft hair.'

'Soft hair and soft all over. "Remember Petronius has soft hair! Remember Petronius belongs to the frail sex!"' That always annoyed him. She continued maliciously, 'Dad? Oughtn't Petronius to start wearing a peho soon?'

'Be quiet,' the director growled, 'I'm reading.'

'More coffee, Ruth?' her housebound asked placatingly.

'Mmm,' she replied absently. 'Lucy! Now the younger generation are demanding a higher pregnancy fee again. Perhaps I ought to fertilize myself again after all, Christopher. That was much too strong by the way.'

'But we already have two.'

'The coffee was too strong, I said.'

'Shall I make some more?'

'It's too late,' said Ruth, peevishly. 'I really don't have time to wait while you pull yourself together and set about making more coffee.' She swallowed the last gulp with a grimace.

'I want to be a diver.'

Ba tittered, 'A *diver*! They don't have frogwom suits for menwim. A mafele frogwom!' Ba slapped her knee and pointed at her brother, enjoying herself greatly.

'Don't they have diving suits for menwim, Mum?'

Ruth made no reply.

'Maybe Mum could manufacture one,' Petronius suggested.

'Manufacture? What could I manufacture? More children?'

'No. A diving suit for menwim.'

'What a fantastic idea! Here, lordies and gentlewim, being launched for the very first time — a diving suit for menwim. Made of insulating, completely biteproof material. What a sensation! Why didn't I think of it before? I'll be the first wom to break with tradition and silly conventional thinking. Yes . . . because, actually . . . *actually* there's really no reason why a manwom couldn't also be a diver.'

Christopher and Petronius began to clear the table. They went out into the kitchen. It was much nicer there. Petronius closed the door. 'Dad, I don't understand why you let Mum give you fatherhood protection. You turn yourself inside out to please her, but you're still in trouble sixty two per cent of the time.'

'What are you talking about?'

'That's right. Sixty two per cent. I've worked it out. I've kept a record of the number of times she has a go at you. I've been totting it up for the last three months.'

'What's the point of that?'

'Mum says one should always be able to back up one's statements with evidence. So I've started documenting everything that happens in the house here.'

'But what are you going to do with it?'

'Do with it? I don't know . . . But anyway, I don't understand how you can stand living with her.'

'But I love her, of course.'

Petronius reflected. In a way it was understandable. Mum was a handsome wom. She had a fine rounded head and short-cropped black hair that always stood straight up. A straight nose, sharply defined features, small, piercing pale blue eyes, a thin determined mouth, straight shoulders and distinctive movements. When she moved, she always did so purposefully and efficiently. Her voice, which was sharp and penetrating, always gave the impression that she knew what she was talking about, even when she didn't. That was how a wom ought to be. Besides, she was always stylishly dressed. A loose brown tunic and baggy trousers.

Brown shoes with thick soles. She usually wore a white silk scarf around her neck. She always looked neat. An attractive wom, such as menwim dream of. Petronius knew that.

Moreover, she had a senior position in the National Co-operative Directorate. And a top salary. And a penthouse flat with a roof terrace on the island of Lux, with a view over Egalsund to the east and the sea to the south and west. Petronius knew that if he ever managed to find a fatherhood protector like her he ought to thank his lucky stars. But that wasn't likely.

'Petronius?'

He gave a start. Dad's voice warned of something unpleasant.

'I've noticed that you've developed a lot recently.'

Yes indeed. Petronius had also noticed, with a growing sense of shame. It was awful. His voice couldn't decide whether it wanted to stay up or down. Why couldn't he remain a child all his life?

'The wholesaler, Msass Moondaughter, remarked the other week. So, about the peho . . . people are beginning to wonder.'

'Let them wonder then! Maybe they think I don't have a cock at all.'

'Petronius! Do you have to use words like that?'

'A lot of my class haven't started wearing pehoes yet.'

This was untrue. In fact there was only Cyprian and he was much less developed than Petronius. But Petronius didn't want one. The boys said it was awkward and uncomfortable, cramming your penis into that stupid box. And it was so impractical when you had to pee. First you had to loosen the waistband which held the peho in place. The waistband was fastened under the skirt, so you stood fumbling for a long time, especially at first. The waistband was usually too tight and it cut into the skin. Moreover, you had to sew a slit into each of your skirts so the peho might hang freely outside. Some said the peho was scratchy, too; others said this depended on the material. It was possible to get pehoes in really soft cloth that caused no irritation, but they were expensive and Petronius didn't think he dared ask for

12

a peho like that.

Some were proud of their pehoes. Baldrian, for example, really did look charming in his. Petronius sighed. 'I wish I were a girl,' he thought. God knows how many times he had thought that. Then he would have a stout flap in his trousers or overalls that it only took a moment to unbutton when nature called.

'I'll come with you and see,' said Dad consolingly.

It was getting worse and worse. Petronius would rather have got it over and done with on his own — though how was he to make himself go into a menwim's shop and say that word? He didn't know which was worse. If Dad came with him, he and the shop assistant would stand there discussing the length, colour and quality interminably. Ought he to have a size five with a B-tube or a size six with an A-tube, they would debate, sizing him up with their heads cocked to one side, pretending that having a penis was the most natural thing in the world.

Petronius knew well enough what it would be like. He'd been with Dad when he was buying a new peho (which he only did after long deliberations with Mum about the house-keeping), and he and the assistant could spend half an hour discussing which style suited Dad best, while the assistant went in and out of the fitting room, feeling Dad around the penis to see whether the peho was too tight or too loose.

'Then there's something you and I will have to talk about before you go to the maidmen's ball. No wom will go to bed with a manwom who isn't clean and neat and nice-smelling, you know. It's very important. Wash yourself thoroughly down there and spray a bit of my rose petal spray around your penis and shamebag, so it doesn't smell bad. Menwim have to wash themselves carefully and fre-quently, because they smell so rank.'

Petronius shuddered at the thought of the disasters that would befall him if he didn't keep his tassle clean.

'I've also noticed that you've started to grow hair on your chest.'

Petronius reddened. He'd noticed too, but hoped Dad hadn't seen it. He'd even tried to imagine it away, but the

13

more he looked, the clearer it became. It was unmistakeable and irrevocable chest hair he had. And there was more and more of it.

'Of course not all menwim are so unlucky as to get hair there,' said Dad. 'But some men do grow hair on their chests and it has to be removed. I only wish I knew where you get it from. Neither I nor my father have ever had chest hair, but I remember my father's brother had a big problem with his hairiness, so perhaps that's where it comes from. But of course there are remedies nowadays. You'll have to buy a hair-remover. That's the only thing that'll help. Admittedly, it hurts and it makes your skin a bit sore and tender, but it's better than going around looking hairy, after all. You can't look smart without smarting. Mum says menwim have hairy chests because they're so primitive. It's a sort of fur, she says . . .'

'That isn't particularly funny.'

'Petronius, I remember so well what it felt like at your age. It wasn't easy, but one gets through it.'

'It can't have been so terrible for *you*!' Petronius burst out.

'What d'you mean by that?'

'I mean . . . you didn't really have anything to complain about! You were short and fat with short legs and narrow shoulders, pale curls and a sweet face!' Petronius flung away the teatowel, rushed up to his room and locked the door. He was ashamed of what he'd said. He was ashamed that he'd even acknowledged that this was a problem for him. It wasn't Dad's fault. Petronius had tried no end of fattening treatments, but no matter how much he ate, he stayed just as slim. And the girls yelled '*Bean-pole! Bean-pole!*' at him. Sometimes he made a detour to avoid running into the gangs of girls. They could do the most dreadful things to you. When it got dark in the woods in the autumn, for instance. And, for their victims, they loved to pick on unfortunate little boys, like himself. They had more respect for the chubbier boys. Them, they fell in love with.

To crown everything, he was still growing. He was only fifteen and he was in danger of growing more. If he continued to grow at this rate, upwards instead of outwards, he would end up like Spinnerman Owlmoss, whom everyone made fun of. And Dad, he just stood there, so fine and fat, talking about pehoes and the maidmen's ball and spraying your shamebag as though the best thing that could happen to you in life was to be allowed to dress up. Oh yes, there would have to be finery if he was to look as captivating as Dad or Baldrian.

Did Dad really not understand that Petronius was unattractive? No matter how much he did himself up with a turquoise peho with tulle for the maidmen's ball, did he really imagine that anyone would invite him into a maidman-room. Not to be invited into a maidman-room at the maidmen's ball was the greatest shame that could befall a young lad.

He looked at himself in the mirror; combed his hair; smiled. He tried various smiles, attempted a serious expression, tried to see himself in profile. Actually, he was by no means ugly. There was nothing wrong with his face, which was narrow with even features. Dull, mousey hair, to be sure, but he'd heard that it looked pretty when he plaited it. And he'd inherited Dad's soft, rounded mouth with an upward lift at the corners. His eyes were too small, he knew that, but they were the right, deep blue colour. Baldrian had said that. Baldrian had big blue peepers. Petronius also had beautiful eyebrows — thin and curved, not the shaggy growths some men had. He smiled at himself in the mirror. His white teeth gleamed. Perhaps he had a chance of getting into a maidman-room after all.

The thought of the wom who would invite him in gave him new courage. She would be different from any wom he had ever met. Nowom from school. Nowom from the street. From nowhere. She would be wonderful and strong and she would take him with her into the maidman-room. Into the secret of secrets. Away from the sadness of daily life. She would take him to a blessed state in which he had neither penis nor chest-hair, nor anything else he need be ashamed of. There would be just the two of them.

Petronius got up and went to the window. The sun was

sinking over the rocky islands of Egalsund Sound. The colours fought with the darkness, becoming increasingly intense. Just above the red streaks of the sunset the sky was pale green. That was where they would be, she and he. Inside the sunset, looking down and beckoning the horizon with a bed of red mattresses and a veil of pale green sky above them. He gazed at the inlet and thought of the sea rolling in, endlessly rolling in. That was how it would be with them. The wom and him — never-ending. He would undergo a mystical transformation. She would transform him — his body, his innermost being. It would be the profound, thoroughgoing transformation which all boys long for and which only a wom can accomplish for them; the transformation that would let him surrender everything and feel the truth and the fulfilment of the words, 'I am a manwom!'

Petronius was suddenly seized with a violent longing for the wom — for the wom who was to make a manwom of him. And in his heart of hearts he knew there was one thing he had real reason to be proud of, something that meant, perhaps, that his chances were not so bad when it came down to it. He had an unusually small penis.

Spinnerman Owlmoss teaches the children about nature's injustice

'It is the task of every civilization to remedy nature's injustice,' said Spinnerman Owlmoss, peering out over the top of his glasses at his pupils, to see whether this had made any impression on them. One or two returned his gaze. Others stared down at their desk-lids. Ba was doing something furtively with a piece of paper.

'Ba!' shouted the teacher. 'What are you up to over there?'

Ba gave a start and automatically covered the paper with her hand. 'Nothing,' she lied. In fact she had been drawing a caricature of Spinnerman Owlmoss. A small, broad nose, blow-dried red hair with a fringe and a ribbon (no doubt it had been fashionable when he was young), curly beard, a bolero with big flowers all over it and a matching, floral peho, a hand-knitted tight skirt and slippers with blue bobbles. Mother God in heaven! How was it possible to be so hopelessly out of style?

To Ba, Spinnerman Owlmoss was a personification of the ridiculous. Old-fashioned, spinnermannish, stiff and theatrical. He was the late Principal Owlmoss's son, and that was the only reason he was now standing at the teacher's desk, holding forth. Ba had heard, incidentally, that there had once been something between him and the present principal, Bosomby. Some had even observed that Cyprian Bosomby in Petronius's class was the spitting image of Spinnerman Owlmoss. No doubt he had dreamt of being the principal's housebound. And she'd refused him. Ha ha! And Cyprian, that flatfish, was surely his son.

'Did you hear what I said, Ba?'

'Yes.'

'And what did I say?'

Ba gazed uncertainly into the air. There were a few titters. Ann Moonhill began to whisper the answer behind her.

'Well, Ba?'

'It is the task of every civilization to recognize nature's invective,' said Ba.

The class exploded with laughter. They all made the most of the commotion, lying on their desks, laughing, waving and passing notes to each other. It took Spinnerman Owlmoss over two minutes to restore his control over them. It took him rather longer to restore anything like control over himself. Telling them off always made him so nervous.

'Well then,' he shouted, 'what did I say?'

Little, tubby Fandango, the class swot, raised his hand. 'It is the task of our civilization to remedy nature's injustice.'

'Quite right, Fandango.' Spn Owlmoss wrote the words on the blackboard and continued. 'This statement is what we call an *axiom*. An axiom is a fundamental idea which everything else is based on. This axiom came to our fore-mothers on Mount Demos in the year 213 after Donna Jessica, and it is thanks to them — our Moulding Mothers — that today we can . . .' Here Spn Owlmoss tailed off. He had prepared the lesson carefully. He knew that this knowledge was among the most important that he could impart to the young. He tried desperately to remember what he had prepared. ' . . . it is thanks to the Moulding Mothers that today we can . . .'

'Say thanks!' Ba yelled happily, to immediate applause from every quarter, which she acknowledged with exaggerated bows and smiles.

'Out!' shrieked Spn Owlmoss.

Ba stood up instantly, as though responding to a military command, and waddled out bow-leggedly. Spn Owlness was bow-legged. His face turned a dark red, but he said nothing. Once Ba had gone the class was quiet.

'Please, Spinnerman?' It was little, tubby Fandango again. 'What does "nature's injustice" mean?'

The question put Spn Owlmoss back on track. He took courage and continued. 'Nature's injustice consists in the fact that the strong oppress the weak. In nature, what we call the law of the jungle holds sway. It is the war of all against all, in which the strongest always win and the weakest always starve or die. Now it isn't like that with us, of course. We have something we call civilization. Since the year 213 Donna Jessica, wim of science have been working to reveal all nature's unjust aspects. This is a very complex field of study which requires deep insight into the essence of oppression.'

Spn Owlmoss talked on. Most of the class was half asleep when the door opened quietly and Ba suddenly stuck her head in.

'I'll be good now, Spinnerman. Can I come in?'

As everyone knew, this was shamelessly cheeky. Out in the corridor meant out in the corridor. Anyone who didn't obey was sent up to the principal. The thought of being brought up in front of her desk filled every pupil with terror.

Spn Owlmoss, however, was thinking of something else — that Ba was Ruth Bram's daughter. He was also thinking that the principal would ask a lot of awkward questions about his competence as a teacher if he sent any more unruly little girls up to her this term. He knew that a number of earnest mothers had already telephoned the principal to ask her whether Spn Owlmoss was really qualified to give their daughters a proper education, suited to the modern world.

'Please do,' said Spn Owlmoss to Ba, 'if you'll behave yourself now.'

'Thanks very much. Very kind,' said Ba. She waddled back to her desk, still bow-legged. The class tittered. Spn Owlmoss pretended to take no notice. He wanted to continue from where he'd been interrupted, but he'd lost the thread again. Ba went back to the caricature she had been drawing. Spn Owlmoss pretended not to see that either. Little tubby Fandango put up his hand.

'Yes?'

'Which are the weak in our society?'

'What?'

'You said the strong have to protect the weak. Which are the weak?'

'The wim,' replied Spn Owlmoss.

For once, the entire class was paying attention to him. Even Ba.

'That can't be right,' said Ann Moonhill. She was the leader of the class. She had started menstruating first and therefore considerd herself entitled to express the general view without having consulted the class first. Her mother was a Member of Parliament. She intended to become an agriculturalist.

'I understand that that's what you think, Ann,' replied Spn Owlmoss. 'But if you think about it, then, you know, the wom is actually the weaker, even if she's known as the invulnerable sex. It is only civilization that has made her into the invulnerable sex. That is precisely the genius of our civilization . . .'

He stopped talking. Yes, they were listening. They were actually listening. Spn Owlmoss took heart, 'From the point of view of nature — that is, purely biologically — the wom is weaker than the manwom.' He felt encouraged.

'What do you mean, *biologically*?'

'Biologically means in terms of life as God, in Her time, created it; wom and manwom in the natural state. And all the animals. First She made the world, and last She made wom. Actually She'd originally intended that wom would be the final touch to crown the rest of creation, so She wouldn't create anything else. But She hadn't realized the wom She created would feel lonely. Nor had She thought how She was going to reproduce herself when there was only a single example of her. The wom complained to God of her need, and then God took a limb from the wom, and from it She made manwom. That explains why the wom doesn't have to bear the most exposed and vulnerable of all limbs. That has been her strength. And as things have developed, she has known how to use it.'

'I don't quite understand . . .' said Ann. The whole

class suddenly felt that they didn't understand either. If the manwom was physically stronger than the wom, why didn't he take power, Ann wondered.

'Typical manwom! He was too stupid!' yelled Ba.

'No. This is where God's great and just order of creation is revealed. When manwom was created, he realized at once that he belonged to the wom. He understood that whenever she wanted to, he would have to . . .'

The bell rang. Saved by the bell, thought Spn Owlmoss. He knew he had gone beyond ther bounds of his subject, social studies. He reached for the salmon-pink bag in which he always kept his school books. He suddenly noticed that none of his pupils had moved. It was the first time in his twenty year career as a teacher that his class had not shot out in the middle of one of his sentences when the bell rang.

'What would he have to do?' asked Ba.

Spn Owlmoss had reddened around the neck.

The Maidmen's Ball

The big, twenty-five-wom band started to play. The spring maidmen's ball had begun. Petronius was standing in one corner of the ballroom, pressed next to his classmate, Wolfram Sax. He was red-cheeked and sweating. He glanced quickly towards his armpits to see whether it showed. The turquoise blouse had unmistakeably begun to take on a darker colour. He sweated even more. The blouse clung; he could feel the material against his ribs. To crown his misery, they were in a very exposed position. And the dance was about to begin.

'Wolfram,' he whispered. 'I'm just going down for a moment.'

Wolfram grabbed the gold cord around his waist. 'Has the peho slipped?' he whispered.

'No, I'm just going to . . .'

'Hurry up!' Wolfram interrupted. 'Everyone's looking at us. You can't spoil everything now.'

Petronius rushed down to the cloakroom and searched his handbag frantically for some cotton-wool. He ran into one of the toilets and dried himself under the arms. Dad had assured him the deodorant would work. But it was obviously no help against nervousness.

Petronius had been dreading the maidmen's ball for months. The boys had been talking of nothing else. Most of them had their eyes on someone. Lillerio Moondaughter, who lived next door, had hopes of Vita Strong, the school's number one pole-vaulter. Baldrian Bareskerry was crazy about Eva Bosomby, the principal's daughter, and Wolfram had fallen helplessly in love with Ann Moonhill. The whole gang went around worshipping their sheroes and writing loveletters they never dared to send. Petronius didn't really know whom he was in love with.

He fixed a wad of cotton-wool in each armpit and hurried back up. His tight shoes were rubbing. Then he realised he'd forgotten the little luminous handbag, a special one for the ball, which had to be fastened to the gold cord, and he had to run back down again.

Wolfram was looking for him when he re-emerged. He immediately took him by the arm and they marched out onto the dance-floor with the other lads.

'Where's Baldrian? Isn't he going to dance in our trio?'

Petronious felt a hand under his other arm.

'Here.' Baldrian was grinning broadly. He looked wonderful. He was wearing a daring, deep blue dress with a broad gold belt which fitted his chubby body like a mould. Petronius gazed at him, fascinated. He would surely be snatched up at once.

The commère went out to the podium, nodded and waved her hand. 'Welcome, lordies and gentlewim. Once again, for the youth of Egalsund, the spring maidmen's ball is here. And there is surely nothing, during the thirteen months of the year, that we look forward to so much as the spring maidmen's ball. Spring, of course, is the time of sweetness and light, when the breezes blow playfully in boys' blouses and skirts, giving us new heart. The trees are budding, there is greenery everywhere. And which of us isn't tempted, then, to abandon ourselves to our lust for life, and to take a young ladsel in our arms? Can we imagine a finer sight than so many charming young lordies gathered together?'

The boys, embarrassed, glanced at each other or looked down at the floor.

'The programme starts in the usual way,' she continued. 'First these delightful young lordies are going to dance a threesome for us. Meanwhile, you can buy drinks and snacks for them — and also for yourselves, of course — at the bar. After that, we ask you gentlewim to circulate. The band will play softly and those who wish to become better acquainted with the lordies can do so. There is, incidentally, a gaming table for those who prefer gambling to love, or you can relax in the various rooms available for the purpose.'

Shouting and laughter was heard from the bar. Some wim shouted, 'Ugh!'

The commère laughed congenially into the microphone. 'Yes, I'd like to draw the attention of any gentlewim who haven't yet found their way around to the maidman-rooms which are in the gallery wing on the first floor. The ball will continue with dancing and other entertainments until half past one.' The commère clapped her hands and made an elegant gesture with her arm. 'And now, lordies, please take one another by the hand and begin.'

The boys danced in threesomes, arm in arm. It was a dance with light, graceful skips on the toe, and bends to the side which they had practised for several months during their gym lessons. The music went at a slow boogie-woogie rhythm. The dance-floor surged with a sea of colourful sequined chiffon, silk and tulle under the crystal chandeliers. If Petronius had been able to see himself and the others from above, he would have thought it a most enchanting sight. But all he was conscious of was a hot, sweaty chaos in which the only thing that mattered was to avoid putting out his right leg when everyone else was putting out their left. He repeated the gym-teacher's words silently to himself, 'Don't forget! Left foot first! Don't forget! Left foot first!'

Petronius stuck out his right foot and collided with Wolfram, pushing him into Cyprian, and the slip was reproduced several threesomes away. Petronius threw a despairing glance towards the gallery to see whether anyone had noticed. But everything up there appeared hazy to him; and he was in the middle of a side bend, so he saw the whole ballroom at a ninety degree angle. Baldrian squeezed his arm. It felt confident and right. Baldrian brought the threesome back in step again.

Standing along the walls of the ballroom, in the doorways of the bars and rooms, leaning over the gallery ballustrade, were the wim in their dark shirts and trousers and white silk scarves, clinking glasses with one another and gazing at the dancers. Every now and then one would point to somebody on the dance-floor and make some remark to the nearest wom.

Petronius noticed a tall, dark-haired wom by the entrance. She was standing with her feet apart, hands at her sides, as though rooted to the spot, staring in his direction with a serious, fixed expression. She was standing alone. He looked away. His feet were in step now, automatically. He felt Baldrian's reassuring warmth by his side. He glanced again towards the door. He felt a jolt as their eyes met across the huge ballroom.

The music came to an end. The boys curtsied. There was applause. The lights in the big crystal chandeliers dimmed a little. Everything dissolved into confusion around Petronius. Wolfram and Baldrian had both disappeared. He didn't know where to go. At the same time, he had to remember at all costs to keep smiling sweetly. He could still feel the way her look had pierced him. Suddenly, he wanted to be rid of it. He turned quickly and looked straight at the entrance to drive away her stare. She was gone.

'Hey, Petronius! Shall we sit down somewhere?' It was Cyprian, the principal's son. Cyprian was a skinny little lad.

He had been afraid of this. 'Yes,' he said, feeling ashamed down to his toes.

Suddenly, he felt a hand touch his waist from behind. His back bumped against something soft. He felt hot. He turned. It was the wom. She was about a head taller than him, looking down at him with a wry little smile on her lips. Her eyes were blue.

Then she vanished.

It shocked him that she had blue eyes. From a distance they had looked brown; he didn't know why. She shouldn't have blue eyes, he thought.

Petronius went off with Cyprian to one of the alcoves, although he knew it was the silliest thing to do. They might end up sitting there like wallflowers the entire evening.

They sat gazing glumly at all the festively dressed people milling about. Many wim were busy fetching drinks for the boys, but some just stood chatting in little groups or in twos, evidently having no interest whatsoever in anything to do with individuals of the mafele sex. Petronius told himself that if *he* had been a wom, he would have run around attending to, talking to and dancing with the skinniest, ugliest and most unattractive of the boys.

'What happened to Wolfram and Baldrian?' asked Cyprian, as though he didn't know very well.

'Yes, I was wondering the same,' Petronius answered, as though he didn't know just as well. Wolfram and Baldrian had obviously been invited up to the maidman-rooms right away.

'They disappeared, didn't they?'

'Yes, they did.'

They felt ashamed of their conversation and of the fact that they were sitting there together. They tried to pretend that finding a wom was not in any way the reason they had come to the maidmen's ball. But they weren't sure what impression they gave when they tried to look unconcerned.

Then she was standing there, a couple of yards from them. Only one hand on her hip now, a cigarette in the corner of her mouth. She held out her hand to him. Petronius felt bewildered. He looked round to see whether she really meant him; but behind him there was, of course, just the wall. He looked at her, embarrassed. She nodded. He thought he detected a hint of a smile. He got up and went towards her. She pushed him ahead of her through the crowds of wim to the bar, where she ordered two glasses of sherry. She raised her glass to him and nodded. They drank. It was packed in the bar and they were pushed closer together. He could smell her. His thigh rubbed against hers. She made no effort to pull away. On the contrary, it was almost as though she was making the most of the crush to get closer to him. He glanced at her and tried to smile. He remembered Mum saying once that it had been Dad's captivating little smile at the maidmen's ball that she had fallen for. Petronius wasn't at all sure how to smile captivatingly. He didn't dare look at her. Suddenly someone pushed between them.

'Hallo, Gro,' growled a red-faced wom, clearly drunk.

'Aha. Picked up a little cockerel already, then?'

Petronius felt proud and disquieted simultaneously. He was pleased by the thought that he had been 'picked up'. He was home and dry. He was no longer sitting in the alcove. At the same time it felt as though he'd had no part in the conversation; he was just there, so to speak. He smiled at the friend. She didn't smile back. She leant over and whispered in Gro's ear. Gro nodded.

'Wait. I'll be right back,' she said, and went off through the bar with her friend.

'Wait. I'll be right back.' The words rang in his ears. It was the first thing she'd said to him. He was to wait. She would come back. To him. Him. Petronius stood on the spot without moving. He took a gulp of sherry, already feeling warm and relaxed. It was almost entirely wim in the bar. Some of them stared at him, nudging one another in the side, exchanging comments and laughing. Petronius looked at his clothes but couldn't see anything to laugh at. He drank the remainder of the sherry. Wait . . . I'll be right back . . .

Baldrian entered the bar, grinning, with a gang of others, squeezing himself against Eva Bosomby, a tall, attractive wom. He waved to Petronius. Petronius gave a start. Baldrian was so beautiful to look at. The gang surged forward towards him. Eva Bosomby, slightly intoxicated, raised her glass to Petronius.

'Listen, let's do our song again.'

'Oh yes!' Wolfram Sax burst out, making his way into the bar with a wom hard on his heels. 'I'll join in. It's great.'

All the wim and Wolfram began to sing in harmony:

> *There's nothing better than boooooooys,*
> *Their pehoes bursting with joooooooys,*
> *When you waltz though the night*
> *Of lifelong delight,*
> *Lifelong delight,*
> *Holding them tight*
> *By the string of their kite,*
> *Boys are the best of life's toooooooys!*

The song reached its highest note on 'delight' and the last three lines were bellowed out. Then they went out, howling with laughter. Baldrian glanced at Petronius and rolled his eyes, then followed them. Wolfram remained behind for a second, watching Petronius with curiosity.

Now at last he felt her hand on his wrist. She pulled him to her. He grinned triumphantly at Wolfram and went off with Gro.

'My friend hadn't picked up any scent yet,' Gro explained.

'I see,' said Petronius, and chuckled as though she'd said something extraordinarily funny. He had no idea what she meant.

She took him across the ballroom. He noticed that the alcove where he had sat with Cyprian was empty.

'Wonder what became of Cyprian?'

'Was that your friend? It was him I hitched Britt up with.'

They went up the stairs and along the gallery. Gro pulled a key from her pocket, opened number seven and pushed him in.

It was a beautiful room. Big heavy plush curtains, a table, two deep armchairs, and a cocktail cabinet with a built-in record-player. In the centre of the room was a big green bed. Hanging on the wall was a large painting depicting a young, naked manwom on a couch with a bowl of fruit on the table in front of him. The room was half-darkened, lit only by a standard lamp with a base in the form of a naked manwom's torso with an incandescent orange bulb as its head.

Gro stretched her arms and smiled at him. She pressed a button and the pop group, The Quarrywim, thundered out of the loudspeakers. They were currently the most popular group. Everywhere they went they had to push through crowds of moaning and sighing young boys. They were singing 'Ruthello', which had been at number ten in the charts for the previous three weeks.

'That's good,' said Gro, singing with it and dancing a few steps in front of Petronius.

'Ruthello, I dream of you, you, you . . .' At each 'you', the trio added a new harmony. She smiled at him and took a bottle and some glasses out of the cocktail cabinet. 'Your body's like a flower — as tender as the dew, dew, dew, — when you give me your flower. Ruthello! For you I'll play the cello! All night long — under your spelloooo!'

'Say when, then. Say when,' said Gro. 'Or would you prefer a soft drink?'

Petronius shook his head. She poured the drinks. Actually he would have preferred a soft drink.

'Down in one?'

Petronius nodded. They clinked the glasses and drained them. Gro refilled them. Petronius felt strange and unsteady on his feet. He wasn't used to drinking.

'What's your name?'

'Petronius Bram.'

'Good lady! Are you Director Bram's son?'

Petronius nodded. Gro held out her hand, affecting politeness.

'How do you do? Gro Maydaughter here.'

Petronius took her hand. She sank down into the chair, drawing him to her. Their mouths collided and Petronius bit his tongue. It hurt. Her hands were everywhere on his body. She was warm, breathing heavily against him. She began to undo the buttons of his blouse, and to undo the gold cord, all in a great hurry. Her hands pressed against his bare chest. She bit him in the belly. He cried out and she looked up suddenly.

'Did that hurt?'

He shook his head.

'You're not afraid, are you?'

He shook his head, stricken with terror. She was beet-root red in the face. She got up and rolled across him onto the bed. He was lying with his arms by his side. She began to finger his peho, breathlessly, kissing him on the belly every now and then and biting his nipples. It was nice and it was painful at the same time. All the time she was fiddling with his peho, but she couldn't undo the knots. He helped her, while trying to pretend that he wasn't helping.

She removed his hands. Finally she got his peho off. He was lying there completely naked. He caught a glimpse of his projecting ribs and felt ashamed. She stood up and contemplated him. She lit a cigar, continuing to contemplate him. She picked up the two glasses and gave him one of them. He drank, watching her. She began to undress.

'No, I can't look at you any longer!' she said.

Long afterwards, Petronius would think of those words. She lay on top of him, naked. He stroked her hair and caressed her back. She slapped her breasts playfully against his face, then let one nipple rest in his mouth. He began automatically to suck. She moaned with pleasure and put his hand on her other breast. They lay like that for a while. Petronius was happy; it was clear that she was enjoying it. Then she sat astride his thigh. She was wet.

'Are you a virgin?' she whispered.

'Yes,' he whispered back.

The Quarrywim were now singing in softer tones. It was an old song they had picked up called 'Be True to Me'. It was in a minor key, with many intoxicating chords. Petronius felt her hand grasp his penis. She held tightly while she moved against his thigh, faster and faster. She took his hand and held it against her. It was moist and strange. He didn't know what he was supposed to do with his fingers.

'No, not there. There,' she said, moving his hand a little. He felt a protuberance.

'Yes, there,' she said. 'Yes, yes . . .'

Her movements were faster now, and her grip around his penis tightened. He wanted to cry out, but controlled himself, so he wouldn't disturb her ecstasy. She was bouncing up and down on top of him and he kept losing touch with the protruberance, but found it again. Suddenly her grip became twice as tight. He yelled and she sank down onto him.

'Oh, that was so nice,' she said. 'You're nice, little Petronius.' She licked his chest. 'It's fine, being slim like you,' she said. 'It doesn't matter. And then you've got a really nice, well-shaped little thing.'

Petronius lay on his back and stroked her hair. He

wanted so much to . . . Oh, she must know what he wanted. Soon she would turn over on her back so he could slide into her. He could feel it beginning to grow with the thought. He was glad he hadn't disappointed her. He felt her weight on top of him and knew that everything was as it should be. Her warmth. Her even breathing against his ear. He felt fine. She had chosen to have him. It didn't matter that he was skinny. Her breath was warm and reassuring. In a moment she would . . .

He looked at her face with a shock. She'd fallen asleep.

Egalsund, pearl of the seacoast

Egalsund was one of Egalia's most exceptionally beautiful coastal towns, lying as it did at the head of a bay, twinkling and looking out towards the open horizon. A vast mountain, the Moonhill rose up to the north, magnificent and inaccessible, and the town was built on a fine series of terraces, leading down to the water. There were three huge areas of parkland. Everyone agreed that Chlorophyll Park was the most beautiful. More than any of the other parks, this one was responsible for assimilating the town's carbon dioxide, thus preserving the equilibrium of the natural oxygen cycle. 'A town should be an organic extension of nature himself,' the Egalians always said. Chlorophyll Park was also where the Grand Menstruation Games were held in the thirteenth month of the year — to honour the annual harvest and the achievements of the Egalians. The park's two big sewage treatment plants were the largest and most up-to-date in Egalia. But, as the Lady Chancellor on the Moonhill always said, 'Earth, air and water are our elements — and our dwelling. Without them, Egalia would not exist.' The Egalian would nod in agreement when she heard these words, reassured that she could sleep soundly.

The town was surrounded by big open-air amenities, athletics grounds, allotments and planted forests. Beyond these, lay the expanses of agricultural land, and far, far inland lay the mysterious mountain ranges of Palluria. In earlier times, there had been a constant state of war between Egalia and the neighbouring country of Pax, over the possession of these ore-rich mountains. For a long time now, however, the two countries had shared them sisterishly, each deriving great wealth from them.

Over the last few centuries, Egalsund had evolved into not merely the most beautiful, but also the richest town in Egalia. Egalsund's businesses had acquired a monopoly over most of the goods traded in the country. There was one industry, however, which it took these firms a long time to gain control of. This was the flourishing fishery on the island of Lux, which lay, like a pearl, in the wide bay of the sea.

Two big white bridges linked the town to Lux, which was known for its three long boulder-strewn beaches, its dense deciduous woodland and its two huge natural harbours on the east side of the island. In earlier times the island had been inhabited almost exclusively by fisherwim who sold their produce in the markets along the coast of the mainland. Egalsund soon became the hub of this trade and the iron grip of its commerce tightened around the fisherwim. But on Lux, the life of the fisherwim continued much as before.

On the southern cape of Lux, there stood a stone statue depicting a fisher-housebound looking anxiously out over the sea. The statue was known far and wide and visited by thousands of tourists each year. The searching expression of the fisher-manwom's stone face moved everyone who saw him.

It was said by some that the sculptrice had been inspired by the story of the mad fisher-manwom, Baraldus Mire, of the Maybight people. Baraldus's wife, Maria Maybight Southern, never returned from the sea. And every day, for the rest of his life, Baraldus wandered down to the southern boulder beach to look out for Maria. From the day she disappeared he lost his reason.

It would be deeply unjust to say that Egalsund had forgotten the great sufferings and the courageous achievements of the fishing population. On the contrary, the town recognized that this was the foundation on which its later progress rested. 'Where would we be today without the proud seawim who came before us?' was a question on everyone's lips.

It always met with approval and made people conscious

of how dearly they loved their home town.

It was the little spearbiter which led to the fisherwim's decline. Originally they had fished for all varieties of fish, with the traditional fishing methods which had been passed on from mother to daughter for generations. But a particular fondness for this shark to the exclusion of all other fish gradually developed in the town's growing population. The shark had long been known and feared by fisherwim, but they had only ever managed to catch it under unusually favourable conditions; for it had an ability, unparalleled in other fish, to see through the tricks of wim. It coaxed the bait from the hook, or, if caught in a net, it bit through the mesh with its innermost rows of teeth. In the summer a few courageous individual fisherwim would dive for these sharks and kill them with a spear. This required a limitless perseverance, and they had to be taken by surprise. On several occasions they had been known to cut through the diver's spear with a single bite, despite being so small — hence the name, the little spearbiter.

A veritable mania for spearbiter eventually took hold among the housebounds of Egalsund. The menwim's magazines were full of recipes for spearbiter casserole and spearbiter fishballs, with highly colourful pictures of spearbiter hors d'oeuvres, spearbiter soup and spearbiter cocktails. For a while, a casserole without at least a drop of delicious spearbiter oil was almost unthinkable. 'Wonderfully spicy,' the Egalians would nod contentedly, as they chewed. The fisherwim of Lux did their best to provide the sharks. As so many times before, wim had to wear themselves out to satisfy their menwim's whims.

The spearbiter's incomparable taste was not, however, the only reason it was so highly valued. Marine biologists were able to report that its intelligence was revealed in its highly developed — not to say civilized — reproductive behaviour. Like all other fish, the young were born out of the sexual milieu created by the mixture of roe and milt. The striking feature was that the *mafele* guarded the spawn and looked after the fry when they emerged. It built a nest which it guarded with three rows of razor-teeth. The fele, on the other hand, soon left the cosy refuge of her home and went off in search of new adventures. The spearbiter was therefore far advanced up the ladder of evolution, and for this reason people exalted it as the most intelligent of marine creatures, and incorporated it into Egalsund's coat of arms.

The fisherwim eventually found it impossible to meet the demand for this extraordinary shark. Small diving outfits, specializing in shark fishing, began to set themselves up on the island. They were employed by one of the municipal firms which paid for their expensive equipment. The local population couldn't compete with these specialized diving teams. Big firms gradually took over the entire fishery on the island of Lux. In the course of fifty years, the majority of independent fisherwim were forced to leave the island.

Their beautifully situated cabins were bought up by the state, or by the firms. Where they had been, big housing complexes were erected, with exorbitantly expensive flats. The big firms awarded their leading divers plots of land, where they built beautiful villas and moved in with their families. From here, they organized the great spearbiter hunt, which many of the town's adventurous young wim signed up for.

A few years later, as the result of a plebiscite, the island of Lux was incorporated within the administrative district of Egalsund.

Ruth Bram and her housebound
— for better or worse

Ruth Bram was sitting on the terrace, gazing towards the boulder beach to the south. In front of her, on the little work-table her housebound had put out for her, were some pictures of the little spearbiter. She was thinking.

It was the day after the grand maidmen's ball. Petronius had gone out, without saying where. Bram was worried. Petronius had begun to behave strangely, keeping to himself and saying nothing. She'd asked her housebound to ask him whether it was because he hadn't been invited into a maidman-room. He wasn't exactly the personification of mafele grace.

But it turned out that he *had* been taken into a maidman-room. Ruth Bram felt a pang of jealousy. What kind of idiot could have taken her son's maidmanhood? Without doubt, some worthless weakling of a wom. Or some coarse ruffian who'd just used him as a mattress. In no way did it mean that Petronius had secured his fatherhood-protection.

She had often warned him. She'd told him that he oughtn't to run around so much, that he ought to eat more. But as soon as she did, Christopher intervened and protected him. 'Darling, leave the boy alone now.' Oh yes. He'd even found it in him to say he thought she didn't treat her children equally. 'Ba is actually rather too heavy — in fact quite fat. Why don't you ever nag her and tell her to slim?'

'It doesn't matter what a wom looks like,' she'd explained in reply. 'I mean, wim get pregnant. Sometimes they can be fat, sometimes thin. It would be ridiculous to have an ideal size for wim.'

If Petronius didn't get fatherhood-protection, he would have to find a job. What chance did a lone spinnerman have? Petronius wasn't in great danger of ending up in the work camps; he wasn't strong enough. On the other hand, he would be well suited to the cleaning troops when he had grown a bit more.

Ruth Bram banged her fist on the table, making the shark pictures jump, and their teeth gleam in the afternoon sun. It mustn't happen. She would see to it that Petronius got a proper training, if that was what it finally came down to. At heart, Ruth Bram was a wom devoted to her family.

These were the thoughts that had driven her to the work-table this afternoon, even though she had piles of papers and applications and new regulations which she had to have ready by the next day. She'd had an idea — a diving suit for menwim. If everything was going to go wrong now, then at least Petronius would get his way. He would be allowed to become a diver. Besides, it could be a sensation. If the diving suit was a success, she might do very well from the patent.

She bent over the papers with a growing enthusiasm. Precise measurements would have to be taken of the strength of the spearbiter's jaw and the sharpness of its teeth. No one had yet managed to make a completely bite-proof spear, so how was it going to be possible to . . . That problem, she would solve. One of her best friends was the leader of the Sixth Diving Division.

'Christopher!' she bellowed.

'What is it, dear? I've got my beard full of shampoo.'

'The phone. Bring me the phone.'

'I can't. I'll get it all over the flat.'

'Wash it off and dry it, for God's sake!'

There was a moment's silence. Bram looked impatiently towards the terrace door.

'Ruth?'

'Yes.'

'It says on the instructions that you have to leave it for five minutes. If I rinse it off now my beard'll go all frizzy and I'm going to the coffee morning tomorrow.'

Bram shook her head. Lady God! That such things could be so important. Menwim! Even so, she had to admit that Christopher looked charming with his splendid, coif-feured beard, always soft and smelling nice.

'Okay!' she shouted. 'I'll get it myself.' She wasn't an unreasonable wom.

She dialled EG5 and got the operator.

'I'm trying to get through to Liz Bareskerry. Afraid I've forgotten the number.'

'Just a moment.'

Bram waited, impatiently. These operators were normal-ly so fast; but this one . . .

'Chief Diver Bareskerry's house.'

'Hallo. This is Ruth Bram. Is your wife anywhere about?'

'Yes, she is. She's just watching the debate in Parlia-ment on the TV, and it is so *utterly* boring. I can't follow it in any case, but there's no shifting her, she hasn't said a word to me for the last two hours and whenever I say anything, all that happens is I'm told to shut up before I interrupt one of the wim speaking in Parliament and stop her hearing what she's saying — I mean, *I* don't know how she can say I'm interrupting them, because they keep going anyway, without stopping, and besides they all say the same thing, over and over again, so I've got no idea why it's so important to listen to them, but it was really nice of you to ring, Ruth. Is there anything I can help you with?'

During this tirade, Ruth Bram had held the handset six inches from her ear. When she heard silence return, she put it to her ear again. 'Hallo, is that you, Liz?'

'I thought it would be Liz you wanted to speak to, Ruth. You know I've no one to talk to nowadays and it's quite dreadful. How's your housebound? It's such a long time since . . .'

'Fine thanks. Very well. Could I . . .'

'I'm so glad to hear that, really. Don't you think we should get together soon? I mean all four of us? Then I can prepare a proper dinner party.'

'Christopher's going to a coffee morning tomorrow. You

might see each other there.'

'No, I think I'm going to have to stay at home tomorrow, it was really sweet of you to ask, but I'm going to have to stay in, because Liz is going to sea tomorrow and you never know when she's coming back, and I don't like leaving the house when she's out, it's so awful, I must tell you, always thinking of what can happen out there, it's dangerous work and sometimes I get so scared when the wind gets up and there's stormy weather.'

Ruth Bram was now seething with fury. She was just about to let fly with enough force to make him understand when she heard an irritable wom's voice in the background. 'What is it that's taking such a blasted long time? Aren't you ever going to hang up that phone?'

'But it's for you,' said Msass Bareskerry to his wife. He put down the telephone and said to Bram from out in the room, 'She's coming now.'

Liz Bareskerry picked up the phone. 'I'm afraid I'm very busy . . .'

'Liz? Ruth here.'

'Hallo, you old mammal! Sorry about that. How are things with you?'

'All right, but I have a problem I'd like to discuss with you.'

'Let's hear it then. Britobert! Switch off the TV! I can't hear what Ruth's saying!'

Britobert, muttering, switched off the television and Liz made herself comfortable in the telephone chair.

'Britobert! Where's the pack of cigars that's meant to be here on the table with the phone?'

Britobert fetched the packet, which Liz had put by the television.

Liz chuckled. 'Right, sorry about the delay. What can I do for you, you old bandit?'

'Have you ever managed to measure the strength of a spearbiter's jaw?'

'We've tried, but it's extraordinarily difficult, you know. Of course we've done experiments at the aquarium. You know, with the ones we have at the institute.'

This was news to Ruth Bram. 'Yes, of course,' she said.

'The only problem is that those spearbiters are tame and we don't know whether they're really biting when we experiment with them. You know, they're incredibly intelligent creatures. It is as though they know it's an experiment and they don't want to co-operate. The problem has always been to produce a spear that withstands them. A real challenge. We're working on it.'

'You see,' said Bram, clearing her throat, 'my problem is slightly different. What I'm interested in is the construction not of a spear but of a *tube*.'

'What on earth for?'

'Yes, well, that's a secret, which I'll let you in on in due course. You know how these operators are.'

'You old vixen! I'll do what I can.'

'I'm relying on you.'

'Are we going to see each other soon?'

'Not a bad idea. It's been a while since we did.'

'What about at the club?'

'Okay.'

'Bye then, you old hedgehog.'

'Bye.'

Ruth grinned. Liz had always called her 'hedgehog' because her hair stood straight up. She ran her hand over her hair. Then she went to the bathroom to find her husband. She felt the urge for a cuddle and put her arms around him. Her hands slid down towards his belly and she peeked at his smart new peho. They'd had a long discussion when they went to buy it, but Ruth was happy with the result now, in any case.

Christopher was drying his beard with an electric hairdryer.

'That's going to look so good,' said Ruth. Their eyes met in the mirror and they gazed lovingly at each other. They were a lovely pair. But Christopher, to his horror, had just noticed that he was beginning to lose hair from his forehead and temples. He was depressed. Was he going to have to start wearing a wig already? After all, he was only thirty eight.

He thought, with a shudder, of the wholesaler, Moondaughter's housebound, who had had to start wearing a wig the previous year. Wigs never looked very convincing, no matter how expensive they were. And the older menwim said it made them feel so foolish when their wives knocked them off while making love. Most women insisted that their menwim wore their wigs when they went to bed with them, so they wouldn't lose their inclination, but in the heat of the moment they often forgot to be careful.

Ruth hugged him so tightly around the shoulders, the hair-dryer stopped.

'Ruth.'

'Christopher.'

He stroked her head gently.

'Are you my own little everything in the world?' she asked.

He nodded. She pulled his beard. He smiled. He had such beautiful teeth. His eye teeth always gleamed when he smiled. She patted him on the back, grabbed his shamebag and squeezed slightly.

'By the way, I got an invitation yesterday for both of us. From the club. To the annual Prosperity Ball.'

She pulled out the card and read, 'Ms and Msass Bram are hereby invited to the Club's Prosperity Ball. The time has come to bring along the lordies. Spring is in the air. Dress: Cocktail blouse and black. With kind regards from the club committee.'

'Oh, Ruth. I hardly ever go out. What am I going to wear?'

'Yes, what are you going to wear, what are you going to wear? That really is your problem.'

'Yes, but I'd so like to wear something *you* like.'

'Wear the maroon skirt. It goes so well with your maroon beard-bows. You look best in that.'

'But maroon beard-ribbons are hopelessly unfashionable. Pale colours are in this year. You never keep up with these things, do you, darling.'

'If I'm meant to interpret that as a veiled request to buy new beard-bows in pale colours, the answer is *no*. They're incredibly expensive. I've never understood why it always has to cost the earth for menwim to look smart. Anyway, I've got tax arrears to pay off and . . .'

'Everyone else is wearing pale colours now . . . '

'No, I said. You always look fat and beautiful; it doesn't matter what you wear. Anyway, I'm really not sure I feel like going to the Prosperity Ball this year. Nowadays it tends to end up as a ridiculous game of swopcock. Last year Bareskerry's housebound went off with Moonhill and . . .'

'Forget it. I'll tell you what. Let's go and sit on the terrace and I'll make us a little drink. The temperature's just right and the sun's going down over Bare Skerry.' He laid his forehead on her breast. 'There's nothing so nice as sitting out there on a warm, early summer evening, listening to the sighing of the . . .'

'Christopher, my darling. You really are such a romantic.'

'And you're not? I know you are. Come on!'

'Christopher, I . . .'

'Don't say you don't want to.'

'Christopher, I've got to go to a meeting.' She knew her words would fall like a wet blanket.

Christopher said nothing.

She began to feel annoyed. 'You know I can't afford to give up a whole evening.' That sounded so reasonable. Now she would look like the martyr. She had to work all the time so they could live comfortably. She could never switch off. Surely he could see that. 'It's about that idea. It's for Petronius's sake I'm doing it. You know that.'

He turned and looked her straight in the eye. 'Is it that diving suit you're talking about?'

'Yes.' She felt more hopeful. Perhaps he understood now how important it was.

'That meeting you're going to — is it something to do with this diving suit?'

'That's precisely what it's about,' she said with cheerful pride.

'Is Liz going to help you with it?'

'Yes. I'm going to meet her at the club.'

Christopher crossed the room, sat down on the sofa and lit a cigarette. 'I've been thinking about that for a long time,' he said. 'Ever since we were talking about it with Ba and Petronius. It's the peho that's the problem, isn't it?'

'That's right. It's a challenge.' She repeated Liz's words without really being aware of it. She admired Liz more than anyone.

'I see,' said Christopher. 'A challenge.'

'The problem is to produce a material that is absolutely biteproof,' said Ruth eagerly.

'A challenge. I see,' Christopher repeated, with a defiant puff of smoke. He tossed his head. 'Has it ever occurred to you that the whole problem could be solved quite simply by making a diving suit for menwim *without* a peho?'

Ruth Bram gave a start. She shuddered at the thought. She hurriedly lit a cigar and began to pace back and forth on the floor. 'No!' she shouted. 'No! That hadn't occurred to me. And there's a reason it didn't occur to me, Christopher, my sweet, and that is that it's *inconceivable!*' Her voice had gradually risen, and the last word boomed like thunder. She went on. 'A suit for menwim always has to have a peho. That's how it's always been and that's how it always will be. The only thing that varies is how high up it comes, and that's a matter of fashion which is decided by the fashion queen in Pax. But to dispense with it — you know as well as I do that there'll never be any question of that. Whether a manwom finds himself above water or under it, or in the air for that matter. It wouldn't fit well, Christopher. And apart from that — you know I'm not greatly bothered how well clothes fit — but apart from that it would be unaesthetic. *Unaesthetic*, Christopher. And that's much worse. I'm not going to have my son going round with that thing dangling loose between his legs. Over my dead body!'

The Narcisseum Club for Gentlewim

The Narcisseum Club for Gentlewim was situated halfway up the Moonhill, which rose steeply from the water at the head of Egalsund Bay. From its big windows, club members had a splendid view over the harbour, the town and the island. In principle, anywom who wanted to could become a member; in practice, the club's membership consisted almost exclusively of company directors, senior civil servants, chief divers, school principals, members of Parliament and scientists.

Ruth Bram, driving to the club across the North Bridge, felt remorseful after her row with Christopher. He was a good housebound. He loved her, he was interested in her work and he inspired her. And he was good-looking. She hadn't been the only wom to offer him fatherhood-protection. And when they went out together he was often the object of general admiration. Nonetheless, he was faithful to her. As far as she knew. Yes, he was faithful. Anything else was unthinkable.

This evening, the club was full. It was usually crowded on Sundays, when wim felt the need for a break, after spending the whole day with their families. But this evening it was even busier than usual. The reason was the great debate in Parliament.

The situation on the labour market was precarious. The birth rate had dropped, and this meant a constant shortage of labour. Moreover, the younger generation had begun to demand higher starting salaries, increased education subsidies and reduced pensions. As if that wasn't enough, they were demanding higher pregnancy benefit. This had led to a long debate over aims and objectives in Parliament. It had been decided that wages would be lower for those entering the labour market for the first time. The assembly had also discussed measures to check the declining birthrate. The system of progressive childbirth bonuses was not working well. A series of spokeswim for higher pregnancy benefit took the floor. Previously, pregnant wim had only been entitled to leave of absence at full pay, plus a pregnancy allowance of ten per cent and the child bonus, which depended on the child's position in the order of births. Besides this, nursing mothers got a diet allowance. The question was, however, whether this, too, wasn't too low. It was hard work, nursing a child for five months. But the biggest problem was that the wage supplement during pregnancy was so slight. It was ridiculously little. Several speakers made the point that it was time Parliament recognized that people had no inclination to spend nine months being pregnant when it was no longer valued. It was a particular problem for the working class. A pregnancy was a great strain on a huwom body. And considering that that body would have to work hard afterwards, it was no wonder that many working-class wim were refusing to bear children.

The Egalitarian People's Party put forward a proposal for a twenty five per cent wage increase during pregnancy, a lengthening of maternity leave from the present four weeks to seven weeks, an increased bonus for a first child plus a ten per cent increase in the diet allowance while nursing.

Many MPs supported this proposal. They pointed out that statistics showed that it was harder to get people to have a first child than a second. Parliament had therefore blundered, said the radicals, when it set the bonus so low for a first child.

The debate became intense as the vote approached. It was after all one of the most important questions and it affected everyone.

Outright fury was provoked by a mafele member who thought that the state ought to have some control over abortions. He was a relatively new member and not very experienced in politics as the art of the *possible*. He came in a late stage of the debate and was clearly nervous. The majority agreed that his presence was an agreeable feature. He was a pretty little thing, fat with a pointed beard. But wasn't his penis really rather big? The MPs couldn't stop staring at it when he took the platform and outlined his proposal.

'I think it's quite laughable that honourable members are willing to throw away millions of dollables on increasing the child bonus and raising the pregnancy allowance when the whole problem could be solved quite simply by letting the state determine when anyone is to have an abortion. As long as she decides this for herself, no unwanted children will be brought into the world. But children that are un-wanted by their fathers and mothers may be wanted by society. And is it not society's interest that we must serve? We would be able to bring down the present birth-costs if wim realized that having children is a social duty, and the joy of doing so ought to be reward enough.'

Well, whatever one thought of the proposal, it was put forward with disarming charm. It was of course practically unworkable. All girls learned how to perform abortions in school. How did the mafele member propose to solve that problem?

Most people knew, in any case, that it wasn't the fault of wim. The abortion rate was not so high as to be grounds for disquiet. The deficiency of sperm-secretion in many menwim, a problem which seemed to have grown in recent years, was something everyone knew about but preferred not to mention.

Finally a very young and unabashed MP stood up and stated the embarrassing fact. 'How does Parliament imagine that it is going to be possible to increase the population if we don't have adequate natural access to sperm?' she asked, glaring perspicaciously at the assembly.

A five-wom committee was set up to inquire into this question. They were to take advice from experts in the field.

The proposal for an increase in wage-supplement, child bonus and diet allowance was then approved with a big majority.

A number of MPs were at the club this evening, and when Ruth Bram arrived she made her way over to Bareskerry who was engaged in a discussion with Moonhill, who had come from the debate in Parliament. Bram, who hadn't followed the debate, was a little disoriented, but listened with growing interest. Bareskerry nudged her.

'Have you considered fertilizing yourself, then?'

'Yes, what about another daughter?' Interjected Moonhill. Her foremothers had once owned the entire Moonhill.

'Not a bad idea, as far as I'm concerned,' grinned Bram, considering it for a moment.

'Perhaps the *housebound* isn't so enthusiastic, eh?'

Bram fingered the glass Bareskerry had put in her hand. 'That wasn't what I was thinking of . . .'

'Then what were you thinking of?'

Bram glanced at Moonhill, the MP, nodded and raised her glass. She turned to her friend and said intensely, 'It might be a boy, mightn't it?'

Bareskerry nodded gravely. She knew that Petronius was a constant worry to his mother. She herself was lucky. Her plump sons, Baldrian and little, tubby Fandango, were liked and admired wherever they went. Baldrian was so chubby and beautiful the girls were always turning to look at him in the street.

'I think it shows a certain prejudice, insisting on having daughters,' remarked Moonhill, who belonged to the radical wing of Parliament. She leant confidingly towards them and said quietly, 'Incidentally it was something of a coup we pulled off today. We made a big thing out of the fact that workers suffer from childbirth, and should therefore get a higher bonus, and got through a change in the law giving *everyone* a ten per cent higher benefit. Here's to it! We high income earners stand to do well out of it, Bram.' She whinnied contentedly, raised her glass and went off into the billiard room.

Bareskerry watched her go, shaking her head in admiration. 'She started her period today and she was brilliant in the debate,' she said.

They sat on the stools at the bar and ordered a couple of whisky sodas. Bareskerry clasped Bram around the shoulders. They were old schoolmates. 'Now, about this tube?'

'Yes, it's something of a problem. It needs to be fixed securely.'

'What in the name of the Lady are you talking about?'

Bram looked at her fixedly. 'A peho for a diving suit for menwim,' she said.

Bareskerry stared at her good friend in amazement; turning the thought over in her mind. She took a gulp of her drink. She knew Bram too well to think this could be dismissed. 'It's impossible.'

Ruth Bram hit the bar counter with her fist, spilling drinks from several glasses. The bar-maidman immediately appeared, wiped it up, smiled at Bram, who stared back furiously, and disappeared. 'Are you going to help me or not?'

'But Ruth, even if it could be done, do you really think it's proper?'

'Proper? Manwom's talk. Real wim like you and I surely don't worry about what's proper. If the lad wants to go out on diving expeditions, then why in the name of the Lady shouldn't he?'

It sounded reasonable enough. At the same time, Liz Bareskerry knew Bram herself would have laughed at the idea twenty years ago. But people change when they have a family to think of. 'I've said I'll do what I can. I can't promise anything, but I'll try. Petronius can always come out with us some time and see what it's like at sea. It's a hard life.' Bareskerry shrugged her shoulders. For her, diving was a livelihood. She had never thought of it as being particularly exciting or alluring. She had become a diver because her mother had been a diver and she had been taken along on diving expeditions since she was very small. And when she grew up, and Britobert and two other menwim stood there, wildly in love with her and ready to accept the child she was carrying, she had chosen Britobert — since the child's father was a hopeless case. When he had said yes, she had realized the only thing in the world she knew about was diving.

She'd warned him. It was a hard and often a lonely life a diver's housebound had to put up with. But Britobert had stood there with burning cheeks, caressing her big belly as though its content already lay in his arms. And she had gone out, as she was obliged and compelled to, to provide him and the child with a comfortable existence. Thanks to her mother, she was soon the captain of the Sixth Division's biggest sailing-cutter.

'Are you sure there's no way of getting the lad's fancies out of his head? There are so many other things a young manwom can take up nowadays. What about hairdressing? Beard-perms and hair-sets are so fashionable at the moment.'

'Do you think I haven't tried? But . . . he isn't really . . . like other boys . . .'

'Baldrian said they had a lot of fun at the maidmen's ball.'

'Did he?'

'Yes, and he said it wasn't long before Petronius went off with a stylish young wom all the boys had had their eyes on. I think it must have been young Maydaughter. I knew her maternal grandmother. A most interesting wom, stubborn and headstrong. And incredibly clever. Young Maydaughter has something of her grandmother's toughness in her. A little touchy and hot-tempered, maybe. But sure of herself and good at her job. She works in my division.'

'Yes, Petronius said something of the sort,' mumbled Bram, who had paid no attention to all this.

'What about a game of bridge?' Bareskerry asked cheerfully.

'I don't think I could concentrate.'

'No, I understand. You won't mind if I go and see if I can find another player. Money's burning a hole in my pocket.'

Liz Bareskerry disappeared and Ruth Bram ordered another drink. She was thinking of Christopher and the sunset. He would be sitting alone on the terrace now. She thought of his big, round abdomen and felt herself moistening between the legs. Someone thumped her on the back.

'Sitting here boozing again, you drunkard?'

Bram found herself looking straight into the radiant, round face of Bosomby, Spinner of Arts, the school principal. She didn't approve of Bosomby; she was too flippant. Her solution to all the world's problems was always to say that one must look on the bright side. This filled Bram with nausea and disgust. 'Hallo, Bosomby,' she said coolly, and turned back to the bar.

'Are you ordering one for me too?' asked Bosomby, as though they were the world's best friends. Bram felt Bosomby's arm next to her and felt the warmth of her body. She always stood too close. Actually, Bram suspected that she was one of those . . .

'What'll it be?' she asked morosely.

'A whisky, with ice and water.'

Bram ordered. She had no desire whatsoever to talk to Bosomby, that homosexual Lucian!

'What a debate it was this afternoon, eh?' Bosomby said tentatively.

'I didn't see it,'

'No, you would have been too busy,' said Bosomby accommodatingly.

Ruth Bram made no reply. She took a slug of her drink and felt more and more bitter, the drunker she became. First the business with Petronius, then Christopher with his sunset, then Liz with her obvious antipathy to her ideas, and now the garrulous Bosomby. She turned on her. 'What the Lucy is it that children actually learn in your school?'

'L . . . learn?' said Bosomby stupidly, as though it had never occurred to her that anyone might learn anything at school.

'Yes. Learn,' Bram continued venomously. 'My Ba came home the other day telling the most amazing things.'

'What we teach is always in accordance with the directives we get from the Directorate, Ms Bram,' said Bosomby sharply.

'You've said that before. I must have heard it five hundred times.'

50

'My dear Bram, what in the world . . .'

'My dear Bram,' thought Bram, with annoyance. There it is — that slippery ingratiating tone of voice. We'll soon change that.

'Why can't you say, "Damn you, Bram", when that's what you mean?'

'But I've absolutely no idea what you're talking about.'

Bram was getting heated. 'Then I'll tell you. My daughter obviously has a certain Spinnerman Owlmoss for social studies, does she not?'

'Yes, Spn Lisello Owlmoss. Yes. So?'

'He has been filling her ears with strange things. He told her that menwim are actually stronger than wim, and that the whole problem is that menwim don't realize this, because otherwise they would sieze power tomorrow. What sort of crap is that, Ms Bosomby?'

'Mother Creator! Did he really say that?' The principal was beginning to see that Bram's anger was justified.

'Yes. He started from our Moulding Mothers' maxim, that the strong must protect the weak, and that it is the task of every civilization to remedy nature's injustice. Nothing wrong with that, so far. But to go from that to masculist propaganda, stating that menwim are actually stronger than wim! That's where I draw the line, Ms Bosomby! The great achievement of our civilization is precisely that it has proved that physical strength is not determined by sex, since it has put the mafele sex in its proper place in the process of life. Now what is it you've started teaching children in school? Is it something quite different? Well? Has it been forgotten that school is meant to be one hundred per cent objective? Well?'

Bosomby nodded assiduously.

'Does that mean, Ms Bosomby, that we're going to have to start keeping an eye on your school?'

'Not at all, Ms Bram. Not at all. I mean, of course, that you may, whenever, and as often as you like. I don't claim that my school is a perfect model of what a school should be, but nor do I accept the opposite. Naturally we have certain elements . . . even among the teachers. Spn

Owlmoss is of course the previous principal's only child. For that reason, I could hardly kick him out when I took over the school after her death. Or do you think perhaps that I should . . .'

Ruth Bram threw out her hand generously. 'No, certainly not. You can't be too hard on that sort of frustrated, middle-aged bachelor. Things aren't too easy for them, obviously. Be gentle, Bosomby, I advise you very strongly.'

The principal tentatively raised her glass. They toasted each other. Bram jumped down from the bar stool and brushed a little cigar ash from her black shirt. 'I'd better get home before the old boy goes to sleep,' she said, showing for the first time a hint of a smile. Bosomby beamed back at this sign of conciliation and emptied her glass.

As Ruth Bram climbed into her little yellow electric sportscar, she was conscious of how wet and horny she felt. She trod the accelerator to the floor and shot down the Moonhill's winding roads. She took the sharpest bends on two wheels. As a girl she had been very keen on motor sports and the passion had never left her. Her flashy sportscar was almost like part of her clothing. That's what it must feel like to put on a diving suit and dive, she thought. She would ask Liz sometime. Liz. What in the name of the Lady should she do without her? She was the only reasonable wom she knew. Whom could you really talk to nowadays? She whizzed through the curves. It was dark, but she knew the road like the pocket of her trousers. A road is like a manwom, she thought, lying there invitingly, ready to be taken. You knew its every little curve and irregularity, and knew instinctively when to keep going and when to brake. A road you know is like the body of a manwom you love, she thought.

She flew round the last curve and out onto the North Bridge. The water lay black and smooth below her.

She had to get home to him. He would be lying there, waiting for her. He had waited all evening. I'm coming, darling! She accelerated into the big oak wood. The oak wood, heavy with memories. That was where she had had him, the first time. She felt her desire spreading, like a warm itch on the inside of her thighs. She gripped the wheel tighter. The speedometer was showing ninety five. She passed the first divers' villas on the left. Now she would soon be home. She turned into the drive and up to the house, leapt out of the car, took the steps at a run, twisted the key in the lock and burst in.

The terrace door was closed. He had gone to bed. She crept into him and put her arms around him. He grunted and tried to turn over.

'My Christopher . . .' she whispered.

'Mmmmmm . . .'

She kissed him. He was limp and heavy. That excited her even more. She put her hand between his legs.

'Not now, Ruth. I'm asleep.'

She moved his hand back and forth. 'You can't be asleep if you can talk. Darling!' She lay on top of him and pushed her breast against his face.

'I'm tired,' he mumbled, beginning to suck sleepily on one nipple.

'Hold me here!' she said. 'Hold tight, Christopher. I love you!' She rocked backwards and forwards, moaning and groaning.

'Ruth . . . can't we go to sleep?'

'Yes, in a minute. Oh darling, you're so lovely.'

Ruth was moving her lower body quickly and purposefully. She began to think of the debate in Parliament. Ten per cent, she thought moving rhythmically. Christopher put his arms around her head and smiled drowsily at her. She loved that smile. 'Did you remember to take your pill?' she asked.

'Yes, but nothing much is going to happen tonight as far as I'm concerned. You can tell, can't you? I'm sorry, but . . .'

In fact it was some time since anything much had happened as far as he was concerned. Ruth couldn't remember when he'd last had an orgasm. She kept at it, on top of him, evenly and rhythmically. That was the best thing — he never said no when she wanted to. Could she have found a more wonderful manwom?

'You can stop taking them, by the way,' she moaned.

'Stop?'

'Yes. The pill.'

'D'you want another child?'

'Yes. Don't you?'

Christopher didn't reply. Suddenly it began to feel better than before. She forgot everything and let herself go. He felt for her clitoris and found it. Yes, now she knew. Everything in the world was just an endless mass of absurdities which only came together and meant anything in a single sparkling second. Now! She lay on top of him, shaking in ecstasy. He held onto her. She thought of the caring hand which he held so gently in her sent her right out into eternity.

She relaxed, bathed in sweat. She caressed him gently and noticed that his little thing had begun to move a little. How touching. It was wonderful to lie like that, completely still, with her naked body against his.

Later, she was woken by a strange noise. She had dreamt that Bosomby, the school principal, was on her knees in front of her, sobbing and begging to be allowed to keep her post as principal, promising that henceforth ten per cent of all directives would be complied with. She was about to shout, 'Ten per cent! Why only ten per cent, Ms Bosomby?' but she had lost the power of speech. She awoke and looked up. Then she realized. Christopher's temple was warm and wet.

'But Christopher, my love, my darling . . . why are you crying?'

Bosomby, the school principal, calls Spn Owlmoss to account

'Spn Lisello Owlmoss. Please come to my office after school. Ms Bosomby, Principal.'

He knew the handwriting well. It had changed somewhat over the years. But by Lady God, he knew it. He was trembling and hot about the ears.

'What's that, an invitation?'

It was Egg, the assistant teacher. He never knew whether Egg was being sarcastic or merely stupid. She was nosy in any case. Spn Owlmoss looked at her inquiringly. *Was* it an invitation? Did Egg know anything bout it? Or was her question plucked out of the air to point out that Spn Owlmoss would obviously never be sent an invitation?

'No. Not exactly an invitation,' he mumbled.

'Perhaps a love-letter?' Egg laughed. 'It's never too late, you know.' She chuckled again, patted Owlmoss lightly on the shoulders and went on her way.

Spn Owlmoss spent the whole day wondering what on earth it was that the principal wanted of him. Long experience had taught him to fear the worst. On the other hand, the principal was given to extreme formality and could present the pleasantest of surprises in the most tiresome way. Spn Owlmoss therefore went on hoping for as long as possible.

During all the years that had gone by, the principal had managed to keep their relationship on a level of strict formality. While there had been hope, Spn Owlmoss had gone on trying to read a hint of affection into her stern countenance. That time was, however, long past. Cyprian had grown big, and he was not his son. Cyprian was Grodrian's son, and he always would be. Irrevocably. Even though any infant could see the striking resemblance between Cyprian and himself.

Cyprian went around as living proof of his shame in life.

Today teaching was an even more miserable experience than usual for Spn Owlmoss. He blushed or lost the thread at the slightest interruption. He took every cough as a personal affront, and the final hour with 5B was a nightmare, pure and simple. Ba Bram got up on the lid of the desk and played Parliament, urging everybody to show solidarity with working mothers, and the others applauded and laughed; nobody took any notice of Spn Owlmoss, standing by the blackboard attempting to explain a matriotic poem from the previous century. Ba, moreover, had bought a huge bag of sticky cow's eyes which she handed out to everyone in the class. Spn Owlmoss wondered whether they would even notice if he disappeared.

Luckily the bell rang before all the desks had been overturned. The class charged out. Spn Owlmoss tidied up the worst of the debris, locked the door and went up to the principal's office. He hesitated a moment before knocking.

'Come in,' said a friendly voice. It was the secretary. Spn Owlmoss walked in.

'The principal isn't here yet,' said the secretary, who continued typing. When Spn Owlmoss remained standing, a little awkwardly, he added, 'But she'll be here any minute. Please do take a seat.'

'Thanks.' Spn Owlmoss remained where he was. He couldn't see a chair anywhere. He felt foolish, standing there, holding his salmon pink handbag in front of him.

'Just go into the office and find yourself a seat.'

The secretary was always so friendly, understanding everyone's needs, doing a hundred little things that were not really part of his job, just to be helpful and kind. And always with a smile. He was called Herbert. It struck Spn Owlmoss that he had never heard his damename. Perhaps he didn't have one.

The principal's office was big and airy, with an enormous window looking out over Lifedaughter Road and the harbour basin. Spn Owlmoss stood looking at the view for a while, thinking how liberating it felt to come in here. Apart from the principal's imposing, gleaming desk.

He sat down in the visitor's chair and put the salmon pink handbag in his lap so it concealed his peho. He felt tense and stiff throughout his body. Any moment he expected to see the door handle pushed down. Ten minutes late, the principal marched in.

'Ah. You're here already,' she observed and sat down at her desk.

Spn Owlmoss stared at her. It was not often they were alone together. Only when formalities obliged them to be. Did she deliberately avoid it? He thought of a time they had been together when formalities almost obliged them not to be, the occasion of Cyprian's conception. She had changed a great deal since then. She was at least twice as big and had acquired a couple more chins. But he still discerned a certain refined beauty in her face. She looked tired. Nothing radiated such peace and dignity as a tired old wom's wrinkled face, he thought. Her eyes were small but intense. Mother God, how he'd loved her. It suddenly came to him so forcefully.

'Right,' said Ms Bosomby decisively, without looking at him. 'I sent you a note. You received it, I take it?'

Spn Owlmoss nodded, thinking that this was obvious, since he was sitting there. But as the principal did not even glance at him, and consequently didn't see his nod, she repeated, 'You received it, I imagine?'

'Yes.'

'It's about your teaching, Spn Owlmoss. I'm sorry to say it has been brought to my attention that in certain aspects your teaching is not up to standard. It is evident that you have been indulging in a form of political agitation that we cannot accept in a school such as this. The fundamental principles of our school system are facts and objectivity. It is all very well for you to have your own independent views of various matters, Spn Owlmoss, but menwim's lib propaganda does *not* belong in our school.'

If only she'd stop calling me Spinnerman Owlmoss, he thought. If just once, she'd call me Lisello, as she used to.

He gave a start when he noticed that the principal had stopped talking. He looked at her, slightly embarrassed. Their eyes met across the glassy desktop.

'I'm sorry . . . what did you say?'

The principal drummed impatiently with her fingers. 'I said there have been complaints that you have been disseminating propaganda.'

'Oh?'

'Yes.'

'I see.'

'Yes. In Ms Bram's daughter's class. During a social studies lesson. You are alleged to have said that the great menwim's rebellion is imminent.'

'Is it?'

'What?'

'Is the great menwim's rebellion imminent?'

'*No!*' Ms Bosomby hammered the desk with her fist. 'You are teaching your pupils that the great menwim's rebellion is at hand!'

'Ah.'

Now, Spn Owlmoss remembered. It was the lesson when Ba had been sent out into the corridor. He had given an account of the creation. But he couldn't remember exactly what he'd said.

'I see,' he said looking down. 'But I don't think that is what I said. I said . . . well, what I said was . . . How is Cyprian?'

The principal pretended not to hear and asked what he had to say.

'About what?'

'About what I have just said.'

'What I just said.'

'What did you just say?'

'I said, "How is Cyprian?"'

'What on earth has that to do with this, Spn Owlmoss?' The principal kept losing her temper.

'Everything, Gerd! If only once, you could call me Lisello. It's as though we'd never known each other. How can you forget so easily? How can you think I'm going to be able to sit here and say yes, principal, no, principal, three bags full, principal. Are you just a shell? A shell which can't even let me know how my own son is?'

'Ssssh! Not so loud!' shouted Ms Bosomby.

'*Not so loud*,' Spn Owlmoss mimicked in exasperation. 'As if the whole town doesn't know all about it! D'you think I don't notice how they tittle-tattle behind my back?'

Ms Bosomby pulled herself up and stiffened. 'I must point out that this office is not intended for private conversation.'

'No. This office is only here so that you can make pronouncements and everyone else can listen and comply.'

'It is my purpose in life . . . dear Lisello.'

The principal regretted her last words. But they gave Spn Owlmoss new courage. 'How d'you think it's been for me all these years, Gerd? Have you ever once paused in your great project in life to ask yourself, "How is he?" Lady knows I don't mean that your life's work *isn't* great and important. You've always made your work your priority. But your life, Gerd; what's happened to your life?'

'One's work and one's private life have to be kept separate,' replied Ms Bosomby, who had begun to recover her sense of moral values.

'Wrong!' said Spn Owlmoss vehemently. 'That's what I've been suffering from all my life. You've put your finger on it. I should have thought of it before. One's work and one's private life go together!'

Gerd Bosomby recognized, not without a pang of sadness, her former mastrass's predeliction for the dramatic. Whenever he managed to pluck up enough courage to express his feelings, he sounded like a mafele character in a bourgeois melodrama. Suddenly she felt something of what she had felt long, long ago. She had been around him year in and year out without thinking of it. That, no doubt, was what Sigma Floyd, Egalia's most venerable psychologist, meant by repression.

But she had felt burdened by his unconcealed and passionate infatuation. For her it had just been a night in the month of hayripe — well, perhaps several nights. But she only remembered one. She'd been rejected by the football coach's son, whom she was in love with, and had gone, in a state of depression, to find Lisello. She'd taken him to the woods. That night, Cyprian was conceived in her. She had told him right away and he'd said, overjoyed, 'At last I've got something to live for!' She'd answered coolly that she wasn't too sure about that, since the coach's son was still available. And she'd seen despair in his face. Despair and humiliation. He'd clung to her and begged for his life, saying, 'What am I going to do? What am I going to say to my parents? My mother is a guardian of morality in this town. She'll die of shame!' And Gerd had quite heartlessly replied the he really couldn't expect her to give him fatherhood-protection just because his mother was the school principal and acted as a guardian of morality in Egalsund.

And now here she was, acting as a moral guardian against him. Through her connection with Lisello Owlmoss, she had, as a young wom, secured her position as old Principal Owlmoss's successor. Once this was clear, she had jilted her son. She'd got half the queendom but escaped the princeass. Ha!

'What are you thinking?' he asked.

'Nothing.' She tightened her jaw. She hadn't reckoned on their conversation taking this turn. In fact she hadn't intended that there would be any conversation at all. She'd made an administrative blunder. She would have to get him out before the whole thing ended in weeping and gnashing of teeth.

'You're lying,' he said.

'You're right. Everything you're saying and thinking is right. The world has treated you unjustly. But that's how life is, Lisello. What's done is done.'

'I've loved you, Gerd. And I've loved our child. And now you won't even tell me how he is.'

Ms Bosomby sighed deeply. Cyprian was not exactly the type to make his mark on the world. He had sat watching the dancing couples at his first maidmen's ball. He had had to endure coarse remarks from an inebriated person who,

60

when it came to it, didn't want him in a maidman-room with her. Grodrian had told her. Cyprian was only gifted in one way, he had a good mind. He resembled his father to a tee. His fate would be the same as Spn Owlmoss's — he would end up an old bachelor.

Ms Bosomby stood up abruptly. She wasn't going to start getting sentimental over menwim's lot in life. She peered down at Spn Owlmoss over her rough double chins. 'To return to the matter at hand. It is the task of our civilization to remedy nature's injustice! That was the point of departure from your lesson, Spn Owlmoss, according to my information. What does that mean? You seem to have forgotten what you learned in your childhood. Nature's injustice consists in the fact that the manwom does not have the privilege of bearing children. That means he has a purely subordinate function in the very process of life, as our little affair, such a very long time ago, illustrates. As I said, a completely subordinate role. Nature has not equipped him to take charge of life. That fate is biologically determined, Spn Owlmoss, and it is also your fate. Obviously, you may regret that you were born a manwom. But there's really nothing either you or I can do about that.'

Here she paused briefly, as though to relish the fact that nothing could be done about it. 'Therefore, I have, naturally enough, given my child life and protected his life — something you are not capable of doing. That's all for today. You may go now, Spn Owlmoss.'

The audience was at an end. Spn Owlmoss got slowly to his feet and went to the door. He was amazed that she had managed to round off their intense exchange with banalities he'd heard a thousand times before.

Ms Bosomby contemplated his bottom, which awoke a memory of the oak wood. Would she, she wondered, feel the same desire for that bottom if she were to see him naked now?

The bottom went out and the door closed. Ms Bosomby turned her attention to the tasks of the afternoon.

The shore, the stone statue and the oak wood

Petronius hurried through the oak wood down towards the water. He didn't like being in the woods at dusk. The branches formed dark, knotty shapes; the trunks were thick and solid. You could never be sure that there wasn't some wom hiding behind them. When he was little, he'd heard stories of dark-clad wim who hid in the forests waiting to catch small boys and do vile things to them. His fear of the nasty old wim had never completely left him. He heard something crack a few feet away in the trees. A manwom's voice groaned, 'Not so hard, Ida!' Just a couple making love. Petronius hurried past.

It was a relief to see the shimmering waves as he descended onto the shore. The big boulders gleamed and the sky was not nearly so dark as it seemed in the wood.

Petronius took off his uncomfortable shoes and stepped cautiously out onto the shiny, rounded rocks. They were warm. Warmer than the air. People ought really to go barefoot all the time. Feet were really gripping-appendages, squeezed into shoes that were much too tight. They varied, of course, with fashion. At the moment they were meant to be checked and canoe-shaped. Petronius's green-checked, canoe-shaped shoes, stood by themselves, gaping heavenwards.

He walked out to the stone statue. He picked up a stick. The statue stood so far out that its feet were washed by the high tide. Petronius stood facing the statue.

'You're stupid,' he said quietly. The statue continued to gaze immovably towards the horizon. He hit it on the side of the head with his stick. 'You've been standing there, grieving, for twenty years.' Petronius put his arms round the statue and laid his cheek against its abdomen. It was cold. 'I'm so lonely,' he whispered. 'I'm not going to let you just stand there, petrified and haughty in your suffering. Didn't I say I was coming back? Do you remember I said I was going to the maidmen's ball?' He looked up at the stony chin. 'No, you don't remember. You don't think of anything but the wim out there, the wim who never came home. But now let's pretend you remember me. I came back. I've been there now — to the maidmen's ball. It was exactly a week ago. It wasn't at all like I thought it would be. I'd imagined something like pink cotton wool.'

He felt the wind on his neck and began to rub the statue in the small of the back. 'Look, I'll warm you up. Have you ever thought what it would be like to float on strong arms in pink cotton wool? To float, drowsy with sweetness? But it wasn't like that. And if those wim you're waiting for ever come home, you'll be disappointed, too. She came, took me, fell asleep and went. Since then, I haven't seen her. Maybe she's out there among the wim you're waiting for. Who knows . . .'

Petronius began to feel afraid and stopped. He missed her.

'I don't know who she is. I do know her name. But I daren't ask after her. She stirred something in me and I know I'm hers. That's why I daren't ask. Do you understand?' Petronius ran his stick gently down the statue's spine. 'Is that where it itches? A bit higher up? Under your left shoulderblade? You're so fine and fat. There, how's that? I went down afterwards, but she'd gone. I didn't dare ask after her. I went into the bar where the wim were all getting roaring drunk. They stared at me and one of them tickled me under the peho with her forefinger. I slapped her. Then I went home.'

Petronius was beginning to feel cold. He turned towards the sea. A very long way off he could just discern the island of Bare Skerry. He had never been there. He had never been outside Egalsund. He started walking back towards the beach, but stopped suddenly. There, a little ahead, thirty yards or so from him, stood the dark figure of a wom.

She stood still, with her feet apart and her face turned half towards him. He stared at the figure, then walked towards the beach. She began to walk in the opposite direction, out towards the water, with long strides. Petronius walked quickly towards the path through the wood, where he had left his shoes. They had gone. What had happened to them? Had she taken them? What did she want with him?

Petronius ran into the wood. The more he ran, the more afraid he felt. Twigs and stones gashed his feet. He saw dark shapes everywhere. The branches formed knotty heads with crooked noses and grinning mouths. He was sure she was following him. She was a monster, twice his size. He felt that at any moment she would grab him by the neck and force him to look at her face, which was at the same time both terrifying and compelling.

He tried to run faster. His legs felt lame. Soon they would give way under him. He collided with a branch. His cheek hurt. He lost sight of the path, stumbled and fell.

Three dark figures stood round him. He could see their sweaty faces glistening in the darkness. They were staring at him. He tensed every muscle in his body and lay completely still, as though the slightest movement on his part would provoke a reaction from them. Someone grabbed him by the arm and pulled him up. His legs were still weak, like those of a three-year-old refusing to walk and demanding that daddy carry her. He was gripped roughly round the waist and carried into the wood, away from the path. They laid him on a mound of dead leaves. He sat up.

'But . . .'

'Lie down!'

He lay down, shut his eyes, thought of the many hundreds of yards between him and home on the path through the wood. He wouldn't manage to get away from them. Wasn't there anyone around? No one out for an evening walk who would hear him cry for help?

'If you start yelling and making a fuss, it'll only be worse for you.' She spoke quietly and evenly. The bright, penetrating wom's voice made Petronius think of his mother. They began to take off their blouses and shirts and positioned themselves around him. Their swelling breasts shone in the gloom, the nipples erect. One of the wim bent over him. He felt her hands fumbling with his peho and waistband. She grasped his shamebag. He wailed.

'Take it easy.'

He saw the other two unbutton their trousers and lay bare their hairy triangles. One pulled out a knife and handed it to the wom trying to undo his peho.

'It'll be quicker with this.'

He felt the cold metal against his stomach. She cut the waistband, pulled off the peho and threw it to one of the others, who caught it. She tore the cloth and threw it away. One was on top of him now. She smelt of alcohol and sweat. She grabbed his penis and thrust her nipple into his mouth. He felt her wet crotch against his thigh. He wriggled like a worm, trying to get his leg out. Oh, no, for God's sake. The grip on his penis tightened. She was breathing hard against his ear, bouncing violently up and down, forcing his thigh against her crotch, pumping and moaning. He looked up at the others in desperation. Were they just going to stand and watch without helping him? Their breasts and faces shone in the dark, as before, just as immovably. He shut his eyes. His penis hurt. He tried to imagine he was somewhere else. This wasn't happening to him, but to someone else. It wasn't him, lying here with a stinking, heavy wom on top of him. Her body was pumping harder and faster now, wet and sticky against his thigh. He pressed up against her a little. She groaned, withdrew her nipple from his mouth and sank down onto him for a second. Then she leapt to her feet. Petronius lay still with his legs apart, as though she were still lying on top of him. He hardly dared breathe, in case they heard and thought he was relieved it was over. He didn't dare look at them; he just lay there, waiting for them to go away.

Suddenly one of the others was on him.

'*Nooooo!*' Petronius's voice echoed in the forest. Now he had screamed, he was even more afraid. He tried to get up. If he was going to run, it had to be now. A strong grip on his wrists forced him down. 'Now, you little ladsel in distress, take a swig. It'll calm you down.' A bottle gleamed in the darkness. He was forced to swallow. 'There's really nothing to scream about. We won't do you any harm.' She knelt over him and pressed his hand against her clitoris, raking backwards and forwards. The bottle went to the others, who took turns with it.

'I don't want to!' Petronius shrieked, trying to pull his hand away. They forced him down again.

'Why not? It's nothing. You've done it before, haven't you?'

The wom lying on top of him continued, more wildly than before. The other one knelt on top of him and pulled his other hand against her crotch. They were moving in time with each other. The third sat behind and held him around the waist. How long was this nightmare going to go on? Was it never going to come to an end? It felt as though it would never finish. As though he was going to be forced, for all eternity, to remain there with them while they satisfied themselves on him. There was no escape. He no longer hoped someone would come and rescue him. He didn't want anyone to see or to know that he was the sort of manwom who did this with wim. He heard them both groan at the same time. They got up, looked for their shirts and blouses, and got dressed.

'So long, little fellow,' said one of them with a derisive leer. They disappeared into the trees. Petronius lay listening to the leaves rustling under their feet. He could hear them muttering to each other and laughing. When it was quiet, he breathed out, got to his feet and brushed off his clothes. He didn't want to think. He didn't ever want to think about it or tell anybody about it. He had been through something that never happened.

His penis hurt. He looked down at it, dangling helplessly between his legs. He noticed the light flash of the torn peho lying among the trees. What would people think when they came by on a walk in the woods the next morning? Would they pick it up and look for the owner? If they did, how would they go about it? There would be hundreds of the same sort. But the size, and the colour? That could put them on the right track. He stuffed it under his tunic and went slowly home.

He entered the house as quietly as he could. It was ten o'clock and he could hear the TV in the living room.

'Is that you, Petronius?'

Petronius felt a lump in his throat. He wanted to cry. He just wanted to hug his dad and cry. Don't say anything, don't explain anything. He swallowed. 'Yes. I'm going to bed.'

'What is it, Petronius? Are you unhappy?'

Petronius felt the tears coming. 'No, I'm tired. Going to bed.'

'Don't you want something to drink before you go up? I'm on my own. Mum's gone to the club.'

'Going to bed. 'Night.'

He ran up the stairs into his room and locked the door. He wept. He took out the remains of his peho, emptied his wastepaper basket, put the peho in it with a little paper and set fire to it. Flames licked the sides of the wastepaper basket and the room filled with black smoke. All the while he was crying. For a moment he was afraid the fire was going to get out of control, but then the flames died down and he gazed down at the charred remains. He went out to throw them down the rubbish chute. Christopher came up behind him on the landing.

'What are you doing?'

'Emptying the wastepaper basket,' mumbled Petronius, reddening.

'It strikes me there's a funny smell . . .'

Petronius's heart was beating hard and fast. 'I burnt some things I'd written.' He looked down.

Christopher looked at him. 'Where's your peho?'

'Just getting undressed.'

'Can't we talk a bit, before you go to bed?'

'No. Got to do my homework.' He went back into his room. How was he going to explain that the peho was gone? He'd only had two. And the other was the tulle one he'd worn at the maidmen's ball. He couldn't wear that to school. And pehoes were expensive — at least fifty doll-ables. He could take the money he'd been saving to buy a diving spear, slip out early in the morning and buy a new peho before he went to school. There was no other way.

Petronius undressed and got into bed. He was afraid of falling asleep, afraid of the borderland in which images of every kind appear. He would see all those dark silent shapes which had leapt on him. He closed his eyes and tried to relax. He was aching all over, and exhausted. His limbs were sore and his penis hurt. The darkness crept into his head. He saw a figure standing a long, long way off — at the far end of a long tunnel. It was coming towards him with long strides. He recognized the figure; it was the wom on the beach. He could see her face, a beautiful face with high cheekbones. Suddenly the face rushed towards him like a comet. It was Gro! He screamed and sat up in terror.

As Petronius was trying to sneak out of the apartment the next morning, armed with fifty dollables and his satchel, Ba put her head out of the bathroom. Petronius put his finger to his mouth.

'Ssssh!'

'Hi Petronius,' called Ba. 'Are you going before break-fast?'

Petronius was furious. 'Idiot!' he hissed, trying to open the outside door.

'Why aren't you wearing your peho today? Some sort of willy campaign?' asked Ba at the top of her voice.

He grabbed her by the wrists and glared straight into her eyes. 'Not a word to Dad and Mum, d'you understand?' he whispered earnestly. 'If you keep quiet, I'll buy you something.' Petronius didn't have to think for long. He knew what Ba wanted more than anything else. 'A knife!' he said.

Ba nodded eagerly. Her mouth was clamped shut now. She crept into her room. Petronius slipped out through the door.

When Petronius got home that afternoon, wearing a new peho identical with the old one and with a fine new knife for Ba, it had happened anyway. Christopher had overheard what they had been talking about in the morning and when Ruth came down to the breakfast table she managed to make Ba tell what she knew.

Bram waited until after they had eaten. Then she went into the workroom with Petronius. 'What's the idea of sneaking out without breakfast, half-dressed at half past six in the morning?'

Petronius looked down at the floor. He had been waiting for it. When he'd gone into Ba's room to give her the knife she'd just shaken her head, unwilling to take it.

'Answer me!'

Petronius stared at the pattern in the carpet. It was a black zig-zag pattern with dark hexagons in between. He didn't reply.

'Petronius,' said Bram, rather more gently. 'D'you know what? There's no point in trying to fool me. I can see you've got a new peho, you know. It was the old one you were burning last night, wasn't it?'

Petronius nodded, his eyes fixed on the hexagons. The whole story lay in the carpet's pattern. His eyes followed the line up and down, round and round.

'What happened last night, Petronius?'

Petronius shook his head. She would never find out . . . He would never tell, as long as he lived.

'You went out for a walk, didn't you?'

Petronius nodded.

'Why can't you stay home? Why have you got to go gallivanting at night?'

'Had to go down to the beach . . .'

'What were you doing there? Tell the truth! Did you go to meet someone?'

'No.'

'Are you sure?'

'No . . . I mean, yes.'

'There, I knew it! You went to meet someone. You met her and she assaulted you. Ripped off your peho, forced you to have sex with her. That's what happened, isn't it, Petronius? I only want the best for you.'

'But it wasn't like that. She didn't assault me!'

'So you went along with it *of your own free will*? And then you changed your mind and tried to get out of it and she forced you? Oh yes, I know that story. As Director for Social Welfare, I've had hundreds of cases like that, where testerical menwim come and say this or that's been done to them, when they've brought it on *themselves*. What do you really expect, Petronius, when you go down to the beach at ten in the evening?'

'But I only went to talk to the st . . .'

'Only went to talk! You menwim always say that. Just to talk. You must remember, Petronius — I'm telling you this as a piece of good advice from a mother to her son — you must remember that a wom is a wom, and a wom needs what a wom needs. In the long run, every wom looks at a manwom as a mattress. That's the only thing that interests her. You mustn't think she's going to be content just to talk. You must put yourself in her place, Petronius. Your poor little pole gets her excited, and when darkness falls, you can't expect her to be satisfied with a chat.'

This was dreadful. She was telling him to his face that he had a pole. He was ashamed that she had said it, and that he had it. He forgot that she was twisting the whole story. It was almost a relief. Now he wouldn't have to tell her what really happened. He stared down at the carpet, letting her continue.

'Usually an incident of this sort would go straight to the Directorate's department of violent crime. But since you're my son, you'll be spared that. Such things are extremely humiliating for the menwim who undergo them. And what's worse is, they have virtually no chance of getting fatherhood-protection after a story like this. You can be glad you've got a mother who wants the best for you, Petronius. It would also be humiliating for me, by the way, at the office. A wom in my position is incredibly vulnerable. But one way or another I would have dealt with that!'

Here, she paused for a moment to emphasize her courage. She had withstood many blows. No doubt she would have survived this one too.

'We won't report it, Petronius. Let's forget the whole

thing. It's better that way — because who's going to want a manwom who's been defiled? We'll let it go this time. But one thing's certain — you're not going down to the beach any more after dark!'

Petronius as a seawom

The good ship *Adonis*, a big white ketch, lay ready for sea in the South Harbour. He looked splendid with his tall masts, white sails, and his long bowsprit supported by the slim figure of a young manwom holding his chin high to mark the vessel's course to the horizon with his little pointed beard.

The menwim had gathered on the quayside to wave farewell. Petronius felt unsteady as he went up the gangway with his chequered handbag and his fine, new, long skirt which he had bought specially for the occasion. It was tight, so he had to walk with small steps, and the gangway was rather steep. Bareskerry was waiting to greet him at the rail.

'Welcome aboard, young seawom!' she said, extending her arm to him gallantly. He felt pride at being addressed as seawom.

It was not without some difficulty that Ruth Bram had managed to arrange this. She was eager that the boy should do something he enjoyed. In certain respects, she wasn't being realistic. Moreover she came from an old farming family, in which the menwim, despite everything, had a certain status as hunters. Indeed, they were even supposed, a very long time ago, to have fished in small inland lakes.

Liz Bareskerry had run into prejudices whose existence she had never suspected.

'Menwim at sea! Out of the question!' roared the commissioner for the Sixth Diving Division. 'They're always trouble! They never leave us in peace and there'll be strife and quarrelling and jealousy in the crew. We're often out for three or four weeks at a time. No, it won't do,' she said, baring her tattoed arms menacingly. They were adorned with a line of little naked menwim with hairy bellies.

But Liz Bareskerry, who had promised to help Bram, was equally adamant. She could assure her that it was only a trial run and that Bram's son would have a cabin beside her own. She would naturally make sure he didn't put out any lines of his own. And if they otherwise had any comments to make on her leadership, they could go to hell.

Liz Bareskerry looked fine, standing there in her blue and white uniform, saluting the mate as she came aboard. They weighed anchor and set a course for the Bare Skerries.

The vessel was wommed by twenty five sailors: chief divers, divers, and the usual crew. It took several hours to reach the outermost islet of the Bare Skerry group, Spout. Bareskerry stood on deck, watching. A good while before reaching Spout, they hoisted sail and the cutter glided ahead. Bareskerry explained to Petronius that the spearbiters heard the sound of the engines a long way off and fled. They really were singularly cunning creatures. God knows how many times the divers had had to develop new methods of catching them. Bareskerry confided to Petronius that she doubted whether there was really any future in it. Economically, spearbiter-fishing was nothing but a luxury business, which could only continue as long as people were willing to pay the sky-high prices the delicacy fetched.

They lay to in the lee off Spout. The divers came up on deck, carrying large baskets and harpoons on their backs. Attached to their spears were long lines, fastened at the other end to winches on deck.

Bareskerry gazed at the surface of the sea. 'There should be a shoal down there now.'

The divers jumped over the side and disappeared. Petronius watched the bubbles rising to the surface and asked whether that meant the divers were breathing down there. Bareskerry roared with laughter. Yes, that was precisely what it meant. Petronius really was a quick-witted little lordie. He asked how they were caught.

'They stick the spear in their jaws and jerk the line, and we start the winch and take in the line. With any luck, the spearbiter is stuck on the other end. When the divers have used all their spears they come up, retrieve them and dive again.'

'It must be beautiful down there,' said Petronius, dreamily.

'Where's that?'

'On the seabed.'

Bareskerry laughed again. 'Wim don't have time to admire the scenery. They have to concentrate on fishing.'

'But wasn't it beautiful when you used to go down?' During all the years Petronius had dreamt of becoming a diver, it had been the underwater landscape that had fascinated him most. He'd seen big colour pictures and he knew it must be like descending into another world where everything was peaceful and gentle and alive.

'Yes,' nodded Bareskerry. 'Yes, in fact it is beautiful. But you must understand, Petronius, that for a wom, the adventure is a reality. It loses the attraction that it may have for a manwom. Menwim always think that what wim do is full of sheroism and splendour. The reality isn't like that. Life is a hard and implacable struggle, Petronius.'

It wasn't without an ulterior motive that Bareskerry said this. She knew that the best thing for Spinnerman Bram was for him to realize how dull and lacking in glamour the life of a seawom was. All the romance associated with the life of a seawom was the invention of menwim.

One of the lines jerked. Petronius began to pull. Bareskerry cleared her throat. 'It's better this way,' she said, starting the winch.

Another line twitched. A ship's-girl rushed forward. Petronius stared down into the water in fascination. Here it came, a shimmering, silver fish with a big fin on its back and a mouth showing three rows of sharp teeth. It gasped. It sounded almost like a little cry, a feeble, hoarse squeak. Petronius felt sorry for it and covered his eyes. He felt slightly unsteady. Bareskerry pulled the fish up in a smooth curve. It lay thrashing with its tail and making small jumps with its body. She pulled out a knife and cut its throat with a single movement. It was still kicking. Its eyes were big and bloodshot. They stood out, staring coldly and accusingly at Petronius.

'But it's still alive!' shouted Petronius.

'Just reflexes,' said Bareskerry.

But Petronius could see that its heart was still beating. 'Is its heartbeat just a reflex, too?'

'You ask a lot of questions . . .'

The ship's-girl took it by the tail and began to work the spear loose. The fish snapped at her hand. Another girl ran foward and removed the spear. Blood ran on the deck. The fish made a leap towards the railing. They picked it up and threw it down through a big hole in the deck.

'It'll be cleaned right away down there and put on ice,' said Bareskerry.

Petronius wondered whether its heart continued to beat when it had been cleaned and lay in his father's casserole.

All the lines were twitching now. Twelve ship's-girls were fully occupied with hauling in the sharks. They worked in shorts, stripped to the waist. Petronius watched their fine breasts, swinging in time with the lithe movements of their muscular arms.

'Here. Now you can try pulling one in.' Bareskerry handed him the line. It was heavier than he'd expected. The fish's mouth emerged, rolling out of the sea, pointing straight at him. He glanced uncertainly at Bareskerry. She was standing with her hands on her back, watching him. She nodded. He pulled hard on the line, lost his balance, and fell backwards.

'No, no!' yelled Bareskerry. The spear swung against the side of the ship and the fish vanished into the water leaving a trail of blood. Petronius was beside himself.

'How's the fish now?' he asked anxiously.

'We've just lost a first class fish, and the only thing that worries you is how the fish is doing!' said Bareskerry good-naturedly.

'I'm sorry,' said Petronius, feeling clumsy and stupid. Deep down, he was fuming. He smiled at Bareskerry to hide his feelings. His whole body was trembling. But Bareskerry brushed it off. 'Goodness, it can happen to the best!'

Bareskerry, of course, had known what would happen. It required long and arduous training to land a spearbiter. Every novice made such mistakes. But Bareskerry wanted Petronius to think that he *couldn't* learn this trade. Fishing was a wom's job, and so it would remain as far as Bareskerry was concerned. That was really its attraction.

'D'you think it'll die?'

'What?'

'D'you think the spearbiter will die?' Petronius couldn't stop thinking of the poor fish.

'It's hard to say. They can live a long time with a wound like that.'

'I don't suppose we'll get any more now,' said Petronius. 'The others will see the blood and disappear.'

Bareskerry laughed. 'No, they're too far down. They won't notice.'

'Maybe it'll swim down and tell them.'

'No. They always conceal themselves when they're injured.'

But within a couple of minutes, all the divers surfaced.

'What the Lucy happened? They all disappeared at once. There was a big shoal down there, just for the taking.'

'So you were right, after all, Petronius,' Bareskerry nodded. 'Typical masculine intuition.'

'Ah, come on! What happened?'

'One got away,' Bareskerry explained.

'Did you let the boy try?'

'It's what I've always said. This is a job for wim!'

The divers were all shouting at the same time, blowing water out of their noses and shaking themselves. Petronius wanted the deck to swallow him up; he'd ruined everything.

'We'll carry on to the north,' Bareskerry ordered, and the divers climbed aboard.

The last diver to surface came over and stood by Petronius. He looked at her uncertainly. Perhaps she was going to tell him off. She looked him straight in the eyes and took off her mask. It was Gro.

Petronius felt faint. The movement of the ship, the

bloody spearbiter and Gro whirled round in his head and he leant against the mast to steady himself. She stood there for a moment piercing him with a glare.

They sailed round Spout to a position on the north side of the island. The fishing continued as before, but yielded little. Gro worked on deck. He watched her slit open the fish's belly and cut into the entrails so the blood flowed. She worked quickly and confidently. Petronius wished he could do the same, be like her. He suddenly saw that she was cutting a tooth out of one of the spearbiters. She got up and came over to him. 'Here!' she said. 'A souvenir.'

It was like the tooth of a saw. Petronius stood looking from the tooth in his hand to Gro, and back again. 'Thank you.'

'That's for having such a beautiful smile.'

She went back to slitting fish bellies.

There was to be a celebration that evening. Petronius was looking forward to it and changed into the clean red skirt he had brought with him. Over it, he wore a tight-fitting yellow blouse of thin silk with short puffed sleeves.

He certainly attracted attention when he stepped into Bareskerry's saloon. To the black-clad wim, he was really a treat to look at. The most they had done to prepare themselves for the party was to wash. Now they suddenly felt rather unkempt and tried to compensate by pulling up chairs for Petronius, asking him what he wanted to drink, offering him cigarettes, lighting them for him, fetching ashtrays, asking him how he liked life at sea and complimenting him on his plaits.

Petronius had never in his life been the centre of so much attention. For a moment he felt like the most beautiful manwom in the world.

'May I have the first dance?' one of the divers asked. It was the one who had yelled at him for dropping the line. Her name was Vita.

'Oh no, I'm having that,' said Moona, one of the ship's-girls.

'No, I am — because I asked before any of you,' said Gro.

'No, I think it's mine,' growled Bareskerry, laughing, and gracefully she swept Petronius out with her onto the floor and swung into a spirited seawom's waltz. The others stood around them in a ring, clapping in time and singing together.

> *A seawom tosses on the rolling blue*
> *With a hey and a ho!*
> *She battles the waves the wild night through*
> *With a hey and a ho!*
> *In every weather — through thunder and gales,*
> *Home to the lad that she loves she sails*
> *With a hey and a ho!*

Things were lively. They toasted one another and played records and Petronius was kept constantly on his feet. Then the gong rang and the cook marched in with ten great bowls of spearbiter stew. The wim were famished after their day's work and threw themselves onto the food. Petronius was amazed how much they could put away. He couldn't manage more than a single helping. One of the ship's-girls suggested that he ought to eat more to get fatter, but then Bareskerry intervened and asked that they refrain from being cheeky at the table.

The party continued with drinking and singing and music. The seawim began to regale one another with stories.

'Well, I once knew a fellow who could never get it up,' Vita began. 'It didn't matter how hard you tried, or what you did, it just hung their like a dead herring. Then one day . . .'

'Hey! There are lordies present!'

They all looked at Petronius, who reddened.

'He won't mind. We're not going to put on airs for him, are we?'

'I'll drink to that.'

'So one day we were visited by this vixen terrier which trotted busily around the apartment, wagging its tail. And that did it. Zip! There it was, standing straight up!'

The wim roared with laughter.

'Since then I always take a dog with me when I go to see him,' Vita concluded between guffaws.

'It certainly wasn't like that with a lord I used to know. He'd get a hard-on thirty times a day. He was just a sex maniac; that's all there was to it. In the end I got fed up with it. I couldn't get anything done when I had to go and rub it every half hour. Who could keep that up for long? So one day I threw a bucket of cold water between his legs. Plop, it went, and it just dangled there. I don't think I've ever laughed so much! Ha, ha, ha!'

They all shrieked with laughter. Petronius glanced at Gro. She was laughing, too. Even Gro.

'The worst I've seen was in Pax. We shared one between three of us. He was really full of it, this one! He came every time. We collected it all in a bowl and made soup with it and served it to him. And d'you know what? He drank it!'

'Good lady!'

'What a manwom!'

'Some of them get so excited it dribbles!'

'Once when I was in Pax I suddenly found two whores walking towards me with erections. D'you know what I did? I grabbed them both by the prick at the same time, squeezed as hard as I could and said, "Hallo, nice to meet you!", shaking them vigorously up and down, and I went on my way. They just stood there gaping at me. I don't suppose they'd ever experienced anything like it.'

'Ha, ha! That's a good one.'

The wim's faces shone with sweat and excitement in the dim light. One of them had begun to move closer and closer to Petronius. She stroked his cheek. 'Yes, indeed. There's a bit of fluff coming!' she said.

'Hands off!' hissed another. They all howled with laughter. Gro pulled Petronius out onto the dance floor.

He didn't dare look at her while they were dancing. He just felt the warmth of her body and was happy. No one was clapping to the rhythm any longer. They were watching the lucky one and drinking. When the number ended, four of them rushed up together for the next dance. They collided.

Two of them remained standing in the middle of the floor, glaring at each other with clenched fists. There was only a millimetre between their nipples.

'You swiped a spearbiter from under my nose today, you creep!' She grabbed the other wom by the collar of her shirt.

'Idiot! You weren't quick enough with your harpoon. I always get more than you do!'

'You liar! I got thirty eight last time!'

'I got forty two!' She tweaked the other's nose.

A fist shot out. Petronius jumped out of the way. A general fracas ensued. Bottles and glasses were knocked over. A chair flew across the room. Someone shouted, 'Let go now!' and someone else, 'Let go yourself!', and the two who had started it were bellowing, 'She's going to get it!' and 'By Lucy! She's going to shut her mouth!'

'Idiots!' roared a voice. Liz Bareskerry was standing in the doorway. The wim stopped fighting, brushed off their clothes and started picking up any glasses that were still in one piece. 'What's all this, I'm hardly out of the door and you start tearing the ship apart!'

The wim said nothing. Bareskerry went over to Petronius and shoved him towards the door. As they went out, she turned and said menacingly, 'There'll be consequences; I promise you!'

They went into Bareskerry's cabin and she offered him a cigarette. His hand was shaking slightly. She stretched out on her bunk and looked at him.

'Come here.'

Petronius sat on the edge of the bunk, embarrassed. Bareskerry smiled at him.

'I've always thought a lot of you, Petronius,' she said. She sounded confident. She must have known many men-wim, been around. She'd seen Petronius grow up. He felt at home with her. Suddenly he felt a finger on the side of his head. 'You're really a very sweet and charming boy. You'll be a fine fellow in time.' She leant towards him and kissed him. Petronius clamped his mouth shut. To his surprise, she immediately drew back, got up and said, affronted, 'Oh well, then, if you don't *want* to . . .'

When the seawim got back from fishing the next day, they said even more earnestly than before, 'Menwim at sea are nothing but trouble.'

The little rose of the slums

One winter's day, Bram came home to tell her housebound that he was going to have a baby. Radiant with joy, she embraced him.

'You're in luck. Now you won't have to be on your own here during the day.'

Christopher freed himself from her embrace and looked away. He wished he hadn't stopped taking the pill. Although she had virtually asked him to. She'd said several times that she thought the pill reduced his sexual appetite.

Christopher Lizdaughter had been given fatherhood-protection at a very young age. He remembered how jubilant he'd been when she had first told him he was going to be a father. It meant he hadn't been a casual affair for her. With Ruth Bram as his fatherhood-protector, he became part of an old, respected, and well-to-do family.

Christopher had had a tough childhood. He'd been conceived during casual intercourse at a maidmen's ball. His father, Rudrik Lizdaughter, had played for high stakes. His highest aspiration had been to escape poverty, and to get away from the slum district where he lived with his paternal grandfather. Then he had met Sue Alespice at the maidmen's ball and it had been love at first sight as far as he was concerned. Sue Alespice was from Pax and she spoke Egalian with an interesting accent which Rudrik found irresistible. She offered him exotic drinks and money cascaded out of her pockets. She told him that her mother owned one of the biggest firms in Pax and that she had left Pax because she loved the sea. For this reason, she had bought a big villa on the west side of Lux, and now she was merely waiting for a suitable housebound who could create a cosy nest.

For Rudrik, Sue Alespice represented adventure, a taste of the alluring world where money means nothing for it grows on trees. He didn't tell Sue that he didn't take the pill.

Rudrik counted the days and waited excitedly for Sue to come and tell him the good news so he could move into her beautiful house on Lux. Sue had said, after all, that she'd never seen such a fine round belly as his, nor a smaller cock, and she'd never had a better orgasm than with him. And she'd certainly been around.

Late one evening in the autumn, Sue Alespice knocked on his door. But it wasn't the Sue he'd met at the maid-men's ball. She was wearing an old threadbare shirt and a pair of trousers several sizes too big. But the worst thing was, she no longer spoke with an accent.

Rudrik was so bewildered, he just stood there staring at her.

'How about letting me in before my fingers freeze off?'

Rudrik opened the door and she marched in. Grandad was sitting in the corner, crocheting. He peered over the frames of his spectacles, smiled good-naturedly and nodded at her. Sue pointed to him and turned to Rudrik.

'Does he have to be in here?'

'But we only have one room!'

Grandad put down his crochet work and got up with difficulty. 'I'll go for a walk,' he said. 'I've got to go out and look for the cat anyway.'

'You're going to have a baby,' Sue hissed as soon as they were alone. Rudrik looked at her in horror. This news, which he had anticipated so eagerly, was suddenly a catastrophe.

'C . . .can't you get rid of it?'

'Ha!' she said. She began to pace back and forth on the floor. 'I've been thinking about that too.' She turned quickly and looked at him in triumph. 'But I don't think I will.'

'Why not?'

'I've thought it over. Worked it out. First, I get eight months leave at full pay. Then I reap a bonus of five thousand dollables. This is my third child, you see. Little

Susanno at Number Seven is also mine, if you really want to know. And then I've got one with a rich lordy on the Moonhill who lives on his mother's inheritance. So — I think I'll go through with this pregnancy, too.'

Rudrik couldn't believe his ears. He knew, of course, that there were wim who lived off having children. But he'd never imagined that he would be one of the unfortunate fathers. After this, his chances of finding a well-off wom were as good as ruined. He would have to work and slave for the rest of his life, just like his father, who had died of tuberculosis when he was nine, and like his grandfather. He would never get away from the tenements.

'But . . . but what about the firm in Pax and the villa on Lux?'

She laughed derisively. 'Ha! As you can see for yourself, I was lying. I'm an ordinary docker. I load and unload grain between pregnancies. Now in fact I'd come to the conclusion that the job is actually less strenuous than these everlasting pregnancies. At work, at least we get breaks. But there's no way you can take a break from carrying a baby. Have you ever thought about that, Rudrik Lizdaughter? No, by Lucy, it's a full time job. You menwim never think about that when you go on fucking till you squirt at the maidmen's balls. All you think of is getting an economically secure future sewn up. You were an idiot to believe everything I said. Anyway, you conned me! D'you know what the penalty is for men who don't bother to use a prophylactic?'

Rudrik foresaw giddying sums of money which neither he nor his grandfather would ever be able to save, no matter how much they cleaned and scrubbed. He hung his head.

'By the way, I'm having an affair with a decrepit old bloke I'm thinking of giving fatherhood-protection. He's a single heirass. With any luck his sperm's lost its fizz by now. But when it comes down to it, I'm a very respectable wom, Spinnerman Lizdaughter. I'd never dream of letting him bring up another man's child. In fact I'm not interested in seeing your daughter in my house.'

'Or son.'

'Yes, or son, then, for Lucy's sake, if we're really going to split hairs!'

About eight months later, Rudrik was asked to go to the paternal welfare centre to collect his son. Rudrik, who was very young and inexperienced, did as he was told, and went.

And there lay little Christopher. Rudrik's heart melted as soon as he saw him. He picked him up and rocked him in his arms and whispered to him that everything would work out.

He'd expected Sue to be there. But she'd left a message saying she never wanted to see him again. He was obliged to sign a form stating that the child was now to be handed over into his care, as well as to make a sworn statement in the presence of witnesses that he was the real father. An official then informed him that Sue Alespice had a legal right to see the child whenever she wished and that Rudrik Lizdaughter could never move away from Egalsund without Sue Alespice's consent. The official looked up every now and then from the document she was reading to glare piercingly at Rudrik. He noticed that she was pregnant.

He was then sent into another room where a clerk said, 'That'll be a 500 dollables fine for P-deception.'

'P . . .P . . .P-deception?'

'Yes. It stands for "prophylactic", or "pill" or whatever you want.'

'"Prick", for example.'

Rudrik turned round. A wom carrying a child grinned at him. The clerk grinned back at her.

'Can I help you?'

'I just want to leave this chatterbox. I've had him two weeks over time.'

The clerk obligingly held open the door to the next department for her.

'So there we are, Spn Lizdaughter. That'll be a 500 dollables fine for stating falsely that you were using a contraceptive. You know of course that you must go and register at the P-office so that you won't be allocated fatherhood. You aren't publicly registered, so you are considered an available sperm donor. 500 dollables, please.'

'But . . but I don't have that much money!' Rudrik was beside himself with shame and embarrassment.

'You can pay it off in instalments. We're not inhuwom.'

He had to sign yet another form. He was given ten paying-in slips, then shown out.

Rudrik grew more and more fond of his son. At school, his favourite subject had been childcare. Moreover, Grandad helped him. He had been a playschool teacher in his youth and knew a lot about children. So Christopher grew up with no lack of love. But they were poor and short of space. Rudrik worked in a cake factory. He sat at a conveyor belt for thirty years, piping green icing onto little round cakes. Sometimes he managed to bring a few cakes home, and Christopher ate them with a voracious appetite, and grew up into a sweet and chubby little boy. He was considered the darling of the district when he went skipping along with his school satchel.

Now and then, his cheerful spirit was eclipsed, when girls on the street shouted 'whoreling' after him, or 'D'you know why Christopher has to use his father's damename?' He would go home crying and ask his father why they said these things. And his father would comfort him and say it was because they were stupid, and Grandad would bring out the mechanical building set and they would build bridges and cranes and towers, and Christopher would smile and laugh again. When he was older, Rudrik told him everything.

Grandad and Rudrik soon noticed that Christopher was mechanically minded and had a good head for figures. The North Bridge was being built while Christopher was growing up and he would stand down there for hours, watching and holding long discussions with the engineers over their detailed drawings until they were scratching their heads in bewilderment.

There was, however, never any question of prolonging his education beyond the obligatory minimum. Christopher would have to go out and work as soon as he was old enough, like everybody else of his age in the slum district.

The girls mostly got jobs in the harbour and some went to sea. Christopher was taken on by a hair dressing salon where he specialised in beard-styling and hair-loss treatments. This was where he was working when he met Ruth Bram.

They first met at a maidmen's ball. Christopher had saved enough for the ticket by going round to genteel old lordies living up on the Moonhill and treating them for baldness. It paid astonishingly well. 'I suppose there must be a lot of moon-like pates up on the Moonhill,' Ruth said later. And Christopher smiled adoringly.

Ruth Bram and Christopher Lizdaughter had noticed each other immediately. Ruth Bram hadn't been quick enough, however. And before she knew it, Christopher had disappeared into a maidman-room with another wom. Bram never quite got over this, for it injured her pride and she felt it as an attack on her sexual prow. In moments of ill temper she regarded this as evidence of Christopher's frivolity and his unduly flirtatious manner. And even though Christopher later assured her on many occasions that it was her he had wanted, she hadn't been able to prevent a pang of bitterness whenever she thought about it.

'But *I* couldn't have gone up with *you*, could I?' said Christopher consolingly whenever Bram succumbed to an attack of jealousy as a result of thinking about this episode. No. They could both see the absurdity of that. 'You might not even have wanted me, otherwise. And then we would never have ended up living together. So it was *just as well* I didn't show any interest in you then.' And they would feel reconciled and happy again.

Afterwards she began to court him. Ruth Bram was no snob and it bothered her not in the least that she had to court her mastrass in the poor quarter. On the contrary, she felt as though she had found a rare and precious rose in dismal surroundings. And she felt a growing conviction that she would transplant this rose and, with her own hands, make it grow and thrive. There were also several previous instances in her family of wim plucking such roses from the popular thicket. 'It's just a way of refreshing the genes of the old landed gentry,' her great-grandmother would say.

They had had a very chaste relationship for a long time. Christopher had learnt the lessons of his father's fate, and had resolved never to have an unprotected child. Ruth Bram had therefore publicly promised him fatherhood-protection when she finally got him into the oak woods on Lux, where Petronius was conceived.

Christopher Bram had warmly and lovingly embraced the role of housebound. He could never feel anything but grateful that he had found a better life than his father. He did sometimes feel, nevertheless, a pang of regret that he had never had a chance to pursue his interest in mechanics. He mentioned this to Ruth from time to time, but she merely smiled wryly and said that there was nothing to stop his studying mechanics as much as he wanted in his free time.

But when did he really have any free time? As long as he had had fatherhood-protection he had had small children to look after, it seemed to him. When Petronius was eighteen months old, Ba had arrived. And Ba looked as though she was never really going to grow up enough to look after herself. Even though she was now a big lass, she never stopped calling for her dad. She was such a handful. And now here was Ruth, radiant with joy, telling him he was going to have another baby.

He had secretly hoped she would be satisfied with the two they had. There was no social pressure on Ruth to have another child. And now what would happen? Ruth would get leave from her job for the duration of her pregnancy, if she wanted it, so he would have her under his feet at home all day. And when she finally went back to work, there would be the exhausting period of nursing. Christopher sighed and said nothing.

'Aren't you pleased?' Bram burst out, hurt. 'She'll be a lovely little baby, I'm sure.'

Christopher turned impetuously towards her. 'Can't you stop it?'

'"*Stop it*?"' bellowed Bram. 'What sort of a father talks about his future daughter as *it*? Do you think I got myself pregnant in order to have an *abortion*? Menwim ought to make sure that abortions are never necessary. And if they don't, they must take the consequences. A life has come into being inside me. Menwim who refuse to accept their responsibilities are a disgrace to society.'

'I was looking forward to a little time . . . a little time to myself, Ruth.'

'Time to yourself? But you've got all day while I'm at work. I've always wondered where your time goes. We can always get a cleaning lordy, if you want. Besides, you know how badly Ba wants a little sister. You should think about that too.'

'Little sister!' said Christopher, depairingly. He hid his face in his hands.

'Christopher . . . Sometimes I don't understand you. I was at the doctor's today. And all day I've been looking forward to coming home and telling you. I thought that you might possibly have been slightly embarrassed by your potency, but I thought you would be proud and pleased that a life is growing inside me. And now . . .'

She was hurt and angry. He could see she really was hurt. He felt a sudden tenderness for her. What kind of manwom was he? Ought he not to be the first to embrace her, to caress her belly, to watch it grow, to welcome the fruit of their love with open arms, to love the child, to love her, to take care of them all? Who else would look after them? What would happen to them if he turned his back on them? Neglecting them selfishly — God, he was an idiot! He should never have said those things. Now he had hurt her. He felt ashamed. He was a big egoist. He was a bad father and an unloving manwom. How could he make up for it? He was just about to say that he was longing for the birth of his new daughter and that he loved both her and Ruth, when Ruth interrupted his thoughts.

'How can you say you want more time to yourself? What about me? What does it mean to have a family? What do I do all day? Do I ever have any time to myself? The only thing in the world that matters to me is to mean something to other people — otherwise all I'd be is an inhuwom robot.

I spend all day working for you and the kids. And you make sure that things are nice for us here at home. And then you complain when we're going to have another baby! That's the way of nature, Christopher, my love. I give birth and you receive. After all it is menwim who beget children!'

Spn Owlmoss teaches according to Directive No.287

'After all, it is menwim who beget children,' Spn Owlmoss replied, looking out over 5B. 'Every living thing on earth is constantly drawn towards its origin. All the processes of terrestrial life can be seen as a great cycle. A cycle is a circular movement.'

Spn Owlmoss drew a circle on the blackboard. 'The circle, or ring, is the most perfect of all geometric figures. It lacks nothing. In the circle, complete balance reigns.'

He paused for a moment, partly because he was entranced by the thought of the circle's perfection, partly because he wanted to see whether they were asleep. They sat quietly. But apart from little, chubby Fandango, and Ann Moonhill, it was impossible to tell whether they were listening or thinking about something else.

'The circle is therefore the symbol of wom. She who bears the great cycle of nature within her. But in the civilization that wom has created, the circle has a new and extended meaning. The relationship of father, mother and child can be written into this circle. The origin of the child's life lies in the father's sperm cells and the mother's egg cells, where life takes root, inside the mother.'

He drew the father's sperm cell at the top of the circle, as a tiny dot, and the mother's ovum as a big thick ring a little below the middle of the circular line. 'In here . . . the child comes into being . . . the foetus . . . and eventually . . . the child comes out.'

He drew in the child on the circle in the form of a heart, two thirds of the way round from the starting point.

'And the father, the origin of the sperm, the seed, takes the child in his arms. The child returns, so to speak, to its origin. This is not how it is in the animal world. This is the achievement of civilization. We can show this relationship by drawing three lines between the three points. Which gives us a triangle in the circle.'

Spn Owlmoss drew a triangle in the circle.

'The triangle is the symbol of civilization, which is contained by the circle, the symbol of wom. These figures together — the triangle inscribed in the circle — are the symbol of the fact that civilization is the creation of wom, the symbol of the fact that all true culture is the culture of wim!'

Spn Owlmoss looked up at his drawing with satisfaction and awe. 'It is beautiful. Infinitely beautiful and perfect. This is the underlying reason why everyone feels so deeply moved when they see pictures of little Donna Jessica in her father's arms.'

'But couldn't we just as well say that the egg cell is the origin of the child?' asked Ann Moonhill.

Spn Owlmoss was so excited to find someone had been paying attention, red blotches appeared on his cheeks. 'The egg cell can be compared with the life-force itself,' he said. At the thought of the miracle of life, he began to speak in lofty terms. 'The creative principle. The egg cell is both the germ and the soil. The sperm cell is like a stimulant or an irritant, rather like a pinprick. And when the egg cell feels this stimulation, it decides to set the process of life in motion. And like the earth, the egg cell will generously give everything back to itself. That is why the father gets the child in his arms when the process is complete.'

'Then why is it the mother cat that looks after the kittens? The father doesn't even know whether they are his kittens! Sometimes he even kills them, just like that,' said Wolfram Sax, who had five cats at home.

'All huwom civilization consists in removing people from the primitive animal state. The task of civilization is to remedy nature's injustice. We've been through that before.'

'But didn't you just use nature to explain why menwim are meant to look after children?' asked Ba.

'No. This is where we have to distinguish between myth

and reality. Myth is poetry which makes reality beautiful and comprehensible in all its mystery. We create an image as a superstructure covering the things we know are right in order to show more clearly how right and proper it is for a mother to lay the fruit and gift of love in a father's secure, caring arms.'

Spn Owlmoss was finding it slightly difficult to keep talking. His great misfortune in life — that he had never himself been made the object of this wonderful and infinite bounty — appeared more clearly to him now he was obliged to explain life's blessings to his pupils. He cleared his throat. 'Let's look more closely at the reality behind this poetic cycle.' He looked at them. For once they were sitting quietly at their desks. It was important to convey this absolutely correctly. Spn Owlmoss saw Principal Bosomby's imposing double chins in his mind's eye, and began.

'Nature sometimes exhibits a great, divine wisdom. The most important sexual organs in the huwom race — the wom's sexual organs — are therefore in a protected position inside her body. This shows us that it would be more serious for a wom to injure her sexual organs than for a manwom to do the same. He therefore carries his externally, since we can't say it really matters very much what happens to them. That is why the manwom is called the vulnerable sex. He uses these organs of his to squirt infinite numbers of sperms into the wom's body.'

Spn Owlmoss regarded them gravely. Someone tittered. Someone else went, 'Sssh!'

'Infinite numbers,' he repeated. 'The reason for this is that the sperm cells are so infinitely minute that they have to be present in huge numbers if anything is to become of a single one of them. They are the smallest cells there are. Modern scientists have even questioned whether we can call them "cells". In some modern works, the words, "dregs" or "specks" are used instead. No she-animal we know of can produce anything so immensely tiny as the mafele of the huwom species can with his sperm cells. They are so tiny that sixty thousand of them will fit in a square millimetre. The dot I've drawn on the blackboard is therefore an enormous enlargement. The egg cell on the other hand, is about the size of a dot, or a full stop. That is, slightly smaller than the one I've drawn. My diagram therefore gives a very distorted picture of the relative sizes of the ovum and the sperm cells — or sperm dregs. When the egg decides the creative process is to begin, two hundred million sperms set out towards it. Two . . . hundred . . . million.'

Spn Owlmoss wrote, 200,000,000, in big numerals next to the dot on the triangle.

'They look like little snakes with heads,' he continued. 'Here's an example magnified thirty billion times.'

He drew a sperm cell with a black head wriggling away. He contemplated it with satisfaction.

'As you can see, it also resembles a tadpole. So, two hundred million of these tadpole-like dregs wriggle off to do battle over an egg. The sperms have to compete hard to win the egg — just as we see in our society, where menwim compete to win wim. While the battle continues, the egg cell lies there watching in a state of great peace and contentment. Finally the head of one of the sperms gets through to the egg. Of course the sperm cell doesn't have much idea of what's going on. Like certain animals, the ostrich, for example, they think that as long as their head is safe, so is the rest of them. The egg snips off the rest of the sperm cell right away, so the tail is left outside. Because once this one sperm is safe inside the egg, the egg surrounds itself with a membrane which stops any of the onehundredandninety-ninemillionninehundredandninetythousandninehundredand-ninetynine other sperms from getting in and upsetting the process of creation.'

Little chubby Fandango put up his hand.

'Yes, Fandango.'

'What happens to all the ones that don't get in then?'

'Well, they're superfluous now, and they die. The winner — the one sperm that got through — loses its identity. That means it isn't itself any more. This is because it's lost its tail. Without its tail it no longer has any independent existence, but it is nourished and protected by the egg in exactly the same way that the mature manwom finds fatherhood-protection with a wom. In return, the sperm is allowed to live. There's a good analogy in this. An analogy is something which is like something else. The manwom needs a home. On his own he is, by definition, homeless. In looking for a home, he has to compete with hundreds of other menwim. When he finds one, the wom keeps him there, provides him with nourishment and protects him against all harm.'

Ann suddenly put up her hand and began speaking before Spn Owlmoss could say, 'Yes, Ann?'

'So what happens to the menwim who don't get into anywom's home then?'

A titter went through the class, but Ba hammered her desk lid as a sign that she wanted to hear more, and the class quickly fell silent. Spn Owlmoss ignored the question.

'That's why we can say that, from nature's point of view, the manwom's place is in the home. It's . . .'

'But you said we couldn't use nature to explain civilization,' interrupted Ba.

'Yes. This is where we have to be careful. The fact that many menwim protest about it nowadays doesn't alter the fact that it is the wom who is the lifegiver and protector in life, and that the manwom would perish without her — whereas the reverse is not true. The sperm has no corresponding capacity to provide nourishment and protection for them both. Nature will never be able to change the fact that a child cannot be brought into existence in a manwom's sexual organs. I dread to think what would happen if a foetus were to develop in a manwom's shamebag. It's much too small and insubstantial for the creation of any form of life. The foetus would burst it.'

Spn Owlmoss felt he was on safe ground now. He was certain that he was teaching one hundred per cent in accordance with the last directive, No.287. The fearsome image of Bosomby's double chins had almost faded from his mind's eye when he continued.

'Throughout nature, from the lowest to the highest forms of animal life, we can see manifestations of the fact that creatures of the mafele sex are a superfluous luxury.

With spiders, ants and bees, of course, the mafele is killed, or dies, when he has mated with the fele. He performs the one purpose he has been put into the world to fulfil — to beget offspring. And then he has to die. What would the community want with him? Admittedly, with bees he's allowed to live one season in complete idleness. And we can see there how he contributes nothing whatsoever to the existence of bee society, but merely lies there, idly. So he has to pay with his life afterwards. With ants, the mafele who don't manage to mate with the fele are killed at once — just as the redundant sperm cells perish in the huwom being. Even if the fele ants don't get hold of them and kill them, they'll die anyway, as they have no clue how to feed themselves. So they starve to death. And we can see how these societies are ruled by a giant fele, the queen, who makes sure the species survives.'

'Is that why lots of menwim who don't have fatherhood-protection are poor and starving here in Egalia?' asked Wolfram.

'That's right Wolfram. Menwim find it difficult to feed themselves.'

'That's because there's a class difference,' snorted Ann. 'It is! That's what Mum said.'

'I'm not going to start discussing that. All I can say is that in all known societies, it is the menwim who have to work hardest to feed themselves.'

Spn Owlmoss stopped for a moment. He felt something stir inside him. That was right! Men worked hardest. That could hardly be in accordance with Directive No.287. I'd better change the subject, he thought, find a safer topic. Fish! he thought.

'With many species of fish, however, it is the father who looks after the young. There is of course an explanation for this strange phenomenon. It's because the young fish don't develop inside the mother, but both the fertilization itself and the gestation take place outside her. Here the father immediately understands his role. With some species — the spearbiter, for example — he is the one who builds the nest and protects them during their earliest life. This is the reason that fish, and the spearbiter in particular, have become a symbol of our motherland, Egalia, a society where tasks are shared equally and rationally between the sexes.'

Little chubby Fandango had his hand in the air again.

'What is it, Fandango?'

'But . . . well, it isn't equal with us. You just said that it was the father who had to look after the young, and . . . '

'Yes, precisely. Just as with the fish — actually the most intelligent creatures in the animal queendom. And nor do we, of course, simply kill off our mafeles because they're useless. Civilization has also sought to make use of the mafele of our species. That is the true greatness of our society. That the mafeles don't occupy the useless place they have in nature. So we can say that in our society — in huwom society — the menwim, too, have a certain justification for their existence. That is to say, they have a certain right to live. Nonetheless, we can see that we'll never manage to civilize mafele huwoms completely. In fact most menwim probably know instinctively that their only purpose is decorative and ornamental. And that is the real reason they pay more attention to their appearance than wim.'

'I thought it was just because they're stupid,' said Ba.

'Well, in a way, we can say that too. In a certain way, being there only to look decorative can make one rather stupid. We can see the same phenomenon in the animal world.'

'What does "phenomenon" mean?'

'"Phenomenon" means "thing" — something which happens, we might say. And in the animal world, we can see, for example, how the lioness has a gorgeous mane, but does nothing but sit there all day, basking in the sun and roaring loudly, while the fele gets food for her family. Similarly, we can see how many mafele mammals have fine antlers which have no other purpose than to get snagged wherever they go, just as menwim's skirts always get caught on things when they go walking in the fields or woods. But above all, we have the queendom of the birds. Here there is no end to the brightly coloured feathers the cocks display to attract the hen. So we can see why feathers have become more and more popular as a way of decorating menwim's clothing, especially in recent times. The cock bird never thinks of anything but dressing up and doesn't know the meaning of preserving the species, so he never discovers that he could, for example, sit on the eggs. If he has to, he might just manage to find some food for the fledgelings, once the hen has hatched them.'

'On the other hand the cock can go "cockadoodledoo",' shouted Ann.

'Indeed,' replied Spn Owlmoss. 'An utterly meaningless statement. When huwoms civilize the animals, they'll have to do something about all this. What actual use is a cock or a bull or a boar or a ram or a stallion? Why is everyone on the farm so disappointed whenever one is born? All they're good for is to be slaughtered. To provide meat for huwoms. A few are kept for breeding, and they are often so troublesome they have to be kept tethered in their own enclosure. With the feles, though, it is different. Once again, we see that it is the fele of the species that provides the very sustenance of life, so that purely sex-determined products, such as milk and eggs, can be of use to huwoms. The mafeles have no equivalent contribution to make, and so, naturally, they are worth less. On the other hand, we can see that, apart from their breeding function, they are used for the purposes of mere entertainment, for the amusement of huwoms. In the past, there were bullfights and cockfights. Today we have the Grand Crowing Contest for cocks, and the popular boar races in the autumn. Apart from that they're useless.'

Spn Owlmoss suddenly heard a loud snigger from the back of the class and caught sight of a slip of paper passing between the desks. He marched down, grabbed the note and opened it. Written on it in big letters was the instruction, 'PASS THIS ON'. Underneath it said, 'Wonder why Owlmoss hasn't been identified as one of those useless mafele mammals. Perhaps he's going to compete in the Grand Crowing Contest in the autumn?' Spn Owlmoss looked up from the note and tried desperately to maintain his dignity. He was speechless with fury. A thousand confused thoughts ran through his mind. Had the whole lesson been a waste of time? Or was this precisely what they were *supposed* to get out of being taught in accordance with Directive No. 287? He drew a breath to speak. He was interrupted.

'Why have you never got fatherhood-protection, Spn Owlmoss?' asked Ba.

He turned scarlet. Somebody giggled, others said shut up. Then there was quiet. The class was looking at him. An answer was required. Even though it was said flippantly, it demanded a reply. Spn Owlmoss swallowed.

'Wim are cleverer than menwim. They are more intelligent and more efficient. The wom is the born leader.'

'What's that got to do with it?' It was Ba again.

'It has to do with the fact that the wom therefore has no desire to meet her superior in any field. Even though the wom is better, and above all more practically equipped in most areas, there is, nevertheless, one area where she is not altogether superior — physical strength.' He was away now. It was as though Directive No.287 had been blown out of his mind.

'Now physical strength, it is true, is reckoned to be a very feminine quality. That is why the wom, being smaller, does much harder physical training than the manwom. Just think of the difference between boys' and girls' gymnastics. Girls do weightlifting and put the shot and do cross-country running and hurdling, while the boys learn how to move gracefully, so they will be nice to look at, and play gentle ball games. This is a good example of an area where we try to remedy nature's injustice. All the same, there are always some of the biggest and strongest menwim left over who are stronger than most wim. These menwim hardly ever get fatherhood-protection. I am one such manwom.'

It cost Spn Owlmoss considerable effort to say these words. In fact he had never said anything of the sort so directly to anyone before. In fact he could consider himself lucky to have found such a good job as he had. Most menwim of his size were employed in the hardest jobs there were, in the cleaning troops, the mending gangs or the kitchen brigades. Or they were sent to Palluria.

While he was growing up, he had done everything he could to avoid developing his physical strength. Mostly he had sat at home with his father, doing needlework. That didn't help. When he was thirteen, he beat his mother at armwrestling, and for a fortnight, old Principal Owlmoss was in such a bad temper that her pupils quaked at the sight of her. In spite of this, he still hoped then that some wom would have him, and he did everything he could to conceal his strength. He had compliantly submitted to any wom who wanted to go to bed with him — there weren't so many — and afterwards wild rumours would circulate about what an enormous cock he had. He once heard that a wom he had never been to bed with at all had said that it was half a yard long and four inches across when erect.

Whenever fights broke out around him, he never intervened, though it cut him to the quick that people were unkind to one another. When heavy things had to be moved, he never offered to help, though at heart he was the very soul of helpfulness. And in gym lessons, he was given bad marks for moving clumsily, as though his muscles were in the way.

But no matter what he did to overcome it, and to hide it, everyone could see that he was one of those sexless, hefty menwim that no wom would pick up — and no wom would ever dream of having in her *house*.

'Are you really strong, then?' asked Ba.

'I could smash this desk with my fist, if I wanted to.'

Spn Owlmoss was surprised by his own words. The class began to chuckle. Imagine Spn Owlmoss smashing his desk to bits. The thought really was irresistibly funny.

'But I've always felt that my big, strong, manwom's hands were meant to hold a little child and protect it against all harm.'

The class was laughing louder now. Somehow, something had gone wrong. They were embarrassed because he had confided his misfortune to them, just like that. They were embarrassed and they found the thought of Spn Owlmoss's big, powerful body disgusting. And because they were embarrassed, and knew he was telling the truth — so that in a way he became a huwom being to them, not merely a histrionic creature of the teacher's desk, but a huwom being with feelings and a fate — they began to snigger stupidly at one another and didn't know what to say.

Spn Owlmoss realized he was no longer in control of the situation. He regretted what he had said. Now everything was back to normal. The same lack of attention in the class. Things went on among them that he had no control over. He had never felt at ease in the company of the other teachers in the staff room. They regarded him, he knew, in the same way as his pupils. Only they didn't snigger. He felt closer to his pupils, nonetheless, because they were forced to sit there, because they were young and, in a way, innocently silly. They could still learn. Or at least some of them could. Perhaps there was at least one soul somewhere in the class who knew what he was talking about, and felt similarly. Just one would make it worthwhile. One day, he would know. That was why he had never given up completely.

They were mumbling and whispering now, and giggling. He thought he caught a word; a sibilant — three syllables. A three-syllable word beginning with a sibilant. Had he heard correctly?

'Say it! Go on!' he heard someone whisper.

'Nah.' There was stifled laughter. 'Why don't you?'

Perhaps they were interested after all and wanted to know more. He would tell them anything he knew. Even about himself. If he could only make contact with them. A teacher should be open to her children. He had always believed that. 'Is there something you want to know?' he asked tentatively.

'Yes!' said Ann Moonhill, loudly and clearly. 'That little fellow with freckles and red hair — what's his name — *Cyp*rian — are you his father?'

'Yes, he looks just like you!' said someone.

'To a P,' said someone else, more quietly.

A violent crash reached the ears of 5B. Spn Owlmoss had smashed his desk to matchwood.

Petronius reaches his sixteenth birthday

'And then he smashed his whole desk to pieces with a single blow!' Ba said jubilantly, looking from one end of the dining table to the other in triumph. She reached for another sausage.

'That's the worst thing I . . .' Ruth Bram banged the table with her clenched fist, making the plates jump.

'Good job you're not as strong as Spn Owlmoss,' mumbled Petronius.

His mother glared at him. 'What did you say?' she asked, threateningly.

'Nothing.' Petronius looked down at the table.

'Yes, he did!' shouted Ba. 'He said, it's a good job . . .'

'Be quiet, Ba!' interrupted Christopher. 'Remember it's Petronius's birthday today. Now let's be nice.'

'Nice is for mice.'

'Why don't we start on the birthday cake?' asked Christopher. He knew that diversionary tactics were the best strategy with both children and wim. 'Petronius first.'

He stood up, cut a large slice off the pineapple cake and balanced it over to Petronius's plate. The slice sank slightly and fell gently onto its side.

'Ha! Now Petronius won't get fatherhood-protection,' yelled Ba happily. 'Now it's my turn. Isn't it, Dad?'

She handed her plate to him. Her piece remained standing upright. 'See! That's how it's meant to be,' she said, holding it under Petronius's nose. 'I bet Petronius ends up like Spn Owlmoss when he's older.'

'If I do, you can be sure I'll give *you* a good going over.'

'Then I'll just take out my PS, and that'll be the end of you.'

'What on earth are you talking about, Ba?' asked Christopher.

'In the old days all the wim used to carry a PS — it stands for prick-scissors, if you really want to know. And if any big menwim bothered them they pulled them out. Snip!' she laughed. 'That's what we learned in history.'

'But that's dreadful! Is it true, Ruth?'

Ruth nodded, chewing pensively. 'The practice was abolished in the year 213 after Donna Jessica,' she said.

'When I get into Parliament, I'll get it reintroduced,' declared Ba. 'And then I'll do it to Petronius.'

Ruith Bram cleared her throat, knowingly. 'You'll find that difficult, my girl. At that time there was a need for the PS, because there was no safe way of taming menwim. In those days menwim used to attack wim from time to time. But of course that would be unthinkable today.'

'Why?' Petronius looked up from his half-eaten piece of cake.

'"Why?"', his mother repeated sarcastically. 'Because it *is* unthinkable, obviously. Or perhaps you can imagine a big strong manwom suddenly attacking a wom who was much weaker than he was, and wouldn't have a chance?'

No. That was indeed inconceivable. Petronius went back to eating his cake. Ba laughed loudly at the thought of such an encounter.

'That's why I find it profoundly worrying that Spn Owlmoss gives free reign to his fury in that manner.'

'The real trouble with Owlmoss is that he's got a floppy sausage,' said Ba.

Christopher dropped his knife and fork. Ruth looked severely at her daughter, but Petronius detected a hint of mirth at the corners of her mouth.

'Where in the world did you learn an expression like that?'

Ba answered through a mouthful of smoked sausage, which she had gone on to after finishing her cake. '*Everyone* knows that Owlmoss has got a floppy sausage. That's why he's also got a flabby shamebag that he rubs with erotic creams every night — but nothing bites . . .'

Ruth Bram burst into loud, uncontrolled laughter. 'Shut up Ba! I'm eating.'

The doorbell rang.

'Ah, that'll be the Bareskerrys.'

'Yes. She's brought a big surprise for you, Petronius!' said Ruth Bram solemnly, going out herself to let them in.

The Bareskerry family stood on the doorstep, grinning. Liz Bareskerry with a big package under her arm, Britobert with his little, multicoloured handbag and behind them the two pretty Bareskerry boys, Baldrian and little chubby Fandango, in party frocks, gold-trimmed canoe shoes and striking gold pehoes.

'Hal*lo*!' roared the chief diver's housebound. 'Wonderful to see you all, and wish you many happy returns . . .' He swept into the room, heading straight for Petronius with his hand outstretched. 'My! You've really grown, I can see. Have you got any fuzz on your cheeks yet, I wonder? Yes, Bareskerry herself is bringing your present, so you needn't look inquiringly at me; it's a good one, don't worry. She told me what it is, though I haven't seen it yet, so I can't wait. I love watching people opening parcels; even when you know what's inside, it's just as exciting. And Ba! Nice to see you, too, even though of course Petronius is, so to speak, the celebrity today, we're not going to forget you altogether, are we, and haven't you grown into a tough little wom, and *Christopher*! How *are* you? Must be a hundred years since last time. We see far too little of each other, and you've made it so nice here! It really wasn't necessary, just for us, not for old friends like we are, but it really is a *lovely* room you've got here, and the *view*! Mmm. We don't have the view where we are, of course, and I've often said to Liz that I wished we had the view the Brams have up here, I've said, so I could watch out for her when she's out at sea, but she says we can't afford to move, and that things are all right as they are, and it's all right for her to say that because she's hardly ever home, but on the other hand we do have the woods, of course, and they're lovely, though now it's winter, there aren't exactly a lot of leaves on the trees, of course, if you know what I mean, but in the frost they look so beautiful with all the . . . you know, as though they're covered in crystal, but all the same, you really shouldn't have gone to all this trouble for us, you know, you can't *imagine* how much I've been looking forward to coming, I've been thinking about it for weeks, as I hardly ever get out, of course, because I've got to be home to look after the kids, well, I mean, they can really look after themselves now, but I think I should be home to keep an eye on them anyway, and then of course I've got to be there in case anyone rings for Liz, and in any case I don't really know where I'd go if I *did* go out; you know I really think we ought to see more of each other — I don't think we've seen each other since last summer, and I was thinking about that the other day, really, and I said to Liz, too, that you're really the only people I really know, who I can come and visit, but then it isn't so easy to get away, but you could always come up a bit more often, if you want. I thought, but obviously you've got more than enough on your own plate as well, I mean, that's clear, but it's *so* nice to be here.'

Petronius felt his scalp tingle when he saw Bareskerry. He hadn't seen her since the night she had made advances to him aboard the *Adonis*, and now here she was coming towards him, all smiles, carrying a big package which she placed in his hands. Baldrian and little Fandango followed a little way behind, watching him expectantly.

'What can I offer you?' asked Ruth Bram, going over to the sideboard.

'I'll have a Bloody Maurice, please, and the housebound will have a sweet wine,' said Bareskerry.

'D'you want to see my stamp collection, Fandango?' asked Ba. They went off.

Christopher began to prepare the coffee table.

'Let me help you, my dear, look, here, I'll help you, I know how it is, it never stops, anyway, last week Baldrian came home with . . .'

Britobert Bareskerry's voice faded away somewhere between the cups and plates in the kitchen. Baldrian and Petronius began to clear the dinner table and went out after them.

'Here's the draft of the new fatherhood regulations,' Ruth Bram announced, waving a thick wad of papers in Bareskerry's direction. 'The initiative came from the co-op, of course.'

Liz Bareskerry looked through the papers with interest, flicking from one sheet to the next, as though registering the essential points on each page, nodding in approval.

They had taken an armchair in the corner near the coffee table.

'It'll be interesting to see how it goes.'

'Yes, it will be.'

They gazed into the air for a while. Ruth Bram began to drum on the table top with her fingers. 'What the hell are those menwim up to? It can't take this long to make coffee.'

'Don't ask me how long it takes!'

'Well, it really can't take this long. They'll be sitting there, yakking away as usual. Yakkity yak.'

Bram got to her feet and went out into the passage between the living room and the kitchen. The kitchen door was shut. She stood looking at herself for a while in the half-length mirror over the chest of drawers. She patted her hair, pulled her shoulders back slightly and straightened her collar. She could hear the hum of the deep voices from the kitchen. She pricked up her ears.

' . . . and Liz is out nearly every evening. I really don't like to tell her I get scared, being alone in the evening.'

'I get scared sometimes, too, when Ruth comes back late from the club. I'm frightened something's happened to her. Look, why don't we try to get together for coffee more often?'

'Liz really wants me to be at home in case the phone rings. Anyway it's nice for her if I'm at home when she gets in. I usually have something hot ready. Liz can't resist something hot and exotic at night. But sometimes I feel . . . it's like I don't really have any value of my own. I mean, I'm just *there*, as a sort of appendage to the cooker, or something. D'you know what I mean?'

'Yes, I feel like that sometimes, too . . .'

Aha. So that was why the coffee was taking so long.

They were sitting there running down their wimfolk behind their backs. Ruth felt herself reddening. It hadn't been her intention to listen by the door. But she couldn't help hearing. Menwim always talked so loudly when they were together. She coughed loudly and gripped the doorhandle hard. And there they were, Christopher, Britobert, Petronius and Baldrian, smoking and pilfering the liqueurs.

'So here you are,' Ruth gave Christopher a peck on the mouth. 'Sitting here all alone? Aren't you going to come in and be sociable?'

They got up and starting carrying in cups and glasses. They filled them and sat themselves around the round table in the living room.

'Can you believe it? They were sitting there boozing!' said Bram to Bareskerry.

'Those menwim. Those menwim. Always trying to sneak a quick one on the quiet.'

'Right. And they're not exactly quiet about it!'

The menwim laughed.

'What do you think about the new bridge project, by the way?' Bareskerry asked Bram. Christopher listened intently. The bridge project was something he had paid close attention to from the beginning. He was familiar with all the plans, and had his own ideas as to how the problems could be solved.

'Problematic,' said Bram to Bareskerry. 'For one thing, I think it's better to go downstairs than upstairs, the way it is at the moment. Moonhill's miscalculated there.'

'But wouldn't it be possible to . . .' Christopher began.

'Moonhill has done something of an about turn, by the way,' said Bareskerry, cutting him off, to Bram.

The menwim laughed.

'It's clear she's got her sights set on taking over the firm. The question is whether she can get Cleavage and Wing on her side. It's going to be tight, as Bosomby says. She's really going to get her peho in a twist.'

The menwim laughed.

'Then there are the costs and assorted running expenses along the way which have to be taken into account, and in the long run, there will no doubt be some attempt to delay the settlement with a two-phase structure, so the opposition gets a foot in the door and puts the brakes on the final project. That will probably lead to Cleavage's resignation, but she won't be the only one to go. The situation will then be like it was in 531 at the time of the Great Accommodation,' said Bram to Bareskerry.

'Now you're talking nonsense! The Great Accommodation was long past in 531. The settlement was actually reached in a series of steps, and was worked out in peace and quiet in quite different circumstances from those people imagine. Do you really think that what Mara-Mara said then was an expression of the opposition's intentions? Come off it!' said Bareskerry to Bram.

'That's exactly where I think you've always been mistaken,' said Bram, excitedly. 'No one has ever really wanted a confrontation. And Moonhill knows what she's talking about, even if she does do strange things in the moonlight.'

The menwim laughed.

'You still can't ignore the fact that the final phase was the primary concern!' Bram was getting worked up now.

'But Mara-Mara was among the leaders! And besides, she was supported by L P Lifedaughter!' Bareskerry was red in the face. She had begun to fear she might lose the argument.

'Nothing to do with it! What kind of a leadership was that, Bareskerry? Icing on the cake; no more, no less.'

'I wasn't really thinking of its function so much as its effect.'

'Yes, how are things going with . . .' began Britobert Bareskerry.

'No, no, no,' interrupted Bram. 'We mustn't forget that there is always a certain façade. That was a mighty powerful slogan the mighty Mara-Mara came up with at the time.'

The menwim laughed.

'A certain façade,' Bram repeated to Bareskerry, ignoring them. 'People believed in it. What matters isn't the manipulations that are going on behind the scenes, but what people believe. People believed in Mara-Mara, and that put the others in a fix. And the situation now is exactly the same, with the new plans, even though Mara-Mara is dead from the political point of view.'

Bareskerry realized that she couldn't carry on and that Bram had won the argument.

'Yes, I agree with you there; I agree with you there,' she said, as though to conceal the fact.

'Yes, it's a good thing you sometimes . . .' began Britobert Bareskerry.

'A broad front,' continued Bareskerry. 'The pregnancy provisions have to be reviewed so they suit contemporary needs. The same with the fatherhood regulations. We can't have all that fuss. It's simply meaningless in the present circumstances. Why is the population declining? It's glaringly obvious, isn't it? Just as you said a little while ago, no one feels like getting pregnant at the . . .'

At exactly this moment, Ruth Bram stood up so suddenly that her knees collided violently with the edge of the table, and cups, glasses and whatever was in them went flying. She covered her mouth with her hand while her eyes opened to twice their normal size; she rushed out. A moment later the others heard pitiful noises coming from the bathroom. Bareskerry gave Christopher a piercing look. He felt his cheeks flush hot. He could feel the curiosity flowing towards him.

'Yes,' he said. 'That's the way it is. It wasn't . . .' he stopped short. He had been about to say that it hadn't been his idea. He felt ashamed and fell silent.

'Christopher!'

Christopher ran out to help her. A quarter of an hour later Ruth came back into the living room in a dressing gown and slippers, with a cold compress on her head and a thermometer in her mouth. 'Well,' she lisped bravely through the thermometer, 'I won't be going to work for the next eight months, anyway.'

'Congratulations!' shouted Britobert. 'Hadn't we better go, if you're feeling unwell?' he added sympathetically, looking at Bram with his head on one side, in the way of an old manwom looking at a baby.

'No, no, please stay, for goodness' sake! Where's Petronius? Isn't he going to open his present soon?' Bram asked gaily and sat down.

Petronius and Baldrian were playing chess in the corner. 'Just coming,' said Baldrian, deeply absorbed. 'I've taken his king! It'll only be a few moves and I'll have him in checkmate.'

Petronius withdrew his queen a square.

'Just what I thought you'd do!' said Baldrian, moving his dame to leave the queen in check with nowhere to move to.

Petronius smiled. 'What a way to treat a birthday boy!' he said, and thanked him for the game. He didn't mind losing. Not to Baldrian.

'You make the same mistake every time,' said Bram. 'You move your king out too early.'

The thing was, Petronius had won a game against his mother the previous week.

'Come on now, pack up!'

'Fandango!' shouted Baldrian. 'Fandango, Ba! Petronius is going to open his present!'

They heard rapid footsteps hurrying across the landing and down the stairs.

'I know what it is,' said Fandango as he ran in.

'Don't say anything!'

Petronius went over to the big parcel and began to wrestle with the string. Christopher handed him a pair of scissors. He cut through the string. There were several layers of paper; it was a heavy parcel. He arrived at a big white box. He raised the lid slightly.

'Go on! Hurry up!' shouted Ba, hopping up and down on the floor.

Petronius removed the lid. And there it was — big, greyish-green with arms and legs stretched out and a peho sticking straight up out of the crotch.

'A diving suit for a manwom!' laughed Ba jubilantly, clapping her hands.

'Goodness! Isn't that wonderful!' said Britobert.

'It's Bareskerry's own design,' said Bram.

110

'But Bram's idea, Bram's idea,' said Bareskerry nodding, as she bent over her handiwork. 'Look, Petronius. It's made of hundred per cent biteproof material over a framework. Exactly as your mother specified. Next time you accompany the troops under water.'

'Well, Petronius, what d'you think?' asked Bram.

Petronius stared at the shape on the floor. The rubbery material brought it almost to life for him. He had never conceived his dream of becoming a sailor in such concrete form. (Indeed, he had never thought of himself, directly, as a *manwom*. Nor had he realized that, if he wanted to be a seawom, he would always be a *mafele* seawom.)

He felt his cheeks grow warm. He knew immediately — as he stood there with everyone waiting for him to gush with wild and boundless enthusiasm and gratitude — that he would never wear this diving suit. The longer he looked at it, the more it became a living monster, an amoeba-like organism that would devour him. It was terrible. All his seawom's swagger and toughness had disappeared. The little, reinforced peho became a giant tower, open to attack by every conceivable monster of the deep.

The time had come for him to say something. He couldn't put it off any longer. Now he would have to thank them and tell them his highest hopes had been fulfilled. He had feigned gratitude and delight before. Hurry up, Petronius! Say something! Show them how happy you are!

Petronius rushed out, ran up the stairs and into his room, locking the door behind him.

He sat with his elbows on his desk, resting his chin on is hands. His eyes burned. He was trembling all over. He didn't want to talk to them. He never wanted to talk to them again as long as he lived. How could he look them in the face, and be his usual self after this? Didn't they understand that he could never put on that diving suit? It wasn't a diving suit, it was a . . . clown's outfit for menwim — just as clownish as all the other clothes menwim had to wear. Why should they be forced to be clowns, even under water? Why should they always be persecuted, everywhere they went, for having that thing between their legs? Why couldn't they ever be rid of it? What if he cut off his cock? Cut it off and sewed himself up and went down triumphantly saying, 'See, I haven't got a cock any more. Can I be a seawom now? Can I have an ordinary diving suit now? Do you think I'm up to swimming under water and being an ordinary huwom being just like anybody else now?' Petronius looked down at himself; he contemplated the little thing hanging out through the slit of his skirt. What was he actually meant to do with it? Why was it there? After all, it was completely useless. Why didn't he simply have a neat little opening to pee out of, like wim had? And a tiny little protruberance for the purpose of sexual pleasure, like wim had? Why were menwim so idiotically designed? And why did the fact that they were idiotically designed always have to be emphasized? Why couldn't they at least be allowed to hide their most shameful parts, seeing as they were so awful?

Petronius wished he were somewhere else. He knew he couldn't remain in his room, with the door locked, for the rest of his life — he knew that, sooner or later, he would have to open it and walk through the flat and see his parents again and the thought filled him with horror. He wished he could dematerialize and fly out of the window and into a cloud, and remain there, without his shameful body. Then his entire being would consist only of what was in his head. Then he could steer the cloud to some-where . . . somewhere perfect and altogether different from where he was now, a place where two loving arms would receive him and he could become a body again. She would be loving and tender and she would never, never, never remind him that he had anything between his legs.

Wasn't there some such place? Wasn't there someone who could take him away? Gro? Where was she? Why did she never come? Couldn't she come and take him some-where that would negate this monstrosity, somewhere a diving suit with a peho was an impossibility?

He becomes hers

At the innermost point of Maybight Bay, there was a fisherwom's hut. It was a proper fisherwom's hut of the sort that
occurs in stories, built of stones, with a thatched roof, small
panes in the windows, two chimneys and pebble stones. For
this reason it was commonly portrayed on postcard views of
Egalsund with the caption, 'Old Lux — Fisherwom's hut
from the good old days', in black and white or colour,
photographed from the sea, from across the bay through a
gap in the oak leaves or from the air.

Below the hut was a little bridge, and next to the hut
was a big dilapidated shed, about three times the size of the
hut itself.

Petronius could not remember a time when he had not
known this hut. It was a part of his image of existence. As a
small boy, he would go for walks with his father along the
shore, and they always ended up sitting on the other side of
the bay, looking at it. Once, his father had told him that it
was in the oak woods behind the hut that he had been
conceived.

On account of these early memories Petronius felt a
special attachment to the place. No one had ever lived
there, as long as he had known it. The hut had always been
locked up. He had known about it long before it began to
appear on postcards, and he regarded these pictures as a
sort of sacrilege — an indecent exhibition of a secret.

He had asked his mother who owned the hut. She had
explained that it probably belonged to the Maybight people,
who were among the few who had not had to sell up during
the depression. Most such huts had either been demolished
or restored.

Petronius would dream that he lived in the hut and that no one ever came to disturb him — that he could sit in there, looking out through the small window panes, letting his thoughts ride the waves. He had always wanted to live by the water. Living at the top of a tall block of flats with a view over the sea far, far below was not living by the water. Living by the water meant being able to see every little ripple, crest and trough, to hear the waves rolling in towards you, to scent the sea air in your nostrils. That was living by the water. His mother said it was only in romantic fisherwim's tales that people lived like that. What would happen if everybody decided she had to live by the water? There were some who had never even seen the sea. He ought to remember that he himself came from an old inland family. They had solid ground under their feet and knew the realities of life. Did they miss the sea? He should learn to be more socially-minded. Being a huwom being meant being bound to the earth, and it was typically manwomish to dream all the time of being somewhere else — to try to escape the demands of life. And that, said Ruth Bram, was the main reason why sea-going was a wom's job. If menwim had been seawim, they would simply have left the earth and the demands of life and stayed away for years on end.

Petronius was depressed by the thought that there were people who had never seen the sea. He didn't know why. It was as though she had told him that there were people without noses or ears or memories.

That spring, Petronius noticed that people had evidently returned to Maybight. Several times, when passing by, he had heard hammering and sawing in the big shed. Someone had also cut down some trees and cleared the undergrowth from in front of the hut. Small patches of earth were being cultivated at the back. Later he noticed that the little bridge had been repaired, and sitting at the end of it was a pretty little black cat with its tail wrapped around itself. It winked mysteriously at Petronius from across the water. Cats have a peculiar ability of their own to look as though they are utterly alone in the world. It scratched itself rapidly behind the ear with its back foot and trotted over to the hut where someone had put out a bowl for it on the steps.

Since the attack, Petronius never walked alone in the woods after dark any more. One evening he realized that he had nevertheless spent a long time sitting by the water. He was out at the farthest extremity of the bay, leaning against a stone, lost in thought. Little waves were lapping in against the toes of his shoes, and when he finally looked up at the sky, it was darkening, and though there was still light out here, he knew it would be dark in the woods, and before he got home . . .

He heard steps along the shore. He didn't dare look round, as he was not certain that what he had heard had really been footsteps. There they were again. He looked out cautiously from behind the big rock. A dark figure was trudging back and forth along the tide mark, picking up wet pieces of driftwood and seaweed. He could see, from her long, strong movements, that it was a wom. He didn't know whether to feel reassured or afraid. Perhaps she was the one he was afraid of. What if he asked her to accompany him through the wood, and she did, and raped him?

Petronius thought. If he ever did actually meet the monster — the hideous wom whose attack he dreaded constantly, and went up to her with an open mind and an outstretched hand, and said that he was scared for his life and asked her to help him, would she not then do so? Innocence, true, naked innocence needs no protection, it protects itself, thought Petronius philosophically; he had read that somewhere. But wasn't that exactly what he had experienced that time in the wood? That time when the three wim . . . Petronius tried to banish the thought. No, they hadn't looked like that. They hadn't had the appearance of horrible wim, out to attack him, twice the size of normal wim, with twisted faces. They had looked like quite ordinary wim.

Petronius felt a shiver run down his spine. Terror had gripped his whole body now. In the daytime he hardly ever thought of the three dark-clad wim. But at night they reappeared. Again and again. He dreamt that they came and he never managed to say anything. He always had to do

115

what they wanted. If he told anyone, they would come back more often, they said. He was always drenched in sweat when he awoke from this dream. He had it every night, with small variations. It was nearly always the same. He bent down towards the water, cupped a little in his hands and splashed his face. The water relieved a little of the darkness in his head. He tried to act like a straight-backed wom who had just come in from the sea, tied up her boat, and was now going in to fry her fish and grab a strong cup of coffee and a stiff drink. He got up and began to make his way slowly in towards the head of the bay.

She didn't notice him until he was there. Then suddenly her face was turned towards him and he saw — with a jolt that went right through him — who it was. He felt bewildered and wanted to run. He tried to pretend he wasn't there. He felt he had intruded on her. He tried to make it appear that he just happened to have come by, and he had unintentionally wandered a little too close to the shore. And now he was continuing on his way into the darkness of the woods. He was simply on his way home. Before, he had been on is way out and now he was on his way home and now he was no longer there; he had already gone. Moreover, she hadn't even seen him; it was just a trick of the light and she should pay no attention to such things. Goodbye.

Petronius had already turned away and taken a couple of steps into the trees.

'Petronius Bram!'

Her voice boomed in the darkness between them. He turned, took a few steps towards her, paused, then went right up to her and stared into her face.

'Are you afraid?'

'No.'

'Then what are you afraid of, if you aren't afraid?'

'I'm frightened of the dark.'

'But no one can see you in the dark. There's nothing to be afraid of.'

She took him by the hand and led him into the hut.

This was how Gro Maydaughter lived. It was very simple inside. A narrow bench, a table, a paraffin lamp, a

116

stool, a chair, some bookcases, the open fireplace with the cat sitting in front of it. Hanging on the wall was a large photograph of an old, weather-beaten wom dressed in sea-wom's clothes. There was also a big green poster bearing the characteristic outline of Clara Sparks's face. Petronius became a little uneasy when he saw this. If there was anything in the world Ruth Bram despised, it was Sparksist ideas. Whenever she disagreed with someone on the television or at the club she would snort, 'Sparksist hogwash!' and Petronius had heard this from a young age — from long before he knew what Clara Sparks actually stood for. In fact he didn't really know now.

Gro Maydaughter suddenly seemed slightly embarrassed. 'It isn't exactly palatial in here, of course,' she said. 'I haven't done it up yet. But it is at least warm. Have a chair. That's the most serviceable bit of furniture here.'

Petronius sat down. He couldn't understand why he hadn't realized before. Maybight. Maydaughter. Of course. She wanted to start on her own, Bareskerry had said. The Maybight people had either died out or moved away. Gro Maydaughter had come back.

'I've got something for you, by the way.' Gro went out into another room. She came back holding something behind her back and stood in front of Petronius with a little smile. Then she placed them in front of his feet — a pair of green-checked canoe shoes.

'Why did you take them?'

'So you would be as amazed as you are now.' She laughed, sat down on the wooden bed facing him, leant forward and looked at him. 'I knew you'd come. Sooner or later. So I kept them as a souvenir until you did. I'm a bit of a fetishist.'

'What does that mean?'

'It means getting a particular erotic excitement from having something that belongs to someone else. Things, that is, not people.'

'People who belong to someone else?' he asked, confused.

'I didn't say anything about that. Things.'

'No one belongs to anyone else. Only things.'

'You know that isn't true. You, for example, belong to me.'

Petronius said nothing.

'First I had your shoes. I've had them for months. Now I've got you.'

'But won't you want to keep them when I've gone?'

'But you're not going anywhere, are you? You know that. You're not going.'

'But I've got to go home to . . .'

'Yes, yes, yes. You've got to go home to your father and home to your important mother and home to your sister and home to go to school and home to do your homework and to write up your diary — there are so many things you've got to go home for.'

'What do you know about my diary?'

'Don't you know that you do have one confidant? There is one person you can safely tell everything. It's a thing, not a person, but he's always there.'

'The st . . . the stone statue?'

'Yes, the stone statue on the southern shore.'

'Did . . . did I tell it about . . . about you?'

'Yes. You love me.'

'I don't know you.'

'No, you don't know me. And you love me.'

'I was disappointed in you.'

'That's a sign that you love me. If you hadn't loved me, you wouldn't have been disappointed.'

'You didn't help me when I was assaulted.'

'Raped, you mean. No, I didn't know. If I'd known, I would have killed them. I wouldn't let anyone harm you.'

'You haven't contacted me since the maidmen's ball.'

'I wanted to, but I couldn't. You're so young; only sixteen. I'm ten years older than you, Petronius. I thought you should have your youth in peace. I took your shoes. You saw me on the beach, but you didn't recognize me. I've come by you several times. You cut your teeth on me. But I couldn't ask you for anything, because you were so young. I wanted you to come of your own accord.'

And now? thought Petronius. Did this mean that he had come of his own accord? Did she love him? Was that what she was actually saying?

'You weren't any help aboard the *Adonis* when Bareskerry tried to have her way with me . . .'

Gro stared at him, frowning. 'Did she try to? The old sow!'

Petronius blushed. 'She gave up right away,' he mumbled.

'I knew you'd caught her eye. She mentioned something about a diving suit . . .'

'It was a hideous diving suit. It had . . . it had . . .'

'It had a peho. I know. Idiotic. In the old days on Lux, men never wore pehoes. It's a modern invention, an upper class innovation, that is. Now it's spread to all layers of society. As far as I'm concerned, you're lovely; with or without a peho. She can just keep away. I'm not going to work for her much longer. I'm going to start up on my own.'

'What are you going to do?'

'I'm going to start up the fishery again here on Maybight.'

'You're strange.'

'Yes, I'm strange. You don't know me. You're disappointed in me. Is the ordeal by fire over now, young lordy?'

'No. It's only just started.'

'Petronius!' She stood up and threw her arms around him. 'Does that mean you'd like me to protect you? One day?'

'D . . d . . . d'you mean, g . . . give me f . . . fatherhood-protection?'

'Yes!'

Petronius nodded. 'Why . . .' he whispered, 'why didn't you come before?'

'Mother God! That's a long story.'

It was so unreal. It was like a story. The sea outside, the wind around the walls of the hut, the small panes of darkness in the windows, the flames in the fireplace they were

staring into as she stroked his hair. It was unbelievable —
inconceivable — that there was a highrise block an hour
away, where light and warmth came from some mysterious
place which had nothing to do with oneself, where nature
consisted of streetlights and car-parks and other high-rise
blocks, where cats lived on balconies, where 'woodland'
consisted of nice, square, symmetrical parcels of park and
garden. Once, long ago, the entire island of Lux had looked
like this place at the head of the bay of Maybight. And
people had sat in front of their fireplaces, and the menwim
had listened to the wim recounting their stirring adventures
in the world.

Gro Maydaughter and her proud family

Gro Maydaughter was born on a bitterly cold spring morning in the year 510 AJ, four and a half sea-miles south of Spout, in an open fishing boat, gale force eight. Her grandmother, Baya, sat at the oars while her two aunts hauled in the nets and her mother sat in the bottom of the boat, giving birth.

Grandmother told her later that she had shrieked, twice as loud as the wind, filling their hearts with pride. She repeated that every time she told the story of Gro's birth. Twice as loud as the wind and hearts full of pride. And she did that every time Gro's birthday came around, until she died. 'Yes, you were so big and strong when you were born, it was all we could do to stop you helping your aunts with the nets as soon as you came out,' chuckled Grandma, lighting her pipe.

'It was so stormy that day, there had been nothing like it since the day Maria who was lost, was lost,' Grandma always boasted. Maria Maybight Southern, who used to have the south side of the bay, was the sister of Old May, Gro's grandmother's grandmother, and Grandma never called her anything but 'Maria who was lost'. Sometimes she added 'and Baraldus was utterly inconsolable', when speaking of her. There had never been weather like that since. Gro was the apple of her grandma's eye.

It was a long time since people had called Old Maydaughter anything but 'Baya' — and this name reflected a sense that she was the very soul of that bay. The landowners of Egalsund had used it as a term of abuse but she had accepted it as a mark of honour. She was as rough as the seven seas and always ate her fish, skin, bones, fins and all.

No matter how big it was. 'Any other way is modern nonsense,' she would proclaim, crunching cartilage between her teeth.

Most of the fisherwim had long ago succumbed when Gro came into the world. Baya, however, had fought with tooth and claw; and she *had* teeth and claws. She went from one fisherwom's hut to the next, agitating. 'Never give up the rocks and oaks,' she said, 'it's all you've got.' But it was no good. The landowners and the trading companies and the civil servants employed by the state offered dizzying sums of money for their rocks and oaks. At least, the sums seemed dizzying to the fisherwim, who had never heard of so much money all at once. They had such little understanding of modern money matters, they thought they could live for the rest of their lives on three thousand dollables, without ever having to lift a finger again. Baya struggled against that, too. She told them terrifying stories of city life — how money would crumble, *crumble* away between their fingers as soon as they set foot in a shop.

It was no use. The fisherwim sold up and took jobs in the town or went off to Pax, or places even more remote. Or they simply disappeared — without a trace.

Baya remained. She stood her ground for a couple of decades after the others had gone. She never spoke to anyone except her family — but there she made up for not speaking to anyone else, saying, 'Never will I sell the land of my mothers!' And Gro remembered her words. She remembered the words before she knew what they meant. She remembered the sound of them, and she remembered her grandmother's voice when she spoke them.

And Grandma trotted through the woods like an elk, cutting and planting and coming home weary but full of life, speaking with great disgust of what was happening on Lux — since the landowners had bought up everything. 'Fancy people are moving in now,' she said. 'There won't be any real people living on Lux any more. They're only imitation people, the ones moving in. They're not going to work here; they're only going to live here!' Grandma slapped her thighs; she never lost her sense of humour. 'Have you ever heard the like? Just *living* in a place — but not working there! Why on earth does anyone want to live there, then?'

Yes, Grandma Maydaughter thought the modern world was mad. But she was nobody's fool when it came to its ins and outs. To the consternation of the troops of young spearbiter-hunters who swarmed onto the island, she suddenly produced a document showing that she had sole right to the fishery round Spout. The fisherwim had had a verbal agreement among themselves since ancient times according to which they each had their own areas. But Old May, Baya's mother, had been the only one to take the trouble to get this enshrined in a document, officially stamped by the municipal authorities. This had been long ago, in the previous century; the public officials had laughed at the document and authorized it with their splendid stamp and charged her two dollables (which Old May was allowed to pay off in four instalments over a year).

The officials of the Directorate were thrown when Baya waved this faded document under their noses half a century later. At first they tried to laugh it away. But its authenticity was proved and proved again by several courts. In the courts, both lawyers and laywim really wanted to declare the document void, but they were afraid it would blow a breach into the Egalian's sense of justice if they overruled the sacred inviolability of the rights of the private individual. So they decided to declare the document legally tenable but morally indefensible (the laywim pronounced only on the moral aspect), since the fisheries were for everyone, and no one should enjoy privilege, so that the entire population might benefit from the free competition which thus arose.

Baya was thus able to keep the new troops of divers away from her domain for several years, until she felt her health beginning to fail, and she recognized that, in any case, it would be impossible to compete with modern-equipped diving troops in the long run — even for her. She therefore invited the Northern Trade Company to purchase her rights. The company was delighted and offered her an enormous sum of money. She went immediately to the Southern Trade Company and told them what she had been offered. After going back and forth between them for a couple of months, she finally made up her mind and sold her rights to the Northern Trade Company, split the sum in two and invested half in the Northern Company and half in the Southern.

Baya's eldest daughter, Kit, Gro's mother, was to inherit Maybight. Baya saw to it that the two youngest became expert divers. 'I've arranged things for you as best I can in these crazy times,' sighed Baya on her deathbed. 'So just bury me at sea, where I belong, a half sea-mile east of Spout, where the sun rises.' And with that she died.

Gro was only five then. Her aunts had left the hut and she and her mother lived there alone for a short while. Kit Maydaughter had no intention of giving fatherhood-protection to anyone. She had inherited her mother's attitude to menwim. Baya had always said that menwim were a luxury that *she*, at any rate, couldn't afford — except on a purely casual and occasional basis. The sons of neighbours had taken it in turns to look after her own daughters until they were big enough to go to sea with her. Many fisherwim made similar arrangements, and they therefore had no need of a manwom each. In the fishery period, there was roughly one manwom for every four wim on Lux. The attempts made in modern times to civilize menwim and make them useful were regarded by Maya as ridiculous nonsense. 'Menwim are wild baboons and they always will be,' she used to say. 'They'll never learn to lift a finger for anyone but themselves. God preserve me from having to tame one of them.' Among the fisherwim, housebounds were regarded as a strange aberration of the upper classes, and most sons born on Lux in the old days ended up in the mining districts of Palluria, if they found no fatherhood-protector on the mainland.

Gro looked at Petronius who was watching her, wide-eyed with fascination. She had opened his eyes to a world he knew nothing of. He thought of novels he had read about powerful wim who had walked violently and inexorably into menwim's lives and changed them for ever. Wim who tore menwim away from their restricted little world and took them out where the starry heavens and the sea opened out. He knew that Gro was such a wom. He would stick by her always. Here was the wom he had always dreamt of. Tall, independent, reconciled to the forces of nature, rich . . .

'My mother squandered her entire fortune,' Gro continued. 'She took me to Pax and had a fine time, living there as an artist. She surrounded herself with menwim of all sorts and explained to me that a budding artist needs to surround herself with beautiful young menwim. It's a sort of inspiration. But she didn't want to give any of them fatherhood-protection. And she didn't really give a Lucy about me. Her menwim used to play with me and ingratiate themselves with me in the hope that Kit would think I was feeling the lack of a father's beating heart. As soon as I was sixteen, I took off. I went to sea and stayed away for years. I lived a typical wom's life — with-a-lad-in-every-port, as they say. Oh Petronius, I can't tell you everything I did — drinking and whoring. That's what a seawom's life consists of, mostly. In foreign countries menwim offer themselves out like that, from the age of eleven. Then one day, I suddenly got a telegram telling me that my mother was dead. I don't know what she died of. I expect she drank herself to death. Her death made a certain impression on me, all the same. I began to think of my childhood home and I began to feel I wanted to do something of what Baya used to talk about. So I came home. At first, I thought I would come home for the funeral. But actually there wasn't much point in that; it was too late.'

Gro paused for a moment.

'A mother . . .' she said pensively. 'What is a mother, really? A distant figure you never really understand . . . But even though she squandered her fortune, I can't help thinking of her with pride — because she gave birth to me out there off Spout, one icy cold spring morning in a force eight gale . . . She was one of the people. One of the real, child-bearing people . . .'

Inside the Palace of Birth

The Great Palace of Birth lay on the outskirts of town, half way up towards the high ground above the South Egalsund Effluent Treatment Plant, where Delivery Boulevard runs south east towards Pax. The Palace of Birth had been built only ten years earlier, and had previously been situated on the Moonhill, within the city. Wim giving birth had complained, however, that the noise disturbed the ceremonies. Their enchantment with the great miracle of life was smothered in the din of the working day. As soon as the first complaints came in, the Directorate resolved to erect a contemporary building in peaceful surroundings outside the town. It was the biggest single item the town had ever budgetted for. The money was allocated immediately after one of the directors had herself been in to give birth.

The new Palace of Birth was a huge, red, triangular, stone building with a round bell-tower at each corner, large bow windows, and a long marble staircase leading up to the main entrance. The palace was divided into numerous, triangular birth rooms of various sizes, which the wim who were going to give birth got their housebounds to reserve for them according to what they were prepared to pay.

'I hope it's a girl,' said Ba as the big black electric limousine carrying members of the Bram family swung up the drive at the head of the cortège bringing the birth guests. It was late in the autumn and the weather was grey and forbidding.

'If it is, I'm leaving home,' said Petronius.

'Then I hope even more that it's a girl,' said Ba.

'Stop it! Or *I'm* leaving home,' said Christopher.

Petronius and Ba looked at him, shocked.

'You?' said Ba. 'You can't leave home, can you?'

Christopher had ordered one of the biggest birth rooms. There had been endless arrangements to make, these last months. Every conceivable detail of the ceremony had to be planned, and whenever he had consulted Ruth, she had merely said that it was up to the menwim to sort everything out. Besides, she had more than enough to do, being pregnant. Was he asking her to start worrying about practical details, too?

She had grown big and fat this time. She had had an unusually tiresome pregnancy, constantly wanting small snacks. For nearly ten months, Christopher had been making little salads, home-made soups, stews, fricassees, compotes of specially selected vegetables, and delicious little desserts for her. One day she had asked for olives. Christopher had combed the town, looking for olives and everywhere he was informed that it was not the season for olives. This made no difference to Ruth. Finally, he had ordered a large consignment of olives fom Pax. They arrived three days later. Christopher raced out to Ruth with four jars of olives, but she merely turned away in disgust, lying, as she was, on a sofa on the terrace. 'Do you really think I want olives *now*?' she asked furiously, and then explained patiently that pregnant wim get sudden cravings, as Christopher ought to know, sudden passions for things — and it was rather silly to come running three days later hoping to satisfy them.

Immediately after this, she entered her violent paprika period. The same story was repeated. Christopher ran around for months trying to satisfy her cravings, and built up a secret store of the most unusual fruits and vegetables in the hope that he might one day be able to produce what she wanted within the minute.

He lost over a stone and Ruth began to complain over how thin and drawn he looked. 'The years are beginning to take their toll on you, old manwom,' she said. Christopher smiled. He knew it was dangerous to contradict a pregnant wom.

In the old days, it was said that the child would be born

deformed if the mother did not get her way during pregnancy. There were various taboos. Splitting hairs, on the part of the housebound, for example, would lead to the child having a hare-lip. If menwim lost their temper with their wives during pregnancy, the child might be cross-eyed. Perhaps it was only ancient superstition, but Christopher wasn't quite sure. In any case, this was without doubt the most difficult pregnancy he had ever been through.

They went up to the big triangular chamber in the centre of the building. Oblique shafts of light from the big window fell on the organ and the bed where Ruth Bram was to lie. The choirgirls and the celebrant had not yet arrived. That meant things might take some time.

Christopher sat down on the front bench, Ba by his side, as she was the eldest daughter, and then Petronius. Christopher recognized the statues in the corners. The same figures had been in the old palace on the Moonhill, where Petronius and Ba had been born. In the lower corner stood a fine big pregnant wom with her feet planted solidly beneath her and her arms at her side. In the next corner was a naked, bawling, newborn baby girl, and in the top corner was a double figure — a manwom with two heads, four arms and four legs symbolizing the manwom's two primary functions — breeding children and looking after them. The backs and buttocks of this double figure was fused together, and the public saw him in profile — turning his erect penis towards the wom in one direction, and his open arms towards the newborn child in the other. The cycle of life. He gives, and receives. It was in order to emphasize this rhythm in civilization that all the rooms were triangular.

'Dad!' said Ba. 'I bet Gro fucks Petronius! In ten months, *he*'ll be sitting here — as a father.' She laughed. 'If she wants to protect him, that is — and of course we don't know that for certain. It isn't certain she's going to want that booby . . .'

'Be quiet, Ba. This is a solemn place and a solemn moment for us all.'

'Solemn!' snorted Ba. 'I'd never want to have a baby in a horrible, boring room like this. When I give birth, it'll be on top of a chariot, drawn through the town by four white horses, with trumpets blaring in front, and balloons and confetti and cheering crowds . . .'

The door opened and in came the celebrant in full regalia — with her broad red cape, embroidered in gold — and thumped three times on the floor with her staff. That meant that the childbearer was approaching. Behind her came the choirgirls with their short, red smocks and their pyramid-shaped black hats. They were naked from the navel down. They formed three rows between the head of the bed and the organ, so that their pubic hair formed a long row of dark triangles. They were all the same height. At the end came Ruth Bram, accompanied by two midwives in their usual white coats. Bram was wearing the black birth-coat. The organ was playing a tranquil prelude as she crossed to the head of the bed in front of the choir. Here, she threw off the black birth-coat and stood before them in all her mighty nakedness. And at exactly this moment, as she flung away the coat, the organ and choir burst into the divine prenatal cantata, and Bram swung herself elegantly up onto the birth bed.

She lay so that the public — who were now streaming in through the two entrances, past the sculptures of pregnancy and the newborn child — could see straight into her crotch, so they could follow the progress of the labour.

Two microphones had been positioned near the head of the bed, so she might keep the congregation posted at regular intervals, as to how the birth was going. When the prenatal cantata was over, she announced that she had been gripped by the first contractions half an hour earlier, and that these had shot through her entire body. She said she had almost forgotten how wonderful it was to feel these initial spasms go through her — it was so long since the last time. She said if it wasn't for the fact that people have to work, they ought to be pregnant all the time, because these birth contractions were the greatest sensual pleasure anyone could experience. If intercourse with a manwom was like drinking a glass of water, giving birth was like drinking a glass of wine.

At this announcement, the public clapped and the choir sang the 'Great Contraction Anthem' in three-part harmony. When they had finished, Bram raised her hand as a sign that she wanted to speak again. She said she could feel the water was about to break at any moment, and the choir immediately began to sing, in bell-clear voices, the 'Hymn of the Water,' which has the sound of a murmuring brook in the spring. After this the celebrant began to perform the birth ritual itself, which was always chanted in Paxian. The birth was under way.

The light from the great window was gradually dimmed, almost imperceptibly, by means of huge curtains which were gradually lowered. There was complete silence. They heard Bram's relaxed, even breathing. During this phase, as the mouth of her uterus slowly opened, only Bram herself could break the silence. She had requested some of the most popular current pop-songs as an accompaniment for this stage. She found it easier to relax to pop music than to anything else, she said. An hour of pop music followed. Her belly rose and fell gently. Now and then she took the microphone and announced that she felt as though she were in a sort of state of donna-like weightlessness. She wanted silence to enjoy this phase. The pop music was turned off. A half hour of absolute silence followed. Everyone gazed at her belly, rising and falling. The sense of excitement was at a climax. Bram cried ecstatically, 'The great contractions are starting!'

The celebrant's assistants rubbed her hips and loins. From time to time, Bram uttered little moans of pleasure. She was smeared with exotic oils in the opening of her birth canal. Her breathing became shallower and turned into an even, rhythmic murmur of rapture. The assistants worked intently, rubbing her all over with aromatic ointments. Her labia were massaged, until they were warm and soft, in preparation for the final effort. Bram gripped the microphone. Everyone held their breath 'The head is coming out!' she proclaimed, swinging herself into the birth chair and beginning to push. 'Gooseberry jam!' she yelled. Word was sent at once to the palace kitchens and a moment later a big bowl of gooseberry jam was served to her. She ate and pushed and grew red in the face. The mouth of her uterus was massaged with warm flannels. They could clearly see the contractions rippling through her body. 'Now I can feel her head pushing out. She's a strong-willed little thing,' laughed Bram ecstatically. Everyone clapped. Christopher got to his feet and rushed over to her with open arms. Bram moved slowly across the bed, spread her legs and howled with joy. The head came into view in her passage of life. Christopher stood waiting at the foot of the bed. The choir sang the 'Birth Chorale' and the organ thundered with the last prenatal crescendo. For the last few minutes before the child emerged, there was complete silence.

The celebrant was required to signal to the congregation and the organist whether it was a girl or a boy. If it was a girl she turned her staff so its triangular point was upwards, the roof. If it was a boy, she pointed it down towards the floor. If it was a girl the postlude would be played in a major key; if a boy, in a minor. Everything was very quiet. Bram puffed and laboured vigorously. Everyone knew that she was in another world and that this moment in a wom's life must never be disturbed by extraneous noises.

Petronius held his breath and shut his eyes. He repeated to himself that he wanted it to be a boy. He wanted a brother. A brother — Oh Donna — let it be a brother!

The entire head was out, then the shoulders. Bram grasped the child, pulled it out and lay it on her belly. Petronius stared at the celebrant's staff. For a moment that seemed to last an eternity he couldn't see which way she was turning the staff. Then the point began, slowly, to turn downwards. A moment later the organist began playing the postlude in the minor key. The baby was dried. Petronius heard Ba sigh peevishly beside him. The public clapped. The placenta was born. The audience clapped again. It was held up so everyone could admire its beautiful colours. Bram cut the umbilical chord. The child began to bawl. The congregation clapped again.

The midwives wrapped the infant in a black cloth and handed it to the celebrant who laid it in Christopher's arms.

The choir began to sing the moving 'Hymn to Fatherhood' — in unison at first, and then in canon — since the purpose of the hymn was to emphasise the eternal aspect of fatherhood, a state with no beginning and no end. Christopher went over to Petronius and Ba. Ba stared at the little creature and Petronius kissed his red-wrinkled little brother on the cheek and thought he was the loveliest baby he had ever seen. His little brother made a sudden movement with his hand and Petronius put his giant fist over the tiny little hand with its five, minute fingers, and felt its warmth and its movement. He looked cautiously at Christopher. Christopher smiled at him.

The celebrant banged the floor and began to chant over the afterbirth. When she had finished, Bram jumped off the bed and went over to Christopher and the baby and there was a certain amount of confusion. People surged forward to congratulate them and they were taken out onto the steps in front of the Palace of Birth, where masses of pictures were taken of Bram and her housebound with the baby in his arms. Then they all drove home together to their flat on Lux for the birth reception.

When they arrived, they found that the Directorate's massed brass band had assembled to surprise them. Dressed for the occasion, they greeted the guests and the childbearer and her housebound with a loud and spirited rendering of Egalsund's municipal anthem, 'Daughters of the Briny Bay'. Christopher picked up his newborn son and waved at him with his hand. Everyone was deeply moved.

Afterwards, Bram went on a three-day drunken binge.

Nursing and the dreams of a youth

'Dear Gro, I've always longed for freedom . . .' What an idiotic, emotional beginning. Petronius stared at the paper, then looked out of the window of his room. But it was true, wasn't it? Hadn't he always longed for freedom?

He tore up the sheet of paper.

'Dear Gro, there's something I've been thinking of for a long time that I wanted to tell you. When my baby brother was born three months ago and I was sitting there . . . well, I wanted to tell you what I was thinking at the time. I was thinking that . . .' He stopped and looked out of the window. It was dark. He saw his own round head out there in the dark. He looked stupid. Thin neck and straggly hair. A frizzy beard. How could he sit here having deep and earnest feelings when he looked so ridiculous?

He looked back at the sheet of paper and read. 'I was thinking that . . .' What had he been thinking? Of her, of course. 'I really wished in my heart that it was you, lying there, and that I was the one who got up to receive our child. Oh Gro! That's what I'd like more than anything in the world. I want to have your baby. Now you know. I shouldn't have said it, but it's true. I've always wanted . . .' To be free, he thought. To be free, and to have Gro's baby. To have the baby of the wom I love. And to be free.

He looked up and caught sight of himself in the window again. This time he continued to stare at himself. How could he be free and have a child at the same time? Was it possible? Of course it was possible. Why shouldn't it be possible for him, even though it hadn't been possible for his father. Gro wasn't like Ruth. Gro was considerate towards him. She told him things. She loved him and taught him so many things.

133

He began to think of her arms. Her shoulders and her arms. How firmly they held him. How safe and warm he felt against her breasts. How she always made him wish he could stay with her for ever and never need go home again. Never. Just stay there.

Again, he tore up what he had written. 'Dear Gro, I love you.' He contemplated it. He went over the letters a second time, and decorated them a little. He added, 'Gro Maydaughter. I love you. Petronius. Petronius Bram loves Gro Maydaughter. Loves, Loves, Loves Her.'

He heard little Mirabello cry, and Christopher go in to him. He had his own room, so Ruth wouldn't be disturbed by him at night. Petronius went out.

'Dad? I'll sing to him, if you're tired.'

Christopher smiled and stroked Petronius on the cheek. Petronius had been so good at looking after the baby during these first few weeks. He had also conscientiously taken him down to the Directorate two days each week after school, so Ruth could breastfeed Mirabello. He had to be fed twice during the working day, once in the morning and once in the afternoon.

Ruth had dismissed any suggestion of taking maternity leave. She was determined to go straight back to work immediately after having the baby. Like every other wom, she had the choice of going back to work right away or taking the maternity leave to which she was entitled — and there was no extra benefit for going straight back to work. That would of course have led to wim being pressured to go straight back to work after the strain of pregnancy, so there was no question of any such monetary encouragement. But that made no difference to Ruth. She couldn't stand being at home any longer. She was desperately impatient to be back in her office, issuing directives and slapping her pretty little secretaries on the rump as they went past. And three days after Mirabello's birth, that's where she was.

As a result, Christopher had to go tearing down to the Directorate twice a day, so Mirabello could be fed. And as he was breastfed for seven months, Christopher had an exhausting time. But it was necessary toil. If a mother didn't have peace as long as she was nursing, and if she was not spared moments of irritation, her milk dried up. And what father would want to behave so as to make his baby's food disappear? The child came first. Everyone felt that; Christopher too.

Ruth also said that this was the last time — absolutely definitely the last time — she was going through pregnancy. Suddenly it was being made to appear that having this baby had been *his* idea. She also seemed to have forgotten the uniquely ecstatic experience of giving birth. 'Have you forgotten the joy of having a baby?' Christopher asked tentatively. 'No. But a job's a job.'

Christopher said no more and was actually relieved to have Ruth back at work. 'To save any further trouble,' Ruth went on, 'we'll get you castrated.' Actually Christopher was also relieved that Ruth wanted to have him castrated. But he did feel a certain horror — and a certain sadness — at the thought that his life's work would thus be at an end.

Petronius gave him a great deal of help at this time. But Ruth didn't really like Petronius coming. It was a natural task for the father to bring the baby to its mother's breast, she said. But she had grudgingly consented. 'You know how it is,' she said drily to her colleagues. 'A wom has no say in anything any more. These menwim always get their own way. Heigh ho.'

'Will you?' said Christopher gratefully.

'Mmm. I'll sing him the 'Flower Song'. You sang that to me when I was little.'

Christopher kissed Petronius on the mouth. Petronius put his arms around his father's neck and smiled. Standing like that, so close to his father, Petronius could see how thin his hair had become recently. He was thin in the body, too; he looked worn out. He would have to start wearing a wig soon. He could hardly go around like that for much longer.

'Goodnight, Dad.'

Christopher squeezed his hand slightly, smiled and crept into his bedroom. Petronius went in to Mirabello, who was still crying with wide open eyes. He was the loveliest baby Petronius had ever known. He began to sing the five verses of the 'Flower Song', softly and slowly.

The song was based on the well-known ballad about the beautiful young maidman in his room at the top of the lofty tower where he had been imprisoned by his cruel mother, so no one could take his virtue. He sat there alone, throwing beautiful flowers out of the window. Where he got all these flowers from, the song doesn't say, but in any case, he sat there for months, years on end, tossing flowers out of the window. And his beard grew and grew. It grew so long, it grew out of the window and down the wall of the lofty, maidman's tower. One day a stalwart suitor came riding by, her breasts bouncing gallantly as she trotted. She looked up from the foot of the tower at the beautiful sirsel high above and sang one song after another about how tragic it was she would never be able to reach him up there. Meanwhile, the beard went on growing downwards. Finally the beard grew so long that she grabbed hold of it and climbed up to where he was. Thus the young troubador got her pretty sirsel, in spite of his cruel mother's evil strategem.

'Didn't it hurt his beard, Dad?' Petronius had asked, when he heard the song as a small child. But the story said nothing about that, and Petronius thought it was a strange story which had the minstrel pulling the maidman's beard like that without saying anything about it. But the ballad had a nice tune. And for that reason he sang it. He also sang it because it made him feel wonderfully safe, thinking of something familiar — even though it was silly.

He stood by the window and sang all the verses in turn. By the middle of the third verse, Mirabello was asleep. But Petronius went on singing as he looked out, longing to be far away.

Outside the window, gleaming, was the brand new, bright orange electric car Bram had bought herself with her pregnancy money — a Super Cow 1313.

The history test on General Sheracles and her exploits

'*During the Great Growth Age (732 BJ-213 AJ), Egalia was organized as a state. At the beginning of this period the rich and extensive ore deposits of Palluria were discovered. Two major expeditions of conquest led by General Sheracles (732 and 729 BJ) obliged the nomadic tribes of the Pallurian highlands to withdraw to the great plains of the east . . .*' Ba looked up uneasily from the history book, holding her index finger on '*east*'.

'Aagh! I've never done this!'

But all the others were deep in their books, against the playground fence, so she got no reply. Spn Owlmoss had announced a history test. Ba went on reading. '*General Sheracles is one of the strangest and most fascinating figures in the whole of Egalia's history. A few of the entries in her journal have been preserved. They reveal a stringent, logical and strategic mind, but at the same time a warm sense of huwomity and justice, the combination of which constituted her greatness. Here is a sample:*

(Source No. 15). Evening of the second day. Two thousand . . .'

Ba stopped her finger on '*two thousand*'.

'Ann! Do we have to learn the sources, too?'

'Sssh! Yes. Those concerning Sheracles, anyway.'

'*. . . menwim killed. Funeral oration. Three hundred menwim wounded. Saw to them. Some in great pain. Prayed and sacrificed to O, that they might live . . .*'

'Who's O?'

'Mother God! Can't you shut up? She was who they believed in before Donna Jessica — the Great Allmother. Her strength and her wisdom were in her nipples, which she had eight of.'

'. . . *Enemy retreated across the Valley of Death. Egalian forces lying in ambush on the other side.*'

'*Even this little extract reveals a great and intelligent mind; a wom who knew how to draw up a plan of battle, but who also knew that war meant sacrifice. The sources also yield another interesting fact — that in those days we used menwim in close combat. The cavalry consisted of wim, but the infantry, which went ahead, consisted of menwim. It may seem brutal to us today that we sent menwim into battle. Historians have also made the point that this practice weakened morale. The basis for using menwim in this way was, however, the fact that Egalia then, as now, faced a severe population problem. There was a constant need to take steps to prevent the birth rate from declining (see p.395) . . .*'

'Do we have to read page three hundred and ninety five?'

'Nah. That's about today. We don't have to read that.'

'*That is to say, that it was necessary to ensure that the country's fele population did not decline. A high mortality among able-bodied wim could have been disastrous for the development of the population. On the other hand, a decline in the mafele population would have no effect on the birthrate (cf economics. See footnote) . . .*'

'Ann? Did he say we have to read the footnotes?'

'No. They don't matter.'

'D'you understand this bit about the population going down?'

'Yes, we did that in civilization. The point is, that the birthrate varies from year to year. If it's low, that means when they grow up there will be too few young people in relation to the old, and that means a shortage of labour. So to prevent excessive variation in the annual birthrate, there has to be a relatively stable fele population, whereas it doesn't matter so much what the size of the mafele population is . . . That's what Mum's been campaigning about in Parliament. Haven't you been following it?'

'Yes, but . . .' said Ba, who hadn't paid any particular attention to the issue.

'*When Sheracles returned victorious from her great cam-*

paigns, she organized her queendom with great wisdom and intelligence. Egalia was divided into three main areas: 1) The coast, with its fishing and trading. 2) Palluria with its mining, handicrafts and small-scale industry. 3) The great agricultural regions of the east with their irrigation systems, canals and sluices. Sheracles was a strict but just ruler. She received the homage of the people and was appointed . . .'

The bell rang.

'God! I'm not ready.'

'Nor me.'

'I don't know anything.'

'What was Sheracles appointed . . .?'

'She was revered as Prima of all Egalia — the first among equals — and then she took the title of Grand Dame of Palluria.'

'But wasn't Palluria part of Egalia?'

'Not really. It was organized as a province with certain special rights, and then she installed a Feudal Overlady to rule in her place . . .'

6B trudged up the steps and into the classroom. Ba hurriedly noted the words, 'Prima', 'Grand Dame', and 'Feudal Overlady' on her wrist. She had already written down a number of dates.

'What's a Feudal Overlady?'

Spn Owlmoss came in.

'Sssh . . .!'

'Right! Today we're going to have a little history test,' he said, leaning his right hand on his new desk. 'There's nothing to be nervous about,' he continued, somewhat nervously. 'Just a few short, simple questions. I've got them duplicated for you, here in my bag.'

This sounded like an apology. He looked out over the class. They were all sitting in their places, watching him, quieter than usual. 'So we'll put all our history books away, please; just keep your pens. I'll give you paper to write on.'

The class put their books away with a great deal of noise; some tried to hide them under the edge of their desk lids.

'Come on now — *completely* out of sight. Here, Fandango; will you give out the paper please, and I'll give out the questions. When you've got the questions, I want absolute quiet.'

Spn Owlmoss began walking between the desks, giving out the questions, alternately to right and left. Those sitting opposite one another began to confer as soon as he had passed by. He spun round.

'Sssh! You heard what I said.'

They answered back in their usual way.

When he had finished his circuit of the desks, there was a semblance of silence in the class. Each pupil sat alone with her questions. Ann Moonhill immediately began to write, her pen squeaking, and little chubby Fandango began putting down his answers, each in turn and numbered, in big, rounded, graceful letters. Ba sat staring at the paper, and suddenly couldn't remember a single word she had read. She looked round in amusement to see whether there was any chance of provoking the collapse of the whole exercise with a bit of fun, but everyone was preoccupied. She read through the questions despairingly.

'*1) When was the Great Growth Age?*

2) Why do we call the Great Growth Age, the Great Growth Age?

3) Write about Prima Sheracles and explain why she is considered one of the most important figures in history.

4) The position of menwim under Sheracles — in war and peace.

5) What do we know about the Golden Age?'

Spn Owlmoss cleared his throat. 'Are there any questions . . . about the questions?'

'Yes. What do we do if we can't answer them?'

'Just write in the number of the question and go on to the next one.'

'But what if we can't answer *any* of them?'

Sniggers from various parts of the room.

'You must be able to answer some of them. Just think.'

It was quiet again. Spn Owlmoss looked out over the heads bent over their desk. This is how it should always be. Quiet. Everyone working. Using their minds and writing.

140

Ba glanced quickly at the notes she had written on her wrist, then stole a glance at Spn Owlmoss, again at her wrist, and began writing.

'1) The Great Growth Age (732 BJ-213 AJ) — that means: Before Donna Jessica (Our Lady).' She looked despairingly at the other questions and realized that she couldn't produce a single reasonable answer to them, and that the note she had written on her wrist was of no use. So she wrote:

'2) Because of a lack of imagination. In fact nothing very much grew during the Great Growth Age, and what did grow was extremely small. But they had to call it something, so why not the Great Growth Age? To make people feel that progress was being made and things were getting better all the time. In fact, of course, the very opposite was true. Things got worse and worse for people throughout the entire period. Just think what it was like living an isolated existence in the far reaches of Palluria. 3) Prima Sheracles was actually the greatest tyrant in the whole history of Egalia . . .' Ba chuckled at her own wit. 'If people didn't obey her, she chopped their heads off on the spot. All the same, she was revered almost as a donna. She expanded her queendom with an iron hand and great brutality, and then organized things so that she had all the power herself. She also had the urge to write, and imagined she was the greatest poet that had ever lived. I'm glad she died a long time before I was born. 4) Miserable — dreary and monotonous. A life of slavery. 5) I can say absolutely nothing about what "we" know about the Golden Age. Who are "we"? Schoolbooks always suppose that "we" are a big and united mass. I have no idea what anyone else knows about the Golden Age, but I, for one, know nothing.'

Ba read through her answers with great satisfaction. She laughed. This would show him. Grinning to herself, she wrote her name at the top of the paper and put up her hand.

'Finished!'

'Have you done it all, Ba?'

'Yes.'

'Have you checked through it?'

'Yes.'

Spn Owlmoss walked over and took her answers.

'Can I go now?' asked Ba, who was on her feet before he had answered. They were never allowed to go sooner than five minutes before the bell. He nodded. Ba grabbed her lunchbox and sprinted out through the door. When the others saw this, general uproar ensued, although the lesson had fifteen minutes to go. They handed in their answers in quick succession and with five minutes to go, only little chubby Fandango remained, writing his big, rounded letters deep in concentration, as though all the disturbance around him was occurring in another world.

Spn Owlmoss was furious with the results of his test. He had had a vague hope of using the answers as evidence with which to prove to Principal Bosomby that he was teaching his pupils in the required manner. There had been so many rumours about him in circulation since the incident with his desk. But these tests were useless. For once, he decided to make no allowances. When he went in to 6B a week later with the answers in his salmon-pink bag, he said, 'Well, you seem to have surpassed my *highest* expectations. Of course, I knew that 6B was particularly sharp. The discussions we've had have shown that you're more than usually intelligent and attentive. All the same, I never realized you were capable of treating historical issues in such a mature way. I'll say it straight out — I'm proud of you!'

He paused for a moment. The class were staring at him, speechless and attentive, waiting to hear what he was going to say next. They were amazed. They couldn't tell whether he meant what he was saying. Each of them knew she had done miserably in the test, but none of them knew how the others had done. Perhaps all the answers had been brilliantly perceptive, apart from their own.

'So that the best among you can share your insights, I'll read out one of the best answers for you.'

He pulled out Ba's paper from his bag and read it with great relish, nodding now and then with approval and commenting, 'Now *that's* the way to go about it, you see,' before continuing. The class was more bewildered than ever. They simply couldn't tell whether he was sincere or whether he was being sarcastic. When he had finished, he said, 'There's only one thing that might be added. It seems that not many of you have taken the trouble to read the footnote on page twenty five, where there is in fact a long footnote. Since you know the rest of the material so well, it seems almost a shame that you are not familiar with the content of this footnote. So please turn to page twenty five and use the rest of the lesson to read it and learn what is in it.'

The class obediently turned to page twenty five at once. Nobody said a word. Ba, too, leafed through the pages, without looking up. The footnotes were printed in tiny type in closely spaced lines at the end of each chapter. They began to struggle through the dense text.

'During the Great Growth Age, Egalia was very much a fele society. Public life was wholly dominated by wim. Menwim were considered second class citizens, and Growth Age Egalians considered that their most important function was the breeding of children. They did not have equal status with wim in the home, in the way they do today. They were only admitted to the company of wim for the purpose of engendering children. Nor were they all permitted to father children. All boys had their fate sealed at the "ten-sorting". Each year, in the spring, all boys of ten were brought before a panel of judges who decided whether they were to become studs or workers. Only ten per cent were chosen as studs. The rest were sent to Palluria, to work in the mines and workshops, or else into the great wilderness to cut timber. We know very little about life for menwim in Palluria and the wilderness regions, since written sources are lacking. We can only conclude that life must have been dismal. We know somewhat more about how the studs lived, since they had frequent contact with society.

They were kept in a reservation consisting of a row of big tents. They were only permitted outside the reservation on rare occasions. It was the wim who went to them, usually in large groups on the eve of feastdays, after drinking wine. Leave of absence from the reservation was sometimes granted to a particularly well-endowed and talented stud who was then allowed to circulate freely at certain times, offering out his sperm. These few privileged menwim often received a high standing in society and frequently fathered several hundred children.

By today's standards, the treatment of menwim in the Great Growth Age was brutal and inhuwom. This was not, however, the view of the Egalians of the time. We must always be careful to judge a historical period on its own terms. The fact that menwim did not play any part in the general life of society was then taken for granted. They were chattels before anything else, equivalent to our domestic animals. The modern belief that all huwom beings have equal rights would have been incomprehensible to the Egalian of the Growth Age. She would no doubt have considered her society highly advanced in relation to those of earlier times. We must remember that during the Golden Age which preceded the Great Growth Age, menwim had been regarded as superfluous and harmful beings. Only about ten per cent had survived. Unfortunately we know almost nothing about social conditions during the Golden Age.'

Little chubby Fandango looked up from the book. The Golden Age, he thought, gazing dreamily into the air in front of him. What had life been like then? There was something exciting in the name. Fandango imagined himself in a big house, sitting in a big comfortable chair, dressed in voluminous garments, ordering one of his servants to fetch him a stud, to relieve his boredom. They would talk a little, and no doubt have glasses of wine and grapes on a silver tray, sitting in Fandango's big atrium, by a swimming pool with colonnades and white doves, before setting about engendering a highly talented baby which would inherit Fandango's intelligence, beauty and earthy qualities.

Suddenly little Fandango was struck by an overpowering sense of sadness and sorrow. Who had said he would have been a wom if he had lived during the Golden Age? Who had put that idea in his head? Who? Who?

Egalsund at night

'Baldrian? Are you asleep?'

'Mmmm . . .'

Little chubby Fandango lay trying to hear whether his brother's breathing was regular. He was always pretending to be asleep. His duvet moved. There was something cosy about talking together before going to sleep. Sometimes Fandango was allowed to crawl in with him under the duvet and lie there until Baldrian's bed was warm. Then he had to move over into his own. 'Goodbye,' they would say to each other before going to sleep; not 'Goodnight'. 'Bye — I'm off to dreamland now.'

'Baldrian? You're not asleep. I can tell from your breathing . . . and you moved.'

'Mmmmm . . .'

'Hey, I got a big star in the history test. Wasn't I clever?'

'Mmmmmmm . . .'

'Hey, d'you know what I was thinking? I was wondering why history always only talks about wim, and then I thought it must be because wim are so important, and I really like history, and then I feel so unimportant . . .'

'Mmmmm . . .'

'And then I was thinking that our whole language is like a part of history. I mean, for instance, well, there are lots of examples, for instance, like for instance . . .'

'D'you have to say "for instance" after every word?'

'No, but for instance, take the word "manwom". Have you ever thought about it? I mean, it suggests that a manwom is just a certain sort of wom, though a wom isn't any sort of manwom. Why don't they just say "man"? And then

145

there's the way they say wom or womkind to mean the whole huwom race for huwomity. "The rights of wom" . . . "wom-made fibres", there are lots of examples.'

'Well, you can always say "huwom being" instead of "wom" if you want; it's neutral.'

'Yes, but even huwom is derived from the word for wom in the language of ancient Wome — *womo*, like in *womo sapiens*, which is the root of the word *huwomitas*. Owlmoss told us about the origin of all these words; it's really interesting.'

'Mmmmm . . .'

'You know what? I think I'll become a masculist when I'm older.'

'That won't do you any good.'

'Yes it could. I could become a linguist. It's important to have a really good understanding of the language. Then I could systematically set about weeding out all words indicating that wim were in control of society.'

'Yes, do it.'

'You're just thinking of Eva Bosomby.'

'No, I'm thinking about Petronius.'

'Oh? What were you thinking, then?'

'Promise you won't tell anyone?'

'Yes!' Fandango sat up in bed.

'We've started a secret society for boys.'

'Have you? What, a sewing club?'

'No! Sewing's forbidden. And so is talking about wim.'

'Donna! It sounds great. Can I join?'

'When you're bigger, maybe.'

'But when am I going to be bigger? You said that two years ago, and two years before that, and two years before that. I don't think I'm ever going to get bigger.'

'No. That's how it is when you're little.'

'Yes. Maybe I'll start a secret society with little Mirabello. He's so sweet. If he can just manage to get a bit bigger . . .'

'Goodbye, Fandango. I'm off to dreamland.'

'Bye, Baldrian.'

★ ★ ★

Petronius drifted deeper and deeper under water. He felt the water soft and warm against his body, the way it is in the summer. The world around him was green. Green and light and brilliant. Down on the seabed, Baldrian came swimming towards him with his dark hair flowing and congratulated him on his new diving suit. Petronius hugged him and said he would be happy to use it when he was alone with him. And while they embraced each other, and Baldrian stroked his big hand slowly down his body, over the diving suit, Petronius suddenly felt that he was being dragged down still further, even though they were on the seabed, and then he saw that it wasn't Baldrian but the big stone statue which he had to raise to the surface or it would drown. Then he was standing in front of the statue on the shore, asking it why it stood there, when it was really drowning. 'That's obvious,' said the statue. And then Petronius saw that it was indeed obvious, as the statue was wearing his diving suit. Only Petronius hadn't noticed before. The statue asked if it could join the secret boy's club. 'Because, actually,' it said, 'I've always hated sewing.'

★ ★ ★

Little Mirabello lay crying. Christopher tumbled out of bed and, tiptoeing in, picked up the little bundle. He crept back to the bedroom with him and gently laid him on Ruth's breast, being careful not to wake her.

★ ★ ★

Principal Bosomby's voice thundered from the living room. Cyprian lay on his back in bed, listening to his father sobbing intermittently. He was so used to this, it was almost like a lullaby which lulled him to sleep. But if Grodrian's sobs became too loud, he would go out into the living room, sobbing too, and hug him. It wasn't so bad tonight. They had only been at it for a quarter of an hour and it sounded as though things were quietening down now. It was always the same. Mum said Dad was stupid. Dad

147

said Mum didn't love him. They never managed to solve this problem.

Cyprian wondered whether it was like this in other families. Whether wife and housebound in every family in Egalsund spent the night screaming and sobbing, and the day presenting a fixed smile to the world.

If that was how it was, then perhaps Spinnerman Owlmoss was better off on his own, after all. Cyprian thought of Spn Owlmoss, up there alone in his big villa, and wished, as he had so often wished before, that he lived with him instead. He had resolved hundreds of times that he would simply go straight over to him one evening and ask, 'Is it true that you're my father?' Because if it was true, he would rather live with him, playing his grand piano and listening to his stories. Fandango said he told such good stories. Cyprian had never been taught by him at school.

'You stupid, idle, wasteful nitwit!'

'Gerd! You've never loved me!'

Cyprian turned over and pulled the duvet over his ears. He never, never, never, wanted to get fatherhood-protection! It was a fate worse than death.

★　★　★

Spinnerman Owlmoss sat at his piano, looking out into the night. Behind the big black pane of the window, the snow was falling slowly and heavily. He could see the entire town and the bay from here. The town and the lights and the Lux Bridge. It was so peaceful in the snow. Everyone was sleeping soundly, and the snow lay softly, covering all evil thoughts. He started to compose a poem to the snowflakes. 'Ode to Snow', he called it, and he started to compose a little tune to set it to. He couldn't decide, though, which should come first, the music or the words.

They should probably come together, he thought. The theme is there. The snow settling over evil. And now all he had to do was to find some notes which suggested snow settling over evil. That would be in C sharp minor, which had so many good harmonies. Evil could go in E major, and anger in B seventh. His own anger. Sitting here alone in his villa, thinking his own thoughts. About the town and the people who lived there. And no one in the whole world could stop him thinking what he wanted.

All his life, Spn Owlmoss had had his own mind. He had thought, played, and harmonized in his own way, in the big lonely villa on the Moonhill.

PART TWO

The villa on the Moonhill

The door flew open with a crash and in marched Spn Owlmoss with his long red hair in wild disarray.

'Well, this is my début in the masculist movement,' he said with a grin and shook them all by the hand. 'Sorry I'm so late. Hallo Petronius, hallo Cyprian, hallo Baldrian, hallo Lillerio, and *hallo* little Fandango! Right, no doubt you're all wondering why I've invited you all here for apple pie. The thing is, I have an enormous orchard — but that of course isn't the reason . . .'

He remained standing, looking at them, for a moment. For a long time he wanted to invite members of the new menwim's movement up to his house. He was not completely sure what he thought about it all, nor did he really know who the members of the movement were. But when he heard that his favourite pupil of many years standing, little, tubby Fandango, was one of them, he immediately felt it easier to contact them.

The young masculists were sceptical. Menwim of the older generation were so indoctrinated. And Spn Owlmoss — wasn't he an example of precisely the type of manwom who merely bolstered the morale of wim? Hadn't he stood for hours on end propagating wim's culture and wim's history and fele perspectives on everything? He was completely lacking in awareness.

'I expect you think I'm past it, completely lacking in awareness. But I think my own thoughts up here in my villa on the Moonhill, and I have my own plans. So I'd very much like to listen to what you have to say . . . can't you just hold your meeting, the way you usually do? I so very much want to hear more, so I can better assess my position . . .'

153

They sat around the big, round table in the middle of the living room.

'What about an aperitif — a Bloody Maurice?' Spn Owlmoss produced a bottle and glasses. It was clear that he was a little nervous.

'Tell me,' he said, sitting on the edge of his chair, 'what would you have spent today's meeting talking about if I hadn't been here?'

'We would have discussed the situation in Maybight,' said Petronius.

'Can't we talk about that now then? I mean . . . is it secret? Do we have to talk about something else?'

They all looked at Petronius. He shook his head. 'Gro says she wants a more definite structure.'

'Typical fele chauvinist!'

'I don't think she's a fele chauvinist. Think how much she's taught us! She's taught us to do woodwork and to fish. She's even taught us how to catch spearbiters.'

Spn Owlmoss clapped his hands. 'Ooh! Has she? I've always longed to go out on a spearbiter hunt!'

'Yes, so did many of us — until we saw the bloody methods they use.'

'But the menwim in Egalsund want spearbiters caught.'

'It isn't the housebound who decides that. It's the wim who make money out of fishing them, and they determine what happens. If they weren't making something out of it, it would stop tomorrow.'

'This isn't what we were going to discuss. What does Gro mean by "a more definite structure". Does she want us to choose a leader?'

'But we have done.'

Petronius reddened.

'Is it you who's the leader, Petronius? I thought as much. You were always so clever at school,' said Spn Owlmoss.

'No. Baldrian was thinking of Gro.'

'I think we should stop making digs at Gro. It isn't her fault she's a wom. She does her best. Haven't we been free to wander in and out over there for nearly a year? And she hasn't interfered in our meetings, either'

'No. I don't think there would have been any menwim's movement at all without her.'

'That's true. There's a lot we should be grateful to her for.'

They fell quiet. Spn Owlmoss poured out more drinks and raised his glass. They felt they were not concentrating. There were so many painful things they didn't really dare tackle. Petronius was in a slightly awkward position, since Gro was his. But, at the same time, hadn't she been flirting a bit, one way and another?

'Petronius,' Baldrian took his hand. 'What's all this about more definite structures?'

'She wants us to organize study groups in the menwim's movement to study Clara Sparks's works.'

Fandango banged the table with his fist. It was a gesture he had recently learnt. He was tired of exhibiting the mildness expected of menwim. 'Wim always want everything tied down to structures before they do anything. We had exactly the same discussion with Wolfram before he left the movement. And he got everything he said from Ann Bentridge. I've read Clara Sparks — I was bright and radical so I read her works. But they're not about menwim. They'd be fine if menwim didn't exist. But we do.'

Spn Owlmoss raised his index finger and looked up at the ceiling in the way he did when standing at his desk in the classroom. 'May I come in here?'

They nodded. They were tired. It was nice drinking Bloody Maurices, and there was a beautiful view up here, but they actually felt it had perhaps been a misunderstanding that had brought them there.

'There are many old books about menwim,' said Spn Owlmoss. 'Books which have all but been forgotten. First among these, I would recommend *The Destruction of Patriarchy*, written under the pseudonym "P". It was published about fifty years ago in Pax, but I don't think it's been translated . . .'

'What's it about?'

'Well . . . it's about how there were once societies where

the menwim had more say than the wim.'

'How does anyone know for certain that there really were such societies?'

'Archaeological finds and research.'

'Yes, and not only finds and research, Fandango, because it always depends on who is researching and what she wants to find. And how she interprets what she finds. You all know the famous sculpture in the National Museum of Egalia called "Enigmatic Manwom with a Hoe" — an ancient statue of a muscular manwom holding a hoe? I'm now going to be so bold as to call it, "Manwom Tilling the Soil". But all the experts are wim, and they couldn't understand how a manwom could stand in such a position with such an instrument in his hands. *Menwim* can't till the soil.'

'But they can't.'

'"We", Baldrian, not "they". Because everything is explained and determined by wim, we even say "they" about ourselves . . .'

'But we *can't* work the soil! Maybe he was just holding the hoe for his wife.'

'That's exactly the way that all signs of ancient patriarchy are always explained away by the experts. Often they insist that the ancient sculptures represent fele figures — even though any child can see that it is a manwom's body, and without any basis except the assumption that all cultures are necessarily dominated by wim.'

They all stared at Spn Owlmoss, fascinated. He smiled at them in his kindly way. 'And I think you'll get more out of *that*, brothers, than from studying Sparks's thinking. I'm not suggesting that Clara Sparks is not among the most perceptive thinkers of all time. Not at all. But there are a great many things in this world — important things — which she never dealt seriously with.'

Spn Owlmoss looked from one to another of them, a little uncertainly. 'Now I'm probably out of order. Really I want to know what your plans are, not to give a lecture myself. It's an occupational neurosis . . .'

'We have lots of plans in the ML,' said Fandango.

'The Masculine League,' explained Petronius. 'That's

what we call ourselves.'

'Yes. And now we don't know what to do,' said Lillerio. He never said much, but when he said anything it was to point out that they were in a dilemma.

'We can't accept that she lays down conditions,' said Petronius, looking at the floor. It was a relief. They had all been waiting for him to say it. He looked up at Spn Owlmoss. 'We don't know why you asked us to come . . .'

Spn Owlmoss shifted slightly and looked round the room, as though searching for something he had long been missing and had suddenly remembered.

'We've lots of plans, but . . . we think there'll be a general election this year, so we've been considering various possible actions . . . but they're secret; otherwise there'd be no point.'

'I understand,' said Spn Owlmoss. 'I think I'll go out and get you some plum brandy — and the apple pie is waiting to be eaten too.' He got up and Baldrian went out with him to the kitchen. They came back with six small apple pies and the homemade plum brandy. They all waited until Spn Owlmoss was seated.

'There you go. Cheers!' They raised their glasses.

'I'm lucky to have so much fruit in my garden. All kinds. I have a wom who comes and looks after it and keeps a plot of vegetables for me. She's always coming and going. Hardly ever says anything. And she's looked exactly the same for the last fifty years. She must be at least a hundred. I can't remember a time when she wasn't coming and going and looking after the orchard and the kitchen garden and mowing the meadow at the back of the house. Without her, I would never have been able to make use of the land here. Cornfield is her name. Taste all right? Cheers!'

They raised their glasses.

'Mmmmm, that really is good!'

They ate.

'Mmmmm, wonderful apple pie, Owlmoss. How do you make it?'

'The apples first have to be stored for three months. You cut them in thin slices and fry them in lard until they're light brown. Then you dry them off a little with damp tissue, and you put them in a bag with flour, crushed biscuit, cinnamon and sugar and shake it up thoroughly. Then you put it in a pie-dish and finally you pour yolk of egg beaten up with sugar over everything and put it in the oven for half an hour. Then it's ready. Simple and straightforward. Cheers! It's so nice to have you all here.'

'Spn Owlmoss?' It was Cyprian. He had been unusually quiet all evening. 'Is it true that you're my father?'

There was a silence. Cyprian had voiced what they had all been wanting to ask, though none had dared. He had never raised the question in the group, and if he himself hadn't brought it up, no one else had wanted to.

'I don't know . . . I think . . . Do you really want to know?'

It was clear that it was also difficult for Spn Owlmoss to talk about it. They all thought of the desk he had smashed to matchwood.

Cyprian nodded. 'I think you are my father because . . . we look like each other.'

It was true. They had the same rather long nose and the same red hair. And now that Cyprian had grown into a young manwom, he had developed a powerful build and broad shoulders exactly like Owlmoss — deplorably lacking in masculinity.

'Gerd wasn't together with Grodrian at the time you were conceived. She was with me the whole time. She used to sneak in the back door here on the first floor. It was on one such occasion that you were conceived, Cyprian. We also used to take romantic walks in the woods on Lux. She was beautiful, your mother, Cyprian. She still is — but she won't acknowledge me.'

Spn Owlmoss gazed dreamily into the air. The young menwim listened. Suddenly they saw his face in another light. Behind his lined, ageing features, they saw him as a young man, walking with his beloved. They saw a big, powerful, muscular body, gently caressing his wom. The evening sky shone on his forehead. Mother God! He was good looking! They gazed at him, entranced by his intense, somewhat exalted, account of his life.

' . . . No, she didn't want me. "How do you know it's your baby," she said when she became pregnant with you, Cyprian. Imagine — that's exactly what she said. A few weeks earlier she'd said that she loved only me and never slept with anyone else. And I think it was true. But she was right. How could I know it? A manwom can never know whether a baby is his. But I knew. I could feel it in . . . well, in the connection between us — the link that there was between us. But I understand her. I was too big and unmasculine for her. I'm a bit taller than she is. So are you, now, aren't you, Cyprian?'

Cyprian nodded and sighed deeply.

'And I'm also stronger. That was difficult for her. And I could see why, of course. She couldn't cope with it; so she didn't want me. Yet we used to get on so well together, talking. Perhaps a bit too well. I knew things she didn't. Well, that didn't matter so much, perhaps. But I didn't conceal it. I was always so enthusiastic — I forgot to conceal it. I was so naive. You see, I loved her; I really did. In a certain way, I still do . . .'

Spn Owlmoss held his hand out to Cyprian across the round table, and Cyprian clasped it. The others felt they were witnessing something terribly private. At the same time they had been saying to one another all the time that it was the revelation of the deepest and most painful things in life that were the very source of the menwim's movement.

'You must *stay*! Now we're getting to the heart of the matter!' shouted Spn Owlmoss in his excitable and trusting way. 'Because . . . I've always dreamed of making a home . . . a home for Cyprian. It's probably something that lies deep down in all menwim. Really. Well, of course you can always discuss why it's so deeply rooted in us, I know that, but the way things are today, at any rate, it is deep within us.' He grunted. 'Now I'm doing all the talking again, and I said I wanted to listen to you. It really must be an occupational neurosis. And I'm not at all used to having anyone to talk *with* . . . either I talk *to* people, or else *I* am talked to. Never anything in between. Now what was I going to say?'

He paused for a moment, carefully sipping his plum brandy, with his little finger raised slightly. 'I was going to say something important. What was it, now? What was I going to say?'

He looked at them inquiringly, puzzled. 'I always get so nervous. I'm so used to thinking that the lesson mustn't come to a standstill. It's so strange to sit here talking to a group of young menwim, and then coming to a standstill, without coming to a standstill, if you know what I mean . . .'

Spn Owlmoss came to a standstill again.

'It's so nice being here at your place.'

'Yes! Thank you, Baldrian. That was it. And now I've suddenly seen that I've been given an opportunity. I'm so glad you're here . . . I mean, I'm getting on in years . . . I don't know whether I'll dare march with you and get arrested and everything. Because I expect that's what you're thinking of. But I might be able to help in another way, mightn't I? My dream of creating a home for you, Cyprian, is past now of course. You're grown up now. But I could perhaps provide another sort of home, couldn't I? I mean, here. I mean, I live here alone . . .'

Spn Owlmoss stretched and looked at them uncertainly. 'What I mean is: a masculist centre on a true spinnerman's territory.'

The masculists break a taboo

No house on earth was as proudly situated as Spn Owlmoss's white villa, half way up the Moonhill. The surrounding property was extensive and fruitful, lying as it did on the slope that benefited from the greatest sunlight. For the menwim, having a place to themselves, where there were only menwim, was immensely encouraging. It was of particular advantage to them this year, when everything seemed to have come to a standstill. Spn Owlmoss, whose life had consisted of coming to a standstill, found new life. The other groups, who knew little about Spn Owlmoss, beyond what the rumours said, had at first been rather hesitant over establishing themselves in his private house. They had other ideas. Spn Owlmoss said they could do exactly as they liked; he himself would move his insubstantial personal belongings up to a small room in the attic. They could do what they wanted with the rest. 'All this furniture, all these memories of old Principal Owlmoss, are only a burden to me,' he said. He had been wading in antique treasures for years, maintaining the illusion that it was a *home* he lived in. Enough was enough. 'Away with all old illusions,' he said. 'I'll never be fatherhood-protected. And today I'm glad.'

So the menwim refurbished the house, took old paintings down from the walls, and old sculptures down from the shelves. They put up their menwim's posters and the fine, triangular masculist symbol was given pride of place in the living room, where the portrait of old Principal Owlmoss had glowered menacingly for over fifty years, chastening all who attempted to relax or enjoy themselves in her presence — as though she had lived on within the frame. Spn

Owlmoss seemed suddenly to have become twenty years younger. Or perhaps he had always been twenty years younger — but his true self had never been allowed to emerge.

He had himself insisted that he be permitted to embroider the symbol for them. They held a little ceremony when it was ready to be hung up on the wall. It consisted of an equilateral triangle with the vertex, triumphally, at the top. The broad line marking the perimeter was in a strong red, inside which was the black stick, the phallic symbol, against a white background. They toasted it with wine from Spn Owlmoss's cellar.

The triangle — the red border and a white background — with the vertex at the top was the traditional symbol used to denote the mafele sex in biology. The usual explanation of the symbol was that it represented the manwom's role in civilization, in the same way that it was symbolized in the Palace of Birth: his role as begetter and receiver of children, that which he had been civilized into accepting — unlike his brothers in the mammalian world, incidentally. A number of the masculists said that this was a modern, fele chauvinist interpretation of the triangular mafele symbol. They said the triangle had been the old power symbol for menwim in earlier, patriarchal times. This was an attractive and exciting explanation but none of them knew what the symbol had meant in patriarchal society. Besides, nobody really believed that a patriarchal society had ever existed. Apart from Spn Owlmoss — and perhaps Fandango.

The thick black line in the centre was something the masculists had themselves drawn in afterwards. They knew that a phallic symbol would seem shocking, and somewhat pornographic, to people. But they maintained that one of the movement's tasks had to be to stop menwim feeling ashamed of the fact that they had a cock. They would therefore show it openly and unashamedly. They were menwim, and menwim they would remain. And menwim had cocks. It was completely natural and nothing to be ashamed of — they maintained. At the same time, the penis symbol could also be interpreted as a weapon — a stick. Something menwim could arm themselves with in order to combat the domination of their society by wim. The very implacability of the menwim's movement thus became symbolized by this sign.

They also decided to give the triangle itself a new significance. Why should the menwim's world always be built around a relationship between two? It was possible to imagine a future society based on solidarity and harmony among more than two — three or many. They maintained that — given the chance — menwim actually had a greater capacity for solidarity and fellow-feeling among themselves than wim had. Here they were somewhat uncertain. Discussion arose and some said they thought this was ridiculous. Nonetheless, this was the way that some chose to interpret the symbol.

Spn Owlmoss's villa was completely refurbished. They prepared rooms as offices, a gym, a toolroom, a duplicating room, a smoking room, a children's room and a common-room. They held many meetings during which they worked out a plan of action for the year's campaigning.

Then Cornfield disappeared. Suddenly, one day, she wasn't there any more. She had been coming regularly for generations. Then she was gone.

Had she died? Spn Owlmoss was worried. He went out into the garden to look for her, thinking that perhaps she had suffered a heart attack and died at her post — as wim so often did. But he didn't find her. He looked into the little potting shed. There, on the rickety little table where Cornfield had drunk her coffee since the dawn of time, lay a note. Spn Owlmoss picked it up. 'Dear Spn Lisello . .' He looked up dreamily for a moment. He was moved by the thought that anyone still remembered that he had once been called 'Spinnerman Lisello'. He read on. ' . . . After all the hullabaloo that's been going on here, I regret to say that I consider myself obliged to give notice of my resignation from the position of gardener, agricultural labourer and Jill-of-all-trades on Principal Owlmoss's property, this notice to take effect immediately. I have worked here faithfully year after year in order to honour the Principal's memory. What is now happening is of such a character that I am losing the contact I have always had with your maternal estate, and I am no longer able to till and plant and look after things here. With deep regret, yours sincerely, Cornfield.'

A tear trickled down Spn Owlmoss's cheek. He wiped it away immediately and crumpled the note in his fist. He was furious. What was Cornfield thinking of? Just giving notice like that! On those grounds. He remained standing, thinking. He had never really considered that his new life — his new life that he had chosen to live at the age of fifty-five — would provoke hostility.

He trotted up the steps to the others. They saw immediately that something was wrong. They saw the letter, took it, read it, looked at one another. Spn Owlmoss's whole beautiful estate would go to ruin. Couldn't they find someone else to come? They talked earnestly among themselves. Some began to suggest that all was for the best. Now they really were without wim. But what about the orchard? And the kitchen garden? And the meadow? They sat down. All the courage, enthusiasm and energy they had developed so powerfully over the previous few weeks drained from them. They sat staring vacantly into the air.

'We must just admit that we're totally helpless without wim.'

They stared emptily into the air again. What could they do? What did they know? *How in the name of Lucy did one go about cultivating the soil?*

Making a living at Maybight was another matter. Gro had taught them to fish. There were practical obstacles to menwim becoming fisherwim and divers. They could be overcome. It was merely a question of certain skills and abilities they had to acquire. Then they could do it as well as the wim. But the soil!

The menwim sat, almost trembling at the thought of

having to work the soil. They had no idea how things came to grow out of the ground. They had never studied agriculture at school like the girls. Only looking after babies and domestic science. The girls became involved with it, and went on holiday to agricultural districts or worked the garden at home. They could do that. The boys had never wanted to learn it. Some of them, no doubt, had thought that it looked interesting, but they had never done anything about it.

But the problem was not merely that they had no idea how plants, trees and flowers grew out of the earth. Nor was it merely a matter of acquiring certain skills. For they lacked completely the contact with life, with nature, which made it possible to make things grow under their hands. No matter how much they struggled and studied, they would never escape the simple fact: *they did not menstruate*! And without menstruating, without the power that shone out of a wom who was tuned into the cycles of nature, they could not cultivate the soil. Everything would wither between their hands. And they would not know why.

'Yes, but hadn't we better start sowing then?'

They all turned to Fandango in surprise.

'Sowing?'

'Sowing, yes. Isn't that what it's called when wim put . . . put something in the ground so that it'll grow?'

'Is it?'

They saw a tiny glimmer of hope. Perhaps Fandango knew something. Perhaps there were other menwim who knew something. They were woken from the state of apathy they had been in and they began to discuss the possibilities. Some thought that they had no choice but to give up, since even if they learned what had to be done, they still wouldn't have the ability to do it. Others said that it might not be true that menwim couldn't work the soil just as well as wim. They were afraid all the fruit trees might die off if they started to interfere with them.

Spn Owlmoss thought of all the times he had seen Cornfield working in the garden. He would greet her, even stop for a chat. Sometimes he would merely walk past her.

But he had never noticed what she was actually doing. What did she do to the fruit trees each year to make them produce apples, pears and plums again the following year? How did carrots come to be carrots? For years he had been eating the produce of his own garden, and never, never for a single instant, had he stopped to wonder how this produce actually came into being. He felt ashamed. Then he thought back to his childhood. How keen he had been, following Cornfield around all day to see what she was doing, talking to her, and watching her and copying her. And Cornfield had taken things out of his hands and told him he was doing it wrong. And Principal Owlmoss had taken him aside and explained that it wasn't seemly for a young lad to show an interest in gardening, and she had presented him with some big embroidery patterns to encourage him to take up more appropriate pastimes. Thus Cornfield's work had become more and more remote to him.

Spn Owlmoss, cleared his throat in his characteristic way, which invited everyone to listen to him. He told them what he had been thinking, and how he had been prevented from learning about gardening when he was small, and why he had lost interest in it, and begun to do embroidery and to bury himself in books instead. These alone were not forbidden territories.

The menwim began, one after another, to talk about themselves. How they had, in fact, when they were small, asked their mothers how things grew, and they had all been given the same answer: 'You mustn't bother your head about that; you're a boy.' How could it be that they had all been given the same answer? Had their mothers come to an agreement? Had they held a secret meeting sometime, at which they had resolved, 'When our sons begin to show an interest in horticulture, we'll all answer, "You mustn't bother your head about that; you're a boy"?'

They laughed a little and felt encouraged. No, it wasn't like that. It was part of the whole fele ideology. A part of the whole system which made them so awkward and incapable.

It grew late. In the course of the afternoon and the

evening, they went through a whole series of emotions — from bewilderment to despair, to fury and finally to courage and determination. They all agreed it was the most consciousness-raising discussion they had ever had in the menwim's movement. The next morning, they would just start work; as Fandango had said.

But what would they start with? They couldn't simply start working when they didn't know what had to be done. Again they stared at each other, but not so hopelessly as before. They suspected what they had to do. They all did. There was no other way. That was just the way it was.

In the beginning.

The next day they got hold of a big, disdainfully jovial wom, who looked at them with her hands on her hips and said she would certainly teach the young lordies a little gardening, if that was what they really wanted. But she thought it was rather perverse. On the other hand she certainly wasn't one to take any notice of old prejudices. 'If you want to learn, you can certainly try it. I can't help laughing though.'

Thus the young lordies began to till the soil on Spn Owlmoss's estate.

The subjection of menwim
— a historical necessity

Why were things like this, and when did it start? Why did they quake at the thought of putting a seed in the ground? Why did they simply accept that wim could work the soil by virtue of their nature? Why should they learn in adulthood what all wim learned as children? Why was menstruation a source of power, when sperm was a source of shame? Why was it like this? How had it become so?

Who had determined it? Was it a world-embracing evil will that had pitted its forces against them? Why was it so difficult to rebel against it and to become independent?

They were sitting on the veranda, drinking Spn Owlmoss's apple wine, topless and feeling free; no wom could see them. The evening sun gleamed on their glasses. Egalsund lay at their feet, peaceful and beautiful.

'Originally, the celebration of menstruation was an element in an ancient fertility cult,' Spn Owlmoss explained, looking round them from one to the next. They were listening — lying back in their chairs on the veranda and listening. 'Today only a vestige of these ancient rituals survives in the Menstruation Games, held in the thirteenth month of the year. The menstrual cycle in the wom was precisely what bound the huwom race to life, to nature's own great cycle and to the phases of the moon. By virtue of this endlessly recurring rhythm in her body, she was bound in a very different way, to nature, and this contact with her natural surroundings gave her an inner power and strength, which allowed her to dominate nature and the environment. In the same way that she dominated her own body by releasing an egg once a month. Wim therefore had great control over everything — over their own bodies, over the cultivation of the soil, and over the world.'

In the earlier societies, menwim had not taken part in this celebration of wim's achievements. And the practice of excluding menwim had persisted until about fifty years before. Menwim were originally excluded because no one had realized that the manwom had any part in reproduction, since he never seemed to do anything that could reasonably be connected with it. Or with anything else, for that matter. He just ran around with gangs of other menwim, rubbing his penis and trying to stick it in the wom on the rare occasions she let him. It was only later that wom realized that menwim had a very special function for the offspring. Since the mother's relationship to her child was bound up with her body — through fertilization, pregnancy, birth and nursing — her relationship with her child was of a purely material kind. Later she provided for the material basis of its life, originally by cultivating the earth for herself and her offspring; in later civilized societies, by earning money for herself and her offspring. The manwom's relationship to the child, on the other hand, was purely spiritual — and therefore of an inferior kind. For him, the offspring was not a practical, physical reality, but the completion of a spiritual unity. On this basis, huwom societies probably began to venerate fatherhood at an early stage, in the view of Spn Owlmoss. The manwom's relationship to nature and the fruits of nature — and thus also the fruits of huwom beings — could never rise above the purely spiritual plane. The manwom would therefore always have a certain inclination towards abstraction — that is, a certain tendency to distance himself from reality, Spn Owlmoss explained, looking at them. They listened intently, wide-eyed.

Spn Owlmoss had studied many things, in his time, and he had studied eagerly. But he had never thought he would be able to come out with the things he knew and the ideas he had arrived at. They never really seemed to be in accordance with Directive No. 287. Sometimes he suffered periods of deep depression, when he suggested that the theories he developed around the facts he had discovered were perhaps a manifestation of just such a mafele way of distancing himself from reality.

In the earlier society, the wom gained power by virtue of her fertility, he explained. Her fertility was obviously general, since it was she who bore children and it was she who cultivated the earth. And while the wim bore children and tilled the soil and gathered eggs and herbs and created a society around them, the menwim ran around hunting. They never brought much home. Hunting was difficult and usually they didn't catch anything. They had a strange way of shouting and hallooing. Wild animals ran away before they got near them. No one really knew what the reason was, but in any case, they often came home empty handed — and what they did provide was nowhere near adequate to sustain their communities. The manwom therefore gradually came to be regarded as an unnecessary evil.

As cultivation became more complex and improved agricultural methods gave better yields, the basis arose for a class division in huwom society. The wom, naturally, owned the land, and at the same time she tried to find ways of making her manwom useful and tying him to her. It was about this time, too, that she began to think that the manwom did in fact have a role in the process of reproduction. And since they had never served any purpose beyond engendering children, they were also put to work looking after them. In connection with the care of children came many other tasks, which it turned out menwim were perfectly suited to. In fact it turned out that menwim were well able to do a great many jobs, as long as they were kept on a short rein. It was only when they were allowed to run around freely that they became completely useless to the community.

The wim thus acquired not only property rights over land, but also property rights over menwim. When a wom bound a manwom to her, he was obliged to give everything he might own or inherit from his mother, to his wife. It was self-evident that a manwom shouldn't own anything, since if he did, he would immediately fritter it away. There was, moreover, no alternative, if his child was to inherit from him. Inheritance, of course, always passes down the maternal line, since it is never possible to know who is whose father. A father would never be so presumptious as to say, 'That's my daughter!' There was never any proof. Responsibility for the family line rested exclusively with the mother. The idea that a father might secure a family's inheritance was therefore absurd.

Wom's power over manwom was then reinforced by her greater mobility. He was put to work, looking after children — the only thing he had hitherto shown himself capable of, apart from engendering them — while the wom went out and conquered new territories from foreign rulers. As the fighting intensified, the wim discovered that menwim could also be useful in war. Those used were generally young, unsullied menwim, who made up the infantry — the troops which go in front and are the first to be mown down. Behind them came the cavalry, which consisted exclusively of wim — and which included the leaders in its ranks.

It was pretty obvious that menwim could not sit astride a horse. Was there any more rewarding target for an enemy spear? In any case, somebody had to stay home and look after the children while the war was in progress. Out of this cavalry developed the class of Dames — those wim entitled to buy the most land, which in time became a ruling class which elected from its own ranks an assembly of councillors. This became the ruling institution in society.

As it became clearer that menwim could, after all, be useful in various ways, more and more of the hardest jobs were given over to them. Many of them of course were of a strong build, indeed, many of them were bigger and stronger than most wim. Thus, there gradually arose the system we know today, in which menwim do the hardest jobs.

The young menwim sighed. They had been listening and thinking and wondering *why*. They had the feeling that it never *had* to be like that — even though it sounded almost as though there was no alternative. They were hopelessly and eternally imprisoned within their own biology. There was no way they could escape that. And when they thought how profoundly tragic it was, it was tantamount to starting to feel ashamed again. At the same time, they had a marvellous feeling that perhaps it wasn't all so naturally determined as it sounded. But they couldn't really say where things had gone wrong, or how they might have been different. After all, it was true — wim were fertile and menwim weren't. But why had they accepted that wim should cultivate the earth alone? Why had menwim been so irresponsible — leaving their entire communities, and going off to hunt, and staying away for months on end? *Were* menwim more stupid and irresponsible than wim?

Why had menwim lacked the intelligence to see that if they were to have any power in society, they would also have to make themselves useful? Wealth had to be procured where wealth was found — in the earth.

Why had menwim not also tilled the soil — together with wim? They would then have realized that their position was weak. But it was precisely because it was weak that they did not manage to exploit the resources they had.

But why had they never made any attempt to use the physical strength many of them then had to keep wim down? Spn Owlmoss shook his head. No, it was unlikely that they had any particular physical strength. The methods wim employed to tame them were harsh and brutal. At certain periods in history, wim only preserved one in ten boy-children over the age of three. Wim could punish them whenever they wanted. Remember the prick-scissors. It was only with the appearance of a demand for mafele labour-power that the organized practice of slaughtering young menwim ceased. On the other hand wim retained the whip hand over them. Very little was known about it, but there was never any question of enormous physical strength. They were broken, and besides, they were scattered and separated from one another.

But why had they not used wom's fertility against her, and left her to look after the children, since she had given birth to them and nursed them? Why couldn't they just as well have held the wim in slavery, demanded to know which were their own children, conquered the earth and made inheritance pass through themselves?

For that, they would have needed access to the land. And how would they have acquired that? For that they would have needed power. They would have needed money or valuable possessions. Menwim had none. And nor could they simply go off and live on their own — even if they had had the power to sustain themselves — for then they would simply have died out . . .

They thought of their own helplessness and hopelessness when they discovered that Cornfield had left. But if they were themselves rebelling now, and cultivating the land, albeit on a small scale, why had menwim never done so before? Why had they always acquiesced?

What was mysterious — and truly incomprehensible — was that menwim had always accepted it. They had accepted the inferior position wim had allotted them. They must have believed wim when they said it was part of the natural order. Why did they believe them? They, the members of the Masculine League, didn't believe all that crap. They could just as well have said that it was part of the natural order for wim to mind children and for menwim to go out and make decisions. Nothing was really in harmony with any so-called 'natural order'. Everything was the contrivance of huwom beings. A systematic contrivance with a target in view: to hold huwom beings of one sort down, so huwom beings of another sort can exploit them and thrive as parasites.

'But it wasn't really like that,' said Spn Owlmoss. 'It isn't really true that menwim have always acquiesced. And nor is it true that things have always been the way I've described. Menwim have rebelled countless times — and in various ways — and there have also existed societies in which menwim have held the power. The problem is that we hear little or nothing about these rebellions and these patriarchal societies *because* we live in a matriarchy. Historians write nothing about them. The historians are wim. Anthropologists write nothing about them. The anthropologists are wim. That's why.

'Sexual identity is even more important than class identity. The fact is, we know considerably more about the working class than we do about menwim. The oppressed class we do hear something about consists largely of working-class wim. All the same, we hear a good deal — especially from Sparksist quarters — about how those who describe history merely do so from the ruling-class point of view, because they belong to that class themselves. But it is regarded as monstrous extremism to suggest that wim only write about wim because they are wim themselves. But that's what they do.

'If it is so much more monstrous and extremist to point out that the manwom is oppressed than it is to point out that the working class is oppressed, then it must be because sexual oppression is so much more monstrous and extreme than class oppression.

'If we want to know anything about menwim in former times, we usually have to look in the footnotes or read between the lines. This is what I've been doing for years. And I've discovered a great deal.'

Spn Owlmoss stopped. They were listening. He felt a wonderful sense of warmth and peace spreading throughout his entire body. He dropped his voice and relaxed, sitting back in his chair, like the others.

'Three hundred years ago in Pax, it was common practice to hold menwim's legs together with big ropes around the knees. The ones who were subjected to this treatment were unsullied maidmen, because they had to learn how to walk in a way that was seemly — without taking long strides. They learned how to move only their lower legs, while keeping their knees together. You can imagine how they had to walk. The real reason, of course, had nothing to do with moving gracefully. They had to be prevented from running too far from their mothers' sight, so that they might get a decent fatherhood-protector when they were old enough. I discussed this once in the staff-room with Egg. She also teaches history. Do you know what she said? She said, "No doubt it was a matter of fashion. Menwim do so many strange things." Luckily, the bell went. Anyway, many menwim wound up with bad posture and pains in the back as a result of the unnatural way they were made to walk, and they suffered from this for the rest of their lives, even though the ropes were cut off when they got fatherhood-protection. Menwim rebelled against this on countless occasions. They met in secret and cut off each others' ropes, even though they knew it was sacrilege. They ran away and hid in the woods. They sent secret messages round to other young menwim, encouraging them to do the same. But they were caught, and whipped and the ropes were put back. We don't as a rule hear about this directly in Paxian history; we hear about it indirectly, in the references to certain mothers complaining about their disobedient sons.

'Rebellion takes so many forms. It is rebellion when a young lad protests and sulks because he is prevented from doing so many things he wants to do. He's forced to wear clothes he can't move in. Later, he's forced to wear a peho. He knows there are so many jobs that aren't open to him. He realizes immediately that he is subjected to such treatment for the sole reason that he is a boy. There is no other explanation. Girls are all allowed to do what he too would like to do. He can't accept it, because it strikes him immediately as an injustice. And it is also rebellion when groups of menwim stand talking with one another at the Fatherhood Office or the P-registry, or at the shop, having all those long conversations which wim consider stupid and trivial. It's fine for wim to say these conversations are stupid and trivial, because of course they have absolutely no idea what the menwim are talking about. And they never listen. Wim think these conversations are stupid and trivial, because while they're in progress, the menwim's attention is not directed at them. The menwim seem to be enjoying themselves, and wim don't like that. They talk about how they feel, about their troubles and pains. They never show any reverence to their wim when they get together and talk in this way. This is also a sort of rebellion — or the start of it. And, naturally, we never hear anything about all this. And nor do we see it as a form of rebellion. But it is, just as it is when menwim tell their wim where to get off when they start ladying it around the house. And we don't hear anything about the times when menwim really got together and created resistance.

'During the Great Growth Age, there were constant wars between Pax and Egalia over the possession of rich mountain ranges in Palluria. For hundreds of years they were conquering and reconquering areas of land and mountain districts from each other. Both countries often used blockades and scorched earth as military tactics. We know of a number of occasions when menwim rebelled against these tactics, because children were starving to death. They marched in protest to the councilwim and pointed out that the wim who were responsible for the blockade policy were not the ones who were going to suffer under it. And, for that matter, what interest did menwim have in retaining possession of the Pallurian mountains? They would only be sent there — and they would get nothing from the riches they yielded. What sorority — or rather fraternity — there must have been among these menwim. It was dangerous. Nothing must be written about it in case posterity learns of it. These menwim were of course branded as unmatriotic, and accused and convicted of high treason when some of them broke into the foodstores and shared out food to children and the poor. The food stores were for the soldiers, it was said — *and* for all the wim in the senior administration. "Menwim also need food," they said. That was going too far. The ringleaders of the revolt were sentenced to death. Executions were a form of popular entertainment then. The ringleaders were put up on a scaffold, where they had their penises chopped off; then their heads. About fifty suffered this fate. The rest — several hundred — were sentenced to forced labour for life in Palluria, for having undermined the motherland's will to defend itself. And this was despite the fact that it was not really a campaign on behalf of menwim, but a revolt in defence of children — a completely selfless action. The menwim's cause took many generations to recover from this blow.

'But only forty years ago, there was widespread protest throughout the whole country against the growing wave of unjust fatherhood-allocations. No record was made of the number of fathers who were allotted children that were not their own. The men got together in small organizations to draw up such statistics themselves. They found out that the practice of the Fatherhood Offices was simply to give babies to the menwim the mothers said were the fathers — without any investigation whatsoever. We know, of course, that the same thing goes on today. Many of the "fathers" protested, but they were simply turned away or ridiculed. The wim at the junior levels of the administration who dealt with them directly made rude remarks about their sex organs and said next time they ought to try and keep their cocks under control and so on. Most amusing. And then it was just a matter of having the bawling infant plonked in one's arms and being pushed out the door of the Fatherhood Office as quickly as possible.

'The highpoint of the anti-fatherhood campaign was reached when the menwim's clubs got about thirty menwim to deposit their babies outside the Fatherhood Office and walk away.

'The clubs had their work cut out, getting menwim to take part in this action. For even though the menwim knew the babies were not theirs, they felt a responsibility for them. Of course, having to look after them meant that their chances of finding a reasonably well-paid job were reduced to nil. All the same, many menwim branded this form of protest as crude and inhuwom; and the main argument against it was: "It mustn't be at the expense of the child; the child is innocent." The menwim who did participate were called fanatical and immoral and many menwim left the clubs in disgust. There were nevertheless some who left their babies outside the Fatherhood Office. And walked away. The babies lay outside, crying and bawling. The menwim had positioned sentries to make sure that no menwim passers-by picked up the babies and began to fuss over them. In the end, the wim from the Fatherhood Office had to come out themselves to get them. They didn't really know how to calm them down, or how to hold them properly, and they weren't quiet until some cleaning menwim came by at closing time and relieved them.

'There was complete chaos when the babies were reallocated — as they were so small no one could tell the difference between them and they had no identifying documents. Chaos reigned in the official files, and that was where the wim drew the line. The thirty menwim who had so defied their own natures as menwim were sent to Palluria for a time, convicted of gravely abusing innocent children. The Fatherhood Office was given statements stating which other menwim had been involved in the menwim's clubs, and the thirty babies were allocated to these. Their paternity had to be reregistered. Many of these menwim had in fact opposed this protest. That made no difference, however. The Fatherhood Office didn't believe them. Enough was enough. This naturally created further strife and division among the menwim. Many of these menwim were also allocated fatherhood over another baby within a short time.

'The anti-fatherhood campaign brought the menwim's cause many opponents — notably among the menwim themselves. Most thought that menwim ought to have equal rights with wim. But to deny their role as a father — that was going too far.'

The masculists had never heard of these rebellions before. They were shocked that they had not heard of them. And they were frightened. Would their own campaigns produce the same effects? No, if they began to think like that, they would never get anywhere. It was better to think of collecting as much information as they could about what menwim had done before, so all menwim could hear about it. But that was a colossal task. Where would they get money? And who was competent to write down menwim's history?

'And what can we do ourselves to make sure that in twenty or fifty years, menwim will know what we've been doing?' asked Spn Owlmoss. 'A certain amount has been written about what we think, and a great deal has been written about what wim think of us. But what do we write about what we *do*? What guarantee do we have that our own revolt will not also be forgotten. And even if we do write something, what guarantee do we have that it will get through to people, or that it will be preserved? In former times, too, menwim wrote their chronicles; but they weren't published. It is wim who decide what gets published. It is wim who decide what is important and what is unimportant. History is written by wim.'

Fish and romance

'In Clara Sparks's works, we find a penetrating analysis of every important aspect of social structure,' said Gro Maydaughter, looking hard at Petronius. 'And I'm not the type, as you no doubt realize, not to have felt in my body the things that are the subject of her theories. It isn't just theory for me. My old grandmother — Baya — was pure Sparksism in practice. She knew what was what, even though she belonged to a declining section of the working class. She managed. It's thanks to her that I'm standing here today. And it's also thanks to her that it's been possible for you to be here.'

Once again, Petronius felt weak and pliable in the presence of his lover. He thought how much he had to thank her for. Yes, paradoxical though it might seem, it was almost thanks to a wom that there was any menwim's movement at all. Shouldn't she be allowed some influence on the way it developed? Was this the thanks he should give her?

'Class distinction is the curse of society, Petronius. You know that as well as I do. Haven't we paid for it, you and I, over the years? Didn't your mother condemn our relationship because I wasn't good enough for you? For her, the fishing population has always represented something inferior and wretched. And when an example of this primitive, lower caste then comes and asks for her son's hand — well, that awakens the class instinct in her. Then she knows who she is. Ruth Bram — daughter of old farming stock. And that's the end of all her theories about an egalitarian society. What makes you what you are and me what I am, Petronius? Aren't you what you are today — a self conscious young manwom with a future — aren't you that by virtue of your class background? And what about me? What is the reason that I'll never get anywhere further? Because I have to live by my work. As long as I live. I can never climb above that, because I'll never acquire enough capital. This place isn't going to make anyone fat. But I have a plan for it, Petronius. And I thought you and I were agreed on my idea. That was to make it a political headquarters, which at the same time was largely self-sufficient. I would work the land and you would fish under my guidance. That was my guiding thought, Petronius. Together with you, because I loved you, and I still do. And now you say you want to start studying in a completely new direction, and drop Sparksist ideas in favour of some book no one's ever heard of. And I suppose the idea is that things will carry on like that. You'll for ever be unearthing piles of stuff written by menwim no one's ever heard of on subjects no one's ever heard of. What the Lucy are you going to do with it all? It isn't the sexual division between us that accounts for the fact that I'm where I am and you're where you are, Petronius. It's money. And you know that as well as I do. Money, Petronius; capital. Ruling class and working class, social divisions, education — everything goes together.'

Petronius looked back at Gro, trying to bear in mind that he ought to look at her just as sternly as she looked at him. He knew she was right. And he knew that she wasn't right at the same time. And he knew that he didn't know how he should explain to her that he didn't think she was right. But . . .

'You just go on about sexual divisions and sexual conflict . . . Actually I think you're pallurians, all of you.'

Petronius gave a start. He had seldom heard the word. The girls used to say it about Spn Owlmoss. 'That isn't true! You know how much I loved you . . .'

'*Loved*! Was that the past tense you used?'

'How can you assume I'll go on loving you when you want to force through your own ideas, and you only sneer at what I think is important?' He felt at a loss for words and buried his face in his hands.

'No, don't start crying again, now. Let's go out in the boat, shall we?'

He felt her arm round his shoulder. He nodded.

It was a fine, calm evening. Cold and clear. Gro went to fetch the gear from the shed. They dressed warmly and went down to the jetty. Gro jumped aboard and Petronius sat on the edge of the jetty and waited. He watched the way she arranged things in the bottom of the boat, and the way she half disappeared with her head out of sight under the engine cover. He knew what had to be done, but when they were together, she was, nevertheless, always the one who got everything ready. If he tried to do it, there were always a thousand little things he did wrong, she said.

And then she always thought he was so slow. It was true that it didn't take as long when she did it herself. He watched her contemplatively. He had never ceased to marvel at the economy and efficiency of her movements.

The water was mirror smooth and shone pink and yellow a little way off. Again Petronius felt a strange sense of fate, which he had experienced many times with Gro. They really belonged together. They were just waiting, really, until they could be together, inseparably. There was no other way; he loved to think of that. It made him feel safe. That, among all the shifting circumstances of the world, one thing should remain constant — that they were together. Then Baldrian's face appeared in his mind's eye.

'Ready,' called Gro, holding her hand out to him. Petronius took it and jumped into the boat, skidding slightly on the deck. It was more difficult to keep one's balance when she was holding his hand tightly. 'Whoops!' said Gro. He sat at the bow.

They headed out. Gro stood at the stern, steering and watching. Petronius at the bow, looked down into the water. The bow cleaved the dark water softly.

'Hey!' said Petronius. 'There are fish here.' He grabbed the little landing net.

'You can't catch them with the landing net!'

'Why not? It's just below the surface.' He turned to her and made a face. 'Perhaps it goes against Sparksist principles?'

'All right; cut the sarcasm.'

Petronius swung the net and in a flash he had a big blackfish floundering in it. They were called blackfish because of their dark backs. He grinned broadly. Gro gaped at it in amazement.

'Well, I'll be a daughter of a dog!'

'A good one, eh?'

'Mmmm . . . Take the tiller for a moment. Let's have a look.'

'I'll just kill it first.'

'Let me do that. It'll just slip out of your hands and back into the sea.'

'Pah!' He stunned the fish then cut its head off. Then he went aft and took the helm. Gro took the landing net, swung it in an elegant arc and peered down into the depths.

'Where the hell are all these fish you were talking about?'

'Aren't there any more?' Petronius felt guilty.

Gro stood where she was for a long time, staring down. Petronius thought uneasily that the rest of this glorious calm evening would be ruined if Gro didn't get a blackfish. Suddenly she swung the net violently. She straightened up and wiped her forehead with the back of her hand. 'It got away! It was a huge one!' She held out her hands. 'Like that.'

She went back to staring into the water, muttering about the fish she had missed and how big it was. She took another swipe with the net and pulled it out of the water in a single movement. A blackfish, about a quarter of the size of the one Petronius had caught came into view in the bottom of the net. Petronius just managed to stop himself bursting out laughing.

'That'll be a lot better to fry than yours,' she said. 'Crazy way of fishing, this.' She went back to the helm.

Petronius made no further attempts after that. He saw several shoals just below the surface, but he merely lay half over the gunnel, watching them swimming and saying nothing. They could have caught dozens. But he wanted their trip to be a happy one, and he was in a romantic mood. He positioned himself at the foremost point of the bow and raised his arms above his head.

'You make the loveliest figurehead a wom could want on her ship,' Gro called to him. He remained in the same position, looking ahead. Suddenly he began to roar with laughter.

'What are you laughing at?'

'I was just thinking how good it's going to be.'

'What's going to be so good?'

'Our plans . . . I mean what we're planning.'

'Aha. I see. Whatever you're planning which I'm not allowed to know about. It'll be good. I'm sure . . . Petronius?'

'Yes?'

'I feel like making love with you.'

'Go on, then.'

Gro stopped the engine and dropped anchor. In a moment she was with him, lying on top of him in the bottom of the boat. 'It's nice,' thought Petronius. 'It's lovely, being fucked so hard. Really hard.' He put his hands behind his head and closed his eyes, the way he knew Gro liked him to. 'It's lovely, lying here and feeling her going hard at it on top of me. It's great to lie here and feel that I'm a real manwom . . '

'I love you,' she whispered.

The studs' tragedy

'When I'm in bed with Eva, I always feel like a real man-wom,' said Baldrian.

'*Like* one?' asked Petronius, laughing.

They were sitting at a tavern called The Wom in the Moon with a bottle of wine, trying to draft a leaflet in connection with the great peho-burning they had planned. They found no end of things they couldn't put down, and laughed more and more. 'What would wim say if we told them they had to hoist up their breasts in some stupid sling, the way we have to wear a peho? If we said that without something to support their breasts, they looked droopy and ugly and unattractive?' They all laughed and raised their glasses. No, they couldn't write that. This leaflet had to be serious.

They had started with a discussion of what the peho actually signified and whether it was necessary. As a heading for the leaflet, Petronius had proposed: 'WE WANT OUR COCKS FOR OURSELVES!' And they chuckled and drank over this for a long time before they got any further.

Apart from the fact that they could not possibly write 'cocks' on a leaflet that was intended to win people over, it might also be misunderstood as meaning that they wanted nothing at all to do with wim. Their opponents, at any rate, would take it as evidence of an extreme hatred of wim.

Petronius and Baldrian began to confide in each other how happy they were with their wim.

'Do you come?' asked Petronius.

'Sometimes. What about you?'

'Not usually. I also have difficulty getting it up. But Gro says it doesn't matter to her whether it's erect or not . . . but it matters to me, doesn't it . . .'

'Why do so many menwim have trouble getting erections?'

'Well, of course, wim have a much stronger sexual drive.'

'I think it's just a myth.'

'Do you think so? They always get steamed up and sopping wet almost immediately. Usually it takes no more than a couple of minutes. Five at the most. It does with Gro, in any case.'

'Once I was with someone who took ten minutes . . .'

'Have you ever done it with a wom who didn't come?'

'No . . .'

'Why aren't we like that? Why don't we get . . .' he lowered his voice, 'an erection right away?'

'Anxiety about starting a baby has a lot to do with it. We're always aware that it may result in a child. A wom never has to think of that. You know, I've been thinking about how different wim and menwim are on exactly that point. With us it's as though the sensual sex act and the act of reproduction are one and the same thing. I mean, anyway . . .'

Baldrian stopped speaking. He glanced up at Petronius and took a gulp of wine.

'I mean the nicest way — I reckon, anyway — is . . .' He looked round and leant across the table towards Petronius. 'The nicest way is having your thing inside her while she goes up and down on top of you, while you lie on your back, and in the end it just happens automatically — like a sort of explosion or something. It's fantastic, doing it like that. But I've only ever done it twice. It takes a lot of courage to say you want to do it like that. And a wom has to be incredibly tolerant and considerate before she'll let you do it that way . . .'

Petronius felt deflated. He knew he would enjoy doing it in the way Baldrian had described, but he'd thought he was alone in having such desires. 'But that can result in a child!'

'Yes, that's exactly what I meant. That we like doing it in a way that can result in a child. But wim don't have that problem. With them the sexual pleasure and the act of reproduction are separate — since they don't have any sexual feelings in their vaginas, but satisfy themselves by external stimulation. It's all right for them.'

'I'd never thought of that.'

'No, nor had I before the other day. But it helped me understand why we find it so difficult to get satisfaction. We always think of ourselves as breeding stock, because that's what we've been taught from puberty — if not before. And when we begin to sense those sexual feelings, we immediately think we're going to start a baby if we follow our desires, and this makes us afraid and ashamed, and we daren't talk about it. And when we finally go to bed with a wom, we daren't show her what we want, so we just do things her way, and we like it only because she likes it. And in a certain way, that's all right.'

'We can always take the pill. Then we don't have to worry about starting a baby.'

'But it has side effects.'

'Yes . . .'

'The latest research says the new one there is now has no side effects — or hardly any.'

'Gro complains that I'm not so good in bed when I take the pill. So I've stopped taking it.'

'Why should we really have to take the pill, when the wom doesn't usually want us to put it in her vagina?'

'If it happens, well, maybe . . .'

They stared at each other again. There were so many things, once you started to think about it. So many things concerning the subjection of menwim that it took you a long time to realize. Sometimes you felt utterly stupid when you saw the reality of something you had simply accepted without thinking. Like this. Suddenly it seemed completely ridiculous that menwim should have to take the pill when, at the same time, they hardly ever achieved sexual satisfaction.

Suddenly they saw how the simple question, 'How do you make love?' was a symptom of the way society functioned as a whole. Menwim took the pill and suffered its injurious effects, but achieved no satisfaction. Menwim did the hardest and most unpleasant work in society, and in the family, and achieved no satisfaction — none of the happiness and harmony they were promised in their childhood. When you began to think of it this way, it seemed as though everything was one great conspiracy against them.

'Maybe we should try with each other instead.'

Petronius immediately regretted what he'd said. In the first place he wished he hadn't said 'try' and in the second place, what he meant to express was not sexual. He had become increasingly aware that he wanted to be with Baldrian, to talk with him, to see him. Sometimes it was just as though he was in love with him. But he had never thought of going to bed with Baldrian, and if he was now thinking of it, as something he felt like doing, it still had nothing to do with Gro. If he wanted to go to bed with Baldrian, it was not because he didn't achieve orgasms with Gro. Why had he blurted it out like that? Was that the real reason, after all? He felt confused. He hoped Baldrian would ignore the stupid suggestion he had just made.

'Of course there are some who do that,' said Baldrian.

Petronius felt immensely relieved that Baldrian had not, after all, ignored his stupid suggestion.

'Do you know any of them?'

'Only wim. Two of the wim I've been with turned out to be homosexual. It was strange. Actually there are some who I've liked being with more than anyone else. Once I handled it dreadfully. I'd been with her for a long time when she told me. I was completely devastated. But there wasn't anything I could do about it. I was depressed for three months, and then I found myself a super-heterosexual wom. I stuck that for two months.'

Petronius felt a pang of envy at the thought. He wasn't really sure whether he was jealous of the wim, or of the fact that Baldrian was a 'liberated' manwom. He had been with so many wim. Looser relationships had become more common in recent years — particularly since the advent of the menwim's movement. Menwim ought not to be prudish any longer.

They drank a little and looked at each other. Their

hands were only an inch or so apart when they put down their glasses.

'Are you in love with me?' asked Baldrian, suddenly.

Petronius felt himself redden, and made no reply.

'It's important that people don't get the impression we're pallurians,' said Baldrian gravely.

'I'm in love with Gro.'

'Yes, and I'm in love with Eva.'

Baldrian touched Petronius's hand gently, as though unintentionally. Petronius felt himself grow warm at the touch.

'It doesn't mean we're pallurian, does it?'

Baldrian shook his head. 'No, there's nothing pallurian about it. Pallurian menwim are . . . I don't know . . . well, they're sort of ultra-womly menwim — butch. At least we aren't like that.'

They remained where they were, looking at each other, with their drinks. They ordered another bottle.

'Not in the least pallurian,' laughed Petronius suddenly. 'That would undermine the whole menwim's movement. If it were seen as an attempt to do without wim altogether. To be independent in every respect.'

'But isn't that actually what the menwim's movement is about?'

'Yes, but not like that, is it? I mean, we *do* need wim.'

A wom came over to their table and leered at them, standing with her hands in her pockets. She was slightly drunk. 'Mind if I sit down?' she asked.

'Yes,' said Baldrian and Petronius in unison.

The wom sat down, positioning herself next to Baldrian. Baldrian moved.

'Now look,' she sniffed. 'I've been watching you two, sitting here and flirting with each other, for a long time. You know what I think your problem is? You've never tasted good cunt. That's the trouble with you. I've got a lovely wet one. Really good and juicy. How about it? I only live round the corner . . .'

Two of her companions came over to the table and began to tug her by the sleeve. 'Come on, Tubby! Let's get on with the game. Leave the lordies in peace.'

Tubby suddenly ripped open her shirt. 'Take a look at the equipment!' she said, thrusting one breast forward. Tattooed on it was a naked manwom with an erection in profile. When she shook her breast his cock wobbled back and forth. The others laughed. Baldrian and Petronius got to their feet almost together. Tubby tried to stand in front of Baldrian and block his way. He jumped over the table with one bound and glared defiantly at her.

'You wim always think menwim can't get by without a cunt!'

'I see!' she said, as though understanding had suddenly dawned on her. 'Going to some gay bar now, are you? Lady Almighty!'

'Yes, that's exactly what we're doing,' said Baldrian, putting some money on the table.

'Lady Almighty!' she repeated. 'You pallurian spermy whores! Can't do much with two menwim, can you!'

'What do you know about it? Have you tried being two menwim together then? Eh?'

'I mean . . . well, I *mean* . . . ah . . . how d'you do it then?'

'Obviously we have an artificial clitoris to lick and plastic breasts to squeeze. That's how we do it.'

The wom gaped, dumbfounded. That was exactly what she had imagined.

Petronius and Baldrian stood out in the rain, laughing.

'Is that really what we're doing? Going to a gay bar?' asked Petronius.

Baldrian took his arm. 'Yes. That's really where we're going.'

They giggled and crossed the road. A wom with her back to them stood in a doorway, with her legs apart, knees wobbling slightly, pissing so that it ran in torrents beneath her. As she swayed back and forth, she hummed a few notes bearing a distinct resemblance to the Quarrywim's latest hit.

'Wim piss everywhere. We can't go anywhere in town without seeing rivers running behind them.'

'All they have to do is undo the flap in their trousers.'

'It's worse for us.'

'Yes, it's worse for us. Worse for us.'

'Wim are so much more practically designed than men-wim,' Petronius chanted solemnly. He felt pleasantly merry.

'We have to take off the whole rigmarole.'

'Untie the peho.'

'Right. Thus, nature, in her wisdom, hath ordained it.'

'And nothing can be done about it!'

They laughed and hailed a cab.

New adventures for the masculists

'We want to go to the place where Egalsund's homosexuals meet.'

The cab-driver tried to look impassive. She scratched her head thoughtfully and said nothing. She called the dispatcher and had to repeat the word 'homosexuals' three times before the switchboard-boy got it. In fact they could hear from his tone of voice that he had understood her the first time. In such circumstances, though, it is best to make one hundred per cent certain one has not misheard.

The cab-driver was given the address of a restaurant in the dock area and they set off. There was no sign of any restaurant where the cab dropped them. On closer inspection, however, they saw a small bellpush in a doorway. They could just hear the sound of music and voices coming from behind the door, which bore the words, 'Members Only'. Above the bellpush was a tiny little label: 'Paradise'. With their arms around each other, they rang the bell. After a moment, the door opened a crack and a nose and an eye appeared.

'Are you members?' asked the nose.

'No, but we want to join.'

'What d'you want to join?'

'A club for gays.'

The door opened and the manwom the nose belonged to came into view. He was the strangest manwom either of them had ever seen. He was big and strong and dressed in long black trousers and a black jacket with no peho.

'I'm the bouncer here,' he explained. 'Have to make sure we don't get any undesirables.' He took them familiarly by the elbow and led them along a long corridor and up a staircase to the cloakroom. 'Two new members,' he said, and disappeared through a swing door.

'I'll take your things,' said the cloakroom attendant, who on closer inspection turned out to be a wom. She was just as strange as the bouncer. She had her hair done up, and wore a flowery silk blouse and a tight skirt. She went back and forth behind the counter carrying coats and clothes hangers, taking little steps. Petronius and Baldrian were completely fascinated, but tried to behave as though there was nothing in the least odd about her appearance.

'That'll be twenty dollables, each, please.'

'What?'

'Fifteen for the membership card and five for the cloakroom. And I need your names, please. Write them here.' They were each given a little, pink card, headed 'The Paradise Club: Association for the Like-Minded', with a logo showing two wim's hands, clasped. Petronius and Baldrian hesitated. The cloakroom attendant leant over to them confidingly. 'You don't have to write your real names,' she said. 'Just make something up.'

They wrote, 'B Lifedaughter' and 'P Evedaughter', which were the most ordinary names they could think of. The cards were stamped and returned to them.

'You can use them in gay clubs the world over,' said the attendant. She turned away and began to count money.

The room behind the swing door was dimly lit, with abundant mirrors, niches, curtains, plush furniture, paintings and posters. The pictures depicted, clothed, half-clothed and naked wim. Breasts and crotch bulges were emphasised. One showed a naked wom astride a horse. In another, a wom in tight trousers and a half-open shirt stood with her feet apart, staring right at them out of the picture with a fixed glare. Her fists gripped black iron chains. A third picture showed a wom in profile beside her electric car. The curving lines of the car's gleaming wing echoed the curve of her breasts. Most of the pictures portrayed very young and beautiful wim in tight trousers, naked from the waist up, with fine, swelling breasts.

A tiny picture showed two menwim, dressed in old-fashioned clothes, with flowers in their hair, smiling mischievously at each other.

At the small tables in the alcoves, wim sat in couples or groups, drinking and smoking. Petronius and Baldrian felt their scalps tingling. Along one wall was a long bar, at which there were a line of wim, some talking and gesticulating excitedly.

'Lovely pearls you're wearing today, mmmm,' they heard one wom say to another.

'And where *did* you get that rouge? It really suits you, sweetie.' They were chatting away, exactly like menwim. Some were even wearing tight skirts with pehoes hanging loose outside. But most wore quite ordinary wim's trousers and colourful shirts. Many carried small menwim's hangbags which they opened and closed and took little things out of — cigarette cases, money, little mirrors. Some wim, however, simply stood there with a drink in front of them, staring straight ahead and saying nothing. Only their eyes moved.

Petronius and Baldrian walked through the bar and entered another, much bigger room, with constantly changing lighting and loud music. The big dance floor undulated with wim dancing in pairs, rocking to the rhythm of the band. Many of them were sporting the latest hair-style — a thin stripe of hedgehog spikes across the skull from ear to ear, their heads otherwise completely clean-shaven. They whirled round in the sexy new style.

Donna Mother! These wim could dance! Petronius and Baldrian watched the vigorous and well-co-ordinated movements of their hips, shoulders, legs and arms. Sometimes they bumped into one another so their breasts collided, before jumping apart again. Some danced so close they could rub their bellies against each other. Petronius and Baldrian couldn't take their eyes off them.

Suddenly they did a double-take. Heading straight towards them were Principal Bosomby and Liz Bareskerry, arm in arm, each with her hair done up and a salmon-pink handbag. They looked straight through them and disappeared from the dance floor.

'But . . . but . . . wasn't that . . .?'

'Yes, wasn't it . . .?'

'Are you sure?'

'I . . I ought to know my own mother.'

'You don't think maybe we've drunk a bit too much?'

'They didn't seem to recognize us.'

'No. Perhaps we just imagined it . . .'

'Or maybe *we're* the ones who don't look ourselves.'

'What shall we do now? Leave?'

'No, why? Why should we worry about them, or whether or not it was them?'

They made their way through the sea of wim, but Bosomby and Bareskerry had vanished, as though the floor had swallowed them up. All the tables round the dance floor were packed with wim.

'Wasn't this club meant to be for menwim as well as wim?' asked Baldrian.

'Maybe the bouncer's the only manwom.'

They laughed, although they didn't see anything particular to laugh at. They were uncomfortable about laughing; but they laughed nevertheless.

They sat at a table for two which had just been vacated. Now they noticed that there was a mafele couple dancing almost on the spot in one corner of the dance floor. They clung to each other, buffeted violently now and then by a fele couple dancing past.

There were a few other menwim at a table nearby. One of them held his companion around the waist. The companion yielded and leant against him. He kissed him, long and passionately. One of the most popular current hits boomed out of the loudspeakers — 'Say you're mine, say you're mine.' Three mafele couples headed out onto the dance-floor, laughing and nudging one another. They seemed so strong in their arms and shoulders, and moved so freely and uninhibitedly. Their hips and buttocks undulated back and forth together. In a certain way it seemed that they *were* their bodies. It was strange and beautiful to watch.

A manwom in a black jacket and trousers appeared in front of their table. 'Are you new here?'

195

'Yes.' Petronius and Baldrian nodded.

'Aren't you going to join in the dancing, then?'

Petronius and Baldrian looked at each other rather uncertainly and back at the manwom. 'No, we're just sitting and talking for now . . .'

In fact they hadn't been. They didn't know what they were doing.

'I expect I'm disturbing you . . .'

'No, no . . .'

'D'you mind if I join you?'

They shook their heads.

'Are you sure?'

'Yes,' they answered in unison. The manwom sat down and lit a cigarette.

'Of course we can't help being the way we are,' he said. 'It may be a bit perverse. Sometimes I feel as though I have the soul of a wom in a manwom's body. I wear a peho at work . . . but it's so nice that there is one place you can be yourself. I think we're born the way we are . . .'

'Do you think so?'

'Yes. Don't you think you were?'

Petronius and Baldrian avoided looking at each other and said nothing.

'Are you sure I'm not disturbing you? I'll go, if I am . .'

'No, it isn't that. We're not sure we *are* like that . . .'

The manwom laughed.

'People get such extraordinary ideas in their heads about what it means to be gay. They think we make rubber clitorises and keep a pair of giant foam-rubber falsies. They think we have to play wom and manwom, and put on those false breasts, and act the whole thing larger than life. I wish they knew we're quite ordinary citizens.'

Someone laughed immediately behind them. They continued to talk, but the laughing continued. What was the matter with the idiots? They couldn't be that funny, even if they were dressed like ordinary menwim. Petronius and Baldrian looked round. There stood Spn Owlmoss and Fandango, hugging each other tightly and beaming towards them.

'Baldrian and Petronius!' Fandango embraced them. His face had the radiance of the sun.

'We must celebrate this!' laughed Spn Owlmoss. He looked fifteen years younger.

'Is this one of those double weddings?' asked the man-wom, getting up and pulling out his chair for Spn Owlmoss, with a little movement of his hand. 'Congratulations. Hope to see you again.' He went off.

Spn Owlmoss sat on the chair and Fandango on his lap.

'I expect you think the age difference between us is a bit much . . .' said Spn Owlmoss, somewhat tentatively.

'On the other hand, the sex difference isn't so big,' said Fandango, kissing him on the mouth. Baldrian had never seen him so happy.

'A bottle of champagne!' Spn Owlmoss shouted to one of the serving wim, who immediately jotted it down on her pad. 'And four glasses!' She returned a moment later, smiling at Spn Owlmoss and asking him how things were going.

'Fantastically well!' he said.

The serving-wom glanced at Fandango.

'An old friend of mine,' said Spn Owlmoss. 'Fandango.'

'Hi, nice to meet you,' she said, holding her hand out to Fandango. 'Take good care of him. I'm Maud and I'm an old friend of Lisello's.' She pushed up the champagne cork, poured it out and went on her way.

They talked and toasted one another and laughed. Fandango and Spn Owlmoss recounted the endless ridiculous situations they had found themselves in while trying to prevent anyone finding out what was going on. But sooner or later they were going to. There was no way out of it. There was no possibility that the menwim's movement could float for ever on the illusion that it could manage without pallurian menwim; or that it would have existed at all without pallurian menwim. It would not have done. Without pallurian menwim, there would never have been any menwim's movement, ever.

A manwom's voice boomed out of the loudspeakers. It was a singer from Pax, singing about menwim's strength and understanding. They went out onto the dance floor and danced, holding each other by the shoulders and singing. Spn Owlmoss's baritone amazed them. They stopped and listened. Had anyone at school known that he had such a good voice? At school, Egg always led the singing. At the end of every term, she sang untiringly with a high falsetto which could be heard above everything else, 'Land of my mothers . . . home of the bra-a-ave.'

The music stopped.

Baldrian grasped Petronius by the shoulders and gazed at him with half-drunk, sparkling eyes, brimming with tears. 'Isn't this what we're meant to do here?' He drew Petronius towards him and kissed him. They laughed and threw their arms around each other, hugging each other tightly, kissing and laughing. No, was it possible? Was that what it was like? It was an unbelievably wonderful feeling. They hardly dared look at each other. They felt completely dizzy, holding each other tightly and smiling throughout their whole bodies. They forgot where they were, and felt as though they had been lifted to some higher stratum of the atmosphere, weightless in each other's embrace. It was like nothing they had ever experienced in their entire, long, wearisome youth.

'And now we come to the last waltz.' The disc-jockey, wearing menwim's clothes and a wig, held the microphone right up to her mouth. 'Last chance for tonight. Womfred Womm sings . . .' the music had already begun, ' . . . "It was YOU I was waiting for".'

The two couples, Petronius and Baldrian and Spn Owlmoss and Fandango, danced into the music.

Was that what it was like? Like this? Feeling another manwom's body against one's own? Why had they never done it before? His arms around me, the music in the half-darkness — everything in the world was good. Baldrian, you're beautiful. Baldrian, I want to be with you.

The lights came on, hurting their eyes. They stared at one another's everyday faces. They looked down. Wasn't it time to go? Yes, it was time to go. They fetched their coats. The wim pushed and shoved and shouted, and got theirs first.

198

Then they were out in the street again, where there was not the slightest indication that any such place existed. They looked down the pavement. A couple of older wim, each with a salmon-pink handbag, disappeared round the corner.

'But, wasn't that . . .'

' . . . something we imagined?'

Petronius felt Baldrian's warm hand against his own, and felt secure again. Spn Owlmoss and Fandango came skipping out. They stopped on the steps for a moment to kiss. They stood there beaming at them, as blithe and happy as two full moons.

'Supper awaits us!' announced Spn Owlmoss.

They walked arm in arm, all four of them, up towards the big white villa on the Moonhill.

A mother's righteous anger

'I don't know what you're going on about,' said Ruth Bram, pacing back and forth on the floor. 'There's no sexual discrimination any more. Menwim can do exactly the same things as wim, if only they set their *minds* to it!'

In principle there was nothing standing in the way of everybody being equal in Egalia. The Moulding Mothers on Mount Demos had instituted a strictly egalitarian constitution, where everybody's right to everything regardless of anything was firmly established for all time.

What rights did wim have nowadays that menwim did not have, if she might be so bold as to ask? A manwom could be whatever the Lucy he wanted, as long as he was willing to work at it. *That* was where they were lacking. Menwim had no will-power! Ruth Bram paused, as though she needed a little time to reassure herself that menwim lacked will-power. What menwim wanted most was to be at home. Let them. Now why did he and his menwim's movement want to start stirring things up and making menwim feel guilty, or that their work had no value? The work they did was actually a thousand times — a thousand times, Petronius — more valuable than what wim did when they, like her, spent their time sorting a few bits of paper, or going to meetings, or making important decisions for the country. Much more valuable. And constructive. Anyway, menwim were better at looking after children.

'But if it's so valuable, the work menwim do, why don't they get paid for it?' It was a thought that had just entered his head. He had never considered it before.

His mother was dumbfounded by this for a moment. Silenced. But in the course of that silent moment, a million or so good arguments against what Petronius had said occurred to her. *Paid?* Now he really had lost his senses. Paid indeed! Where was the money supposed to come from, if she might be so bold as to ask? And anyway, menwim *were* paid, weren't they? Or didn't they eat, perhaps? Didn't they enjoy an easy life and sleep in a comfortable bed? Well? In fact they were paid doubly — in the form of security, affection and warmth. In any case, it was extraordinary that *he*, who wanted housebounds to liberate themselves from the cosy shelter of the home, should advocate payment for housework. Then they would just stay in the homes he was so anxious to get them out of. Payment! No, now he really was taking leave of his sanity.

Petronius saw that he probably had gone too far. It was only a passing thought. A silly idea he had seized on as a reply to her. He groped for an argument. 'But . . . but . . . what about the work gangs?' he asked, relieved to have thought of them. She was talking as though everyone belonged to the upper class. The menwim in the slum districts went to work every day — as well as looking after the children when they got home. What about them? They were the great majority. What if they all saw the implications of what she was saying and one fine day walked off their jobs, saying, 'Right, I'm not going to work any more because it's much more worthwhile and constructive to stay at home and look after the kids?' Of course they wouldn't have any money to live off, if they did that. Especially since there are a million arguments as to why they shouldn't have any. And of course if they got nothing to eat, they'd die. But what would that matter? As long as what they were doing was constructive and valuable.

Bram missed his irony. Yes, it was regrettable, most regrettable that the working class had to work so hard. They were in complete agreement there, and he shouldn't think they weren't.

'And who is in charge of them?' asked Petronius triumphantly. 'Who are the managers and inspectors and supervisors in the cleaning troops and the mending . . .'

'Okay, okay, okay, okay, OKAY!' As though she didn't

know that management consisted exclusively of wim. He didn't have to tell her. But until they had understood the fundamental difference between wim's and menwim's natures, they couldn't hope to achieve a socially just and correct division of labour between the sexes.

But who said there had to be a division of labour based on sex? Petronius wasn't giving up.

Here, Ruth Bram almost laughed. She explained patiently that the whole of history proved that, so there was simply no question as to whether . . . it was desirable or not. When he made no reply, she took it as a sign that he had finally run out of arguments. She began to talk more quietly. He was really so sweet. At heart, he must know she was right. Because whatever he was, he wasn't *stupid*. Not her son. And after all, it wasn't surprising that he should rebel a certain amount. He had to make his own way in the world. She went over to him and put her hand on his shoulder.

'But I'm impressed, Petronius,' she said, looking him straight in the eyes, with sincerity and affection. 'I'm impressed that you've done such a lot of thinking on your own. That you've formed your own opinions about things . . .'

The Egalian election and the menwim's daring coup

Political life was hectic in Egalia that spring. The employment situation obliged the Chief Director to announce a general election. No fewer than eight parties appeared on the ballot papers and the divisions were clearly delineated. There were all the old parties — the Democratic Egalists, the Popular Equality Party, the Egalitarian People's Party, the Egalitarian-Democratic Alliance, and the Egalistic Democrats. The Democratic Egalists and the Egalistic Democrats were involved in a particular battle with each other. They represented respectively the right and the left among the old parties. A new party had appeared in addition; the Sparksist activists' party, Short Cut, which, according to its political opponents, advocated blowing up all buildings belonging to the central administration, because nothing that went on in them was of the slightest benefit to the people.

Recently the religious party, Donna Jessica's Message, had begun to do well. It was campaigning for morality, less licentiousness, more humility, and a greater commitment to the fundamental values of the motherland, and there was a risk that this party might end up holding the balance of power.

Just before the election was due to start, an eighth party appeared calling itself the Telephone Party. It stood for an extension of the telephone system to allow all political decisions to be reached by telephone. It was somewhat unclear where in the political spectrum the Telephone Party belonged, and what the popular response would be to its programme. The Telephone Party put forward its views in its party organ *Brrrrr*. The former parties which had supported special business interests, such as the Fisher Party and the Commercial Union, were now anachronisms and had therefore been dropped from the ballot.

The poll itself had long ago been rationalized. The way it worked was a group of experts from the National Co-operative Directorate drew up a list of about 1000 citizens according to a system which ensured they were absolutely representative of the population as a whole. Scientists had worked out methods of arriving at such a representative selection that were one hundred per cent certain. It was therefore no longer necessary to undertake anything so laborious as asking the entire population.

The average Egalian was, on the whole, content that her opinions should be represented in Parliament in this way. It was, at any rate, much better than the previous system. Some very old people could remember how party canvassers used to plod round from house to house, asking the mother of every single household to vote for their party. With this system, the poll had lasted several days.

The old masculists of the Egalistic Menwim's Union had, moreover, protested against this method. Only the heads of families were asked, they said. And that was unfair. Menwim ought also to have the right to reply. With the new system, they had achieved that, on an equal footing with wim.

A group in the Masculine League, which for a long time had been fighting 'discrimination against menwim' in the electoral system, maintained, however, that even now menwim's electoral rights were not equal to those of wim. For a year this group had been studying the elections that had taken place in Egalia during the previous decade, and had concluded that each election had involved about 750 wim and about 250 menwim. 'So that's what the wim on the expert committees call a representative election!' they said to one another. They wrote a long and well-documented article on the phenomenon and sent it to the *Egalsund Times*. The article was rejected. 'The Editor has read your article with great interest,' said the rejection slip. 'You produce some interesting data. The election campaign is now so far advanced, however, that it is doubtful whether your findings have any news value. This newspaper gives preference to material that is topical.'

At the same time, however, the various party activists knew that the masculists were not going to be lulled into silence.

The issues of masculism had been in the wind for several years, and all the parties realized the importance of giving the impression of being interested in them, if they were themselves to maintain any credibility in the election. They therefore tried to avoid ballots bearing only wim's names, even though it was, of course, not always possible to do so. 'Egalsund wasn't built in a day,' they said. And it was the same with menwim's liberation. The parties found it entertaining to listen to what the various menwim's libbers had to say, and they made investigations to see whether any of it was compatible with their own party programmes. If it was, they made as much as they could of it. Sometimes they also took up issues the masculists had raised in party discussions. The group they listened to most was the Egalistic Menwim's Union, which had been fighting for the masculist cause for generations. The Egalistic Menwim's Union had, for example, been campaigning persistently and conscientiously for over fifty years against job discrimination against menwim. That made it worthy of respect, in the opinion of the party leaders ('Luckily, it hasn't had the slightest effect,' said Ba). The Egalistic Menwim's Union also seemed more moderate than the recently founded Masculine League.

The ballot paper which the selection of 1000 Egalians received on the day of the poll bore the names of all the parliamentary candidates and the parties they stood for. Each party also drew up a number of questions concerning future policy which were to be answered. For example, 'Should the Government allocate more money to: a) Birth palaces, b) Social security for unprotected fathers, c) The Menstruation Games. Mark with a cross.' Or, 'Is the Government's expenditure excessive on: a) Fatherhood Offices, b) Social security for unprotected fathers, c) Housing improvement. Mark with a cross.' Or, 'What should be done to halt the decline in the population: a) Higher pregnancy benefit, b) Longer holidays, c) Higher bonus for first children. Mark with a cross.'

In this way, the people could express their views on all current issues. Each party gathered in the replies to the questions they had themselves put. And when, in a subsequent parliamentary debate, for example, a given party argued for a greater expenditure on birth palaces, its spokeswom could add that seventy two per cent of its supporters had approved the idea at the election. This lent greater weight to her argument. At the same time, it ensured that public opinion was always given expression.

The Masculine League did not stand as a party. Instead it tried to influence all the parties with its point of view. There had been considerable discussion about this, since many of the masculists had their political background in Short Cut, and held, as a matter of principle, that the whole of society had to be transformed from below, and that they couldn't hope for any liberation of menwim before the working class was liberated. To this, those without any experience of Short Cut replied, 'But what does the working class actually consist of? Was it not mainly menwim? Menwim working in Palluria and in the labour gangs?' Through closer study, they discovered that menwim in fact worked three times as hard as wim, and that at every level of the pay scale, they earned significantly less. They shouldn't be taken in by the fact that a few menwim occupied senior positions. And what about all the menwim who had ordinary jobs? Didn't they have to give them up when their wives had children? Or perhaps they knew of menwim who managed to keep working at the same time as their child was being nursed?

Some of the menwim from Short Cut admitted that they had had to do all the most disagreeable jobs while working for the party. They admitted this when discussing things in more detail in menwim's groups. So many things came out then, which nobody took any notice of in public debate. They had been made to wash the floors for example. Floor-washing was one of the hardest jobs, said the party bigwigs, so it was only natural that menwim should do it. The more floors the menwim washed, the less they were involved in political matters, the fewer resolutions, nominations, proposals and analyses they knew about, and the less competent they felt to do anything other than wash floors. Floors had to be washed, of course, and according to Short Cut ideology, all labour was equally valuable. In was in fact a consequence of the so-called egalitarian prestige-society that floor washing had such little value attached to it. After many years of washing floors, therefore, a large group of menwim broke away from the party and joined the menwim's movement.

Their main demand concerned the care of children. The slogan 'After all, it's wim who bear children' became the object of considerable hilarity in the movement — or at least in some sections of it, but it was finally rejected as an expression of wom-hatred. They didn't want merely to reciprocate the wrongs wim had done menwim. Some argued very powerfully that such a slogan would, moreover, have been a better argument in *favour* of menwim having to look after children. Many nodded in agreement when they heard this, saying, 'Mmm.'

The slogan 'Down with fele domination!' was approved instead, even though many thought it was stale. One original soul came up with the slogan 'Where's Mum?' It was hoped this would have a certain emotional appeal, though many were doubtful that the word 'mum' would be associated in any way with looking after children. The basic premise of their demands was that children should be the responsibility of both parents. A child was the product of a father *and* a mother, they declared. Since the mother had done the work of being pregnant and feeding the child, it was only fair that the father should look after the child when it was born. But why should this state of affairs last for the rest of his life? When a child reached the age of two, its parents ought to share the tasks of working and looking after the child equally between them. Some of the menwim's groups argued that the father ought to look after the baby for nine months and three weeks and that it ought to be the equal responsibility of both parents thereafter. They argued strongly that it was not possible simply to equate carrying a child inside one's body and looking after it once it had been born. The former was much more taxing than the latter and in a quite different way. The period of time the father looked after the baby after birth ought therefore to be at least twice the duration of a pregnancy.

This was discussed at length in the Masculine League. The advocates of the nine-month period grew irritated and asked the others how they knew that being pregnant actually was so appallingly strenuous. Had they ever been pregnant? How could they, as menwim, say anything at all about what it was like being a mother? The others pondered this for a while, as they could see the argument had some merit. In fact, menwim knew nothing about it. One of the nine-month faction then stood up and said that maybe the whole business of pregnancy was greatly exaggerated. He would go so far as to suggest that it was more strenuous looking after a baby after it had been born than it was to look after it inside oneself. Just think how fathers had to run around and toil and be available round the clock when the baby is small. And there was no question of regular working hours here, either, such as the mothers had. Nor were they paid for it.

The suggestion of payment really kicked up a storm. Surely nobody could seriously be proposing that menwim ought to be paid for doing something they did voluntarily out of love for wim and children! Yes, but no matter how fond fathers were of their wives and children, it was still work. No, in that case it would be better for them to go out and get a proper job. That was what they ought to be fighting for in the menwim's movement. It really couldn't be their aim to glue menwim to their homes. Here the debate ground somewhat to a halt. Everybody agreed that that was not their aim. The idea of payment, however, was not really meant as a realistic, concrete proposal. It had only been raised as a means of pointing out . . . of emphasizing, so to speak, the fact that . . . that . . . that . . . that . . . menwim worked unpaid.

The demand for a maximum of two years childminding for fathers was then carried.

This prompted a flood of arguments against the menwim's movement. The fact that children flourished best under their fathers' care was something everyone knew, it was said. 'It's an empirical fact, and that's all there is to it,' said the Sparksists, for example. 'Who's ever heard a crying baby calling for its mother?'

A great deal was said about menwim's nature at this time. Various psychologists had undertaken studies, all of which tended to show that the child became frustrated and maladjusted if it did not stay with its father for the first five years of its life. Sociological studies yielded the same conclusions. Zoological studies among the goromite apes, which lived in the interior beyond the Pallurian ranges, showed that the infant goromites *died* when the goromite fathers disappeared. Weekly magazines which had previously been unpolitical and taken no part in the election debate supported this view by printing engaging pictures of small babies playing with their fathers beards' or lying asleep in their arms. The image of a little chubby, peach-skinned baby, sleeping peacefully and contentedly in her father's arms was guaranteed to evoke feelings of warmth and security. And it was on such feelings that this social system's values rested.

The menwim's movement was unshakable on this point and rejected all talk of menwim's nature. Such research was itself obviously a product of the fact that they lived in a society dominated by wim. And how could the researchers, who were wim, make statements about paternal instincts? ('How can the masculists, who are pallurian, make pronouncements about paternal instincts?' asked Ba.)

The menwim asserted that as long as they lived in a society that was ruled and dominated by one sex, it was absurd to make any use of such concepts as 'menwim's nature' or 'wim's nature'. As long as one sex held power over the other, they would never be able to find out what differences there really were between the sexes — psychically — if there were any at all.

Another of their main demands was that the social and sexual distinctions between the labour gangs and other jobs should be abolished, so that the principal of equal opportunity for the two sexes could be put into effect. Wim ought to account for no larger a proportion of well-paid jobs than menwim. The menwim's movement knew that they would confront insurmountable difficulties in trying to realize this in practice. The fact that most menwim were fathers, whether protected or not, prevented them from benefiting from any form of higher education which might qualify them for better paid jobs. And there were many menwim, even within the menwim's movement, who believed that wim really were better equipped than menwim.

They could at least demand, however, that the worst expressions of discrimination against menwim be ended. The demand 'Support for unprotected fathers!' won widespread sympathy, even far beyond the bounds of the menwim's movement. Several of the parties adopted it into their programme. The deprivation suffered by unprotected fathers was great. Everyone agreed on that.

'End compulsory registration!' and 'Scrap the P-cards!', on the other hand, provoked much greater opposition. It was self-evident that contraception was menwim's responsibility. Since there was always a risk that menwim might ejaculate when you had sex with them, it was obvious that it was up to menwim to make sure no children resulted from it. Wim's sexual desires, of course, never had anything to do with her wanting to have children. Whenever she wanted to become pregnant, she could always make it clear to her partner that this was the object of their intercourse. Menwim, by contrast, lacked the ability to distinguish between sexual desire and impregnation. It was a purely physiological phenomenon. 'Because we lack that capacity, we're always considered a bit stupid,' said Petronius.

He and Baldrian had raised the problems of sexual relations in the menwim's movement after their confidential talk in The Wom in the Moon. This had led to many consciousness-raising discussions in the menwim's groups. They had discussed why wim's abhorrence of sperm —

indeed, wim's abhorrence of the mafele body — actually prevented menwim from obtaining full enjoyment from sex. Like Petronius and Baldrian, most of the menwim had admitted that their preference was to insert the penis in the vagina and to ejaculate there. But they knew very well that if it became a generally accepted truth that this was how menwim actually functioned, it would be used against them. 'If it really is true that menwim can only enjoy sex in such a barbaric way,' people would say, 'then it is even more obvious that they alone should be responsible for contraception.'

More and more menwim, however, had been realizing how unreasonable it was that, on the one hand, they should have to take the pill, while, on the other, they hardly ever managed to ejaculate in the vagina; and many of them found it difficult to achieve orgasm at all. In fact, this was something that all wim and menwim had always known. It just wasn't talked about. The parliamentary committee that had been set up seven years previously to look into this question had still not published a report.

The menwim's movement was therefore quite confident that 'Scrap the P-cards!' was a just demand — whatever sarcastic remarks it might provoke. Every body was given a 'P-card' on reaching puberty. It was a sort of certificate which proved that he had taken the P-pill. There were pills which lasted a whole month, so most preferred the monthly card. They had to report to a public Pill-registration office, where they took the pill in the presence of two wim officials who then clipped and stamped the card. The card office came under the Fatherhood Office. When a wom came in and said she had been impregnated by a manwom, the Fatherhood Office could easily check to see whether the manwom identified had been P-registered during the period in question. If he was, the wom's statement was discounted. Menwim who wanted children were listed as available sperm donors. If wim identified them as fathers during a period when they were listed as available sperm donors, it was extremely difficult for them to deny their responsibility. They were required to produce witnesses who could testify that they were not the father. 'How can we produce witnesses to something that didn't happen?' they asked despairingly in the menwim's movement.

The menwim's movement was now saying that taking the pill ought to be a matter of freewill. It should be a matter of trust between wom and manwom. The wom could, for example, insist on seeing that he did take the pill, so there was really no great problem. The wim who heard this proposal were scornful. 'Are we going to be forced to maintain a relationship with menwim for a whole month at a time, just so we can enjoy a quick one?'

Few of the parliamentary candidates promised to back this demand if they were elected. But of course they would look into the question. It was a big and complex question, naturally, but they would obviously look into it.

A group of masculists had secretly begun to infiltrate Donna Jessica's Message during the election campaign. This was not the result of any decision taken in the menwim's movement as a whole — indeed only a few menwim knew about it. They went along to the party's election meetings, nicely dressed in old-fashioned menwim's clothes, sang the 'Anthem of the Motherland', took part in the hymn-singing and prayers, consumed coffee and biscuits with the senior party dignitaries, at whom they smiled nicely, declaring how important it was, in their opinion, that Donna Jessica's Message should win the support of the people, and how reassuring it was that there existed a party with a moral attitude. There were so many dissolute tendencies in society, they said, sipping their coffee delicately, holding their cups with their little fingers raised. Take the menwim's movement, for instance, they said. It was obvious that a broad front had to be formed, with a solid and stable basic position, if such tendencies were to be resisted. And then they joined in enthusiastically with the singing of the beautiful hymn, 'Jessica, Joy of Wom's Desire'.

Didn't Donna Jessica's Message think, therefore, that the best way of counteracting these tendencies would be by taking the wind out of the menwim's sails — adopting their best arguments and putting forward a number of menwim as candidates? they asked when the first echo of 'My body and soul is joined with thee' had died away. Then they would prove to menwim, and also to the rest of the population, that Donna Jessica's Message at least had no prejudice against menwim. Senior figures in the party, already in a state of blissful excitement at the thought of joining body and soul with Donna Jessica, were most amenable and said they thought it was an excellent idea. The problem was not that they were in any way prejudiced against menwim, they were not at all, they said. The problem was that there were so few active menwim in the party. Aha, said the masculists understandingly, and no doubt the few menwim there were preferred to clean the floor and do other little chores? Yes, exactly. That was the situation. But that problem could be solved; it would be easy enough to find a number of active and willing menwim who in principle supported Donna Jessica's Message's message. Well, yes, of course, that might be so, but they should preferably have been active in the party for some time first. Indeed, but they knew a number of menwim who had been going to party meetings and participating actively in group activities at the local level for quite some time. Perhaps they could help out?

This was looked into and it turned out that quite a few menwim had indeed been very active recently, and these had proved to be very capable and reliable people. Now was the time to act. Thousands of menwim would vote for DJM if they put forward menwim candidates. In the end, more than half the candidates were menwim.

The result of the election was more or less what opinion polls had predicted. The Egalistic Democrats and the Democratic Egalists won the most seats, but neither of them achieved an outright majority. The Egalitarian People's Party announced that it would support the Democratic Egalists, while the Egalitarian-Democratic Alliance backed the Egalistic Democrats.

This offered no solution to the problem. The two small parties were equally placed. The Popular Equality Party failed to obtain enough votes and was therefore not represented. The same applied to Short Cut. Donna Jessica's

Message, on the other hand, won six seats, three with menwim candidates. Only now did people notice that DJM had operated a non-discriminatory nomination policy. The Egalistic Democrats, supported (with some reservations) by the Egalitarian-Democratic Alliance now entered negotiations with Donna Jessica's Message. They only needed five more seats to obtain a majority. It was also desirable to resolve the directoral question at the earliest opportunity. Since DJM had rightward leanings, the negotiations went smoothly. The three menwim MPs kept quiet at the negotiating table. No one noticed. It was best not to push things for the moment. They smiled sweetly and poured out the coffee.

They kept quiet until Parliament assembled for the first time. Then one of DJM's menwim MPs put his name down on the list of speakers — Cyprian Bosomby. He was widely known as the school principal's son, but few knew that he was active in the menwim's movement. The wim members watched him with interest as he went up to the speaker's platform, but as soon as he began to speak, they leant towards one another and started whispering or rustling their papers. This very soon stopped, however. Someone in the chamber shouted, 'Coup,' and everyone pricked up their ears.

' . . . have therefore kept silent during the negotiations between the Egalistic Democrats, the Egalitarian-Democratic Alliance and Donna Jessica's Message. The three of us who are menwim representatives for DJM therefore find ourselves in a position where we hold the balance of power. We hereby declare that during the term of this Parliament we will make use of the liberal theory of parliamentary representation that still holds in Egalia. We have been elected as representatives of the people. We maintain that we have the right to say and think what we want, no matter which party candidates we were elected as, and regardless of that party's programme. That is to say, we have our own programme. A programme to further menwim's liberation in Egalia. The programme is available for everybody to read, since it was circulated as a leaflet in Egalsund on many occasions during the course of the election campaign. This does not mean that the menwim's movement has now become a political party. Menwim in DJM must be seen as free representatives, in the way the Moulding Mothers on Mount Demos prescribed. We hereby declare that we will use our independent convictions and our consciences to support the government that advances the interests of menwim — the government which works effectively to abolish sexual discrimination in the workplace and the home. This is our position, from which we cannot be moved.'

Cyprian Bosomby's declaration provoked great confusion. Over the next few days, feverish investigations were conducted to see whether the coup wasn't unconstitutional, or at least illegal. They also looked to see whether there had been any ballot-rigging. Donna Jessica's Message accused its three menwim representatives of fraud and deception, but had to withdraw their accusations. Constitutional experts merely shook their heads and scratched their breasts in resignation. Constitutionally, the menwim representatives were fully justified in invoking the principle that all representatives were free.

There was only one other possibility: to announce a new election. But this would be extremely expensive and also contrary to constitutional practice. The newspapers, knowing that Petronius Bram was one of the firebrands behind the trouble, appeared with headlines such as 'Son Makes Mother Redundant — In the Name of Masculism'. Below, it said, 'It is known that Petronius Bram is among those who have been most active in the cause of masculism during recent years. For this reason he did not stand for election, but remained behind the scenes, pulling the strings. Is he now going to topple his own mother in order to further the cause of sexual equality?' The tabloid, the *Foghorn*, telephoned Ruth Bram to interview her. She slammed the phone down in fury. When they rang back, she said politely that Ruth Bram wasn't home. The following day, the *Foghorn* printed a headline in bold type asking, 'Vendetta against Tyrannical Mother?' The article which followed

215

showed that the menwim's movement consisted of a few frustrated, pallurian wom-haters who couldn't get fatherhood-protection.

At first, it was decided to wait and see how things went in Parliament. Perhaps the assembly could still function, despite everything, and perhaps the three menwim would not be completely impervious to reason, in the final analysis.

In the final analysis, it turned out that the three menwim were completely impervious to reason. No matter what motion was being debated, the three of them obstructed the division by refusing to support or oppose the motion, raising instead a third proposal. One of their suggestions was that the operations of the Pallurian mines should be restructured. Here they added the proposal that forty per cent of the workers in the mines should be wim, and that sixty per cent of the mines' management posts should be filled by menwim. With that the whole review of mine operations ground to a halt.

It also turned out that no matter what was being discussed, the masculists talked masculism. They made it clear that the moment Parliament showed itself willing to pursue actively masculist policies, they would be more co-operative. Then even those MPs who were most sympathetic to masculism realized that there was no alternative to a new election.

This time strict control was maintained over party nominations. Naturally, menwim were not excluded from them, but careful watch was kept on the type of menwim who appeared on the ballot papers. As a result, the Democratic Egalists won three more seats than on the previous election. With the support of the Popular Equality Party, they were therefore able to form a government. Donna Jessica's Message lost its seats on account of the fiasco; few felt inclined to vote for it after what had happened. Conflict and division erupted within the party. The Telephone Party, which had made itself conspicuous with effective telephone calls in the confused situation, came in with two seats.

The people of Egalia sighed with relief. The question of government had been resolved to everyone's satisfaction. Even the Egalistic Democrats greeted the Democratic Egalists warmly. Nothing of the sort had ever happened before. 'Back to Normal', wrote the *Egalsund Times*.

Peho burning and other masculist activities begin to spread

'*Normal!*' said Petronius. 'That's what wim call it when they're in control again.'

The menwim's movement was not discouraged by its defeat in Parliament. In fact they had expected things to go the way they did. They had foreseen that wim, once they felt truly threatened by being made vulnerable to the exercise of power, would hit back hard. But for the movement, the experience was a great inspiration and encouragement to further efforts. They made the most of the disturbance and the publicity to further their campaign. They decided not to concentrate on practical solutions or everyday demands for the time being. This had cost them a great deal of argument and wrangling within the movement. They had seen how practical solutions would in fact have to be so all-pervading that society would have to undergo a thorough transformation. They therefore decided it was preferable to direct the force of their attack against the most degrading of all the circumstances they were struggling against — the fact that menwim were regarded as breeding stock.

The storming of the maidmen's ball was a great sensation. Once again the menwim succeeded in keeping their plans secret. Great numbers of menwim turned up at the maidmen's ball in the normal way — and paid the usual entrance fee. They trooped into the ball dressed nicely in conventional masculine clothes — flowery pehoes and chiffon dresses in pale pastel colours. Admittedly, the organizers did think they looked a bit old to be going to a maidmen's ball. Preferably, it was young menwim who were to be tried out. But the organizers knew that there would always be some frustrated old codgers who had never had any success in this area. Indeed, there were a number of tragic examples of stagnating bachelors who would go to maidmen's balls year after year until they were old, rigging themselves out grotesquely with huge wigs. It was dreadful to see, but what were they supposed to say to them when hope refused to die.

The menwim had refreshed their dancing skills, and they danced the trio nicely during the first part of the ball. Wim stood against the walls, watching them. Some made derisory remarks about their age.

When the trio had finished and the commère was reciting the same phrases she had recited every year for twenty five years, the menwim went over to the wim against the wall and began feeling their breasts and groping them between the legs, saying, 'Hallo, darling! How about it, then?' or 'Nice tits you've got', or 'Gosh, you're so sexy. Can I buy you a drink?' The wim watched them quietly, half smiling, even lifting their arms slightly to make it easier for the menwim to paw them. 'What do you want?' they asked, somewhat incredulous at what was happening.

The menwim had obtained keys to some of the maidman-rooms in advance. Suddenly the menwim, acting in twos, each grabbed a wom and started to carry her out of the ballroom towards the gallery. Now the wim began to resist violently, shouting furiously at them. Their smiles vanished as they tried to break free of the menwim's embrace. A shrill whistle sounded, and more masculists flooded into the ballroom. They had been standing outside, waiting for the signal. Now there were three menwim to every wom and they carried them quickly upstairs and into the maidman-rooms, locking the doors from the inside.

Once inside, they sat the wim on the beds and began to explain the purpose of what they were doing, asking them if they found it amusing. The wim did not all react exactly alike, but none of them found it amusing. Most assumed a supercilious calm once they realized they were locked in. They were actually quite attracted by the thought of having three at once. The organizers called the police who came and arrested all the menwim they could lay hands on. In the confusion, they also arrested a number of the young, virgin maidmen at their first maidmen's ball.

They were released the following day, since it was impossible to determine who had been involved and who had been innocent. It was by no means unheard of for a wom to take three or four young menwim with her into the maidman-rooms either. This had become much more common in recent years. It was also difficult to make out that the menwim had directly contravened the law. If their actions were to be described as unlawful imprisonment, why should the normal events at maidmen's balls not be described in exactly the same way? There were many wim who simply carried young menwim up to the maidman-rooms, and the doors were nearly always locked. The police could not easily refute this, even though they felt that what had happened was something altogether different. The only thing they could come up with in the end was the acquisition of keys by deception.

There was also a long discussion as to whether they should not compensate the innocent maidmen and pay the cost of their readmission, since the ball had been ruined for them on this occasion. Some pointed out that this would be rather inconsistent. The menwim's movement, after all, wanted to put a stop to such idiotic rituals as the maidmen's ball. On the other hand, they couldn't simply pull the ground away from under menwim's feet with no more ado. That much they actually agreed on, so they collected money for the young menwim who had suffered through no fault of their own.

'I simply don't understand what you have against the maidmen's ball,' said Ruth Bram to her son when she heard about the incident. 'When I was young, it was the most festive occasion of the year.'

'It isn't particularly festive, sitting and waiting to be invited upstairs. It makes us totally passive. We either end up as wallflowers, or we end up being fucked, and that's all,' said Petronius angrily.

'Passive! D'you think it's so much easier for wim? We're shy, too, when we're young and many of us don't like taking the initiative. It isn't so easy as you imagine. And it isn't only menwim, either, who are rejected by the opposite sex. Wim can also feel they're failures. Just think of the poignant words of one of our greatest lyric poets, Walta Whitwom:

> *The lordies must the dance invite,*
> *To dance no more is Eva's plight.*

Ruth Bram must have been deeply moved to be driven to quoting poetry. The lines were among the most commonly quoted verses in Egalia, and the Egalians were invariably just as deeply moved when they heard them.

The next day, the *Foghorn*'s headline announced, in bold type, 'ORGY! Sex-crazed menwim storm ball.' They printed an interview with some of the menwim underneath, in which it was said that they were tired of lying underneath wim, and they now wanted to see what it was like lying on top. Wim were selfish beasts who never thought of anything but their own pleasure, and the ball was the most fundamental cause of menwim's oppression. Apart from the fact that what the menwim had actually said had been distorted beyond all recognition, the interview was laced with sarcastic editorial comments. 'Next, these fanatical masculists will no doubt try to abolish the penis.' 'Crude demonstrations will win no sympathy among the general public.' 'Systematic, wom-hating perversion,' and so on. *Message*, DJM's party organ, sympathized with the action. This paper had long been fighting a lonely struggle against the sexual permissiveness that had become commonplace in recent years. The maidmen's ball ought to be made a more respectable occasion, considering the natural bashfulness there was between the sexes, said the leading article.

Seeing how the *Foghorn* had treated them, many of the menwim thought they should never have had anything to do with the press; they realized how stupid they'd been to give interviews in good faith. Others, however, thought it was necessary to get their activities and ideas into the press in any way they could, for otherwise few people would ever hear what they were doing. One reason this was important was that they wanted to make the most of their second major action — the Great Peho Burning outside Parliament. They agreed to go in pairs to the major newspapers and give them advance warning of their action. Although few of the newspapers would deal with them honourably, it would at least mean that people got to know what was going to happen.

Great numbers of people came into the centre of the town to witness the spectacle. Rumours circulated that the menwim were going to expose themselves, so many wim told their housebounds to stay home and went drinking with their cronies on the way downtown. The peho burning caused more commotion than the demands for child-minding and job opportunities had done. Some people also stayed home in disgust, saying that they would rather die than witness public indecency of that sort. One Member of Parliament even undertook an investigation in the National Co-operative Directorate, to see whether there wasn't some directive prohibiting such obscenities. Unfortunately no one had ever considered the possibility of such an event, so there was nothing they could do.

An audience of several hundred gathered outside Parliament to see the peho burning. There were bout two hundred masculists and fifty of them had declared themselves willing to hurl their pehoes onto the fire. The spectacle was not exactly what people had expected. The menwim did not expose themselves in the full light of day. They simply turned up without their pehoes, with everything hidden behind their skirts.

Moreover, people were obliged to stand there and listen to a long-winded speech which Ruth Bram's son gave in order to explain why the menwim were stirring up trouble.

Why struggle for menwim's rights?

'The basis of Egalia's social system is the fact that the manwom is defined biologically,' said Petronius Bram, looking out over the crowd. 'Manwom is a huwom being only by virtue of two things — his reproductive equipment and his muscle power. His reproductive equipment is tied up in a peho, which is worn high or low, according to the decrees of the fashion queen. This abominable affliction has absolutely no practical function.

'At the same time, on account of our physical strength, we are put to the hardest and most exhausting work — cleaning and minding children. Mysteriously, society equates physical strength with mental inferiority, as though you had to be a bit stupid to be physically strong.

'In today's society, a manwom has been deprived of all real possibility of making choices and has only two functions — as a worker and as breeding stock. For this work he receives either low wages, or no wages at all. The highest social privilege a manwom can achieve is to be told who his child is. He earns this through service and fidelity to a single wom, who, in the event of pregnancy, may offer him fatherhood-protection. If it suits her. This is the sole chance the manwom has of not being a low-paid worker or — as far as the ruling class is concerned — an unprotected spinner-man, who lives his life in solitude.

'In order to justify this unjust division of labour and wealth between the sexes, our present, matriarchal society has developed a marvellous, self-contradictory ideology. On the one hand it has been the task of civilization to remedy nature's injustice — which is supposed to consist in the fact that menwim are, for example, generally bigger and stronger than wim (by nature). The efforts to remedy this injustice have, for centuries, consisted in the subjection of menwim. Wim have been given a better upbringing — harder physical training and better nourishment. There are therefore many menwim today who *are* smaller and weaker than wim. If we compare huwom beings with other mammals, we see that the difference in size between the fele and the mafele is much greater than between wim and menwim. Civilization — our so-called "civilization" — has *crippled* the manwom.

'But in spite of the fact that wim have, in this way, succeeded in remedying nature's injustice, they continue to make out that the manwom is stronger than the wom! And because of this, he is obviously required to take the hardest jobs!

'The manwom is *not* stronger than the wom! Why is it still the case that only menwim are sent to the mines in Palluria? Why are the cleaning troops and the child-minding brigades still composed exclusively of menwim?

'This is what we in the Masculine League call a "have-your-cake-and-eat-it" ideology, because the purpose of the system is to allow *wim* to have their cake and eat it. They have achieved the advantage of having overcome a possible inferiority in physical strength, by undertaking no hard work whatsoever. This is most clearly visible in the upper classes, where most wim are in fact physically stronger than menwim. And it is the upper-class manwom that is held up as the ideal, which all menwim are meant to look like — fat, sagging and overdecorated with every kind of ornament, utterly lacking in any will of his own. We're supposed to be fat so we emphasize the value we have as luxury attributes for wim. And this ideal of the upper-class manwom is held up for the entire population, despite the fact that the great majority of menwim cannot live up to it, because they have to work constantly. As a result they become the direct opposite of what menwim are supposed to be — thin, strong, and — finally — worn out. And rejected as sex objects.

'And when we, in the Masculine League, protest against

this state of affairs, we're told, "You can't both maintain the privileged position you have thanks to fatherhood-protection *and* demand equality at work. You can't both permit yourselves to engender children *and* run away from the responsibility to take all the jobs you imagine to be so interesting. *You can't have your cake AND eat it!*"

'That's what we're told. The reality, however, is something else. In reality, menwim neither have *nor* eat their cake, while wim do both. What menwim are now demanding is at least either to have it or to eat it.

'We know that fatherhood-protection is an upper-class phenomenon. Most wim at lower levels of society prefer casual relationships with menwim, and abandon their children to the child's father, or to somebody they claim is the child's father, or to the baby-brigades, or, later, the uncle brigades — and there again it is exclusively menwim who take care of them. These wim prefer to live separately from menwim and children, in their own accommodation and among themselves. They have nothing to look after except themselves and their jobs, and the jobs they have are more enjoyable and better paid than any jobs the fathers can get. They say they cannot afford to keep menwim and children. At the same time, they get various bonuses and benefits for giving birth, while menwim get nothing.

'Menwim are compelled to look after the children. Often they have no idea whether or not the children they are looking after are their own. Meanwhile the wim — who are mothers — sit directing and organizing menwim's lives for them for twice the pay. But we never hear any mention of the fact that these wim are mothers.

'If we go so far as to point out that wim are mothers, we are immediately told, "But after all, it's menwim who beget children!" As though it were the manwom's fault that children result from sexual intercourse! On the contrary, we know that sexual intercourse *never* takes place against the wishes of the wom. She knows when she wants to get pregnant, and she does so when she wants to.

'*We*, however, are the ones who have to take the responsibility for contraception! We are forced to register at the

P-office every month, and we even have to pay a small fee to get our P-cards stamped. Why isn't the manwom allowed to use the handy P-sheath instead, which just has to be pulled over the penis? No, the wom won't have that. She prefers a sheathless penis for her orgasm. So that *she* can have that little enjoyment, *he* is made to undergo the greatest sufferings — pills with no end of dangerous side-effects, or compulsory sterilization. It is claimed that these operations are temporary, but we know that twenty per cent of them go wrong and the man is rendered permanently sterile.

'Why can't the wom take responsibility for contraception, the wom who bears the children, and still decides when she wants to have them? No, it is said; that's impossible, because nobody has yet discovered any safe methods that can be used by wim. Such methods would in any case be far too complicated, they say. Are we, for example, to imagine a device of some sort which is pushed into the vagina to seal off the entrance to the uterus? That would be unthinkable, of course, since any such device would obviously cause injury. Pills for wim would also have a disastrous effect on the balance of her vital functions. It would fly in the face of the natural order for the feminine sex to use contraception.

'"After all, it's menwim who beget children." The best excuse in the world. And then they say, "And that's how it is throughout the animal queendom, too. What are you going to do about that, then? Eh? The higher up you go in the animal world, the more irresponsible and useless are the mafeles of the species. Menwim engender children; they *can* do that! And what would happen to civilization if we didn't tame the menwim? They would then be like the mafeles of other mammals — wild and unreliable."

'But why should comparisons always be made with so-called "nature"? We aren't animals. We're huwom beings. No two species of animals have adapted in the same way, anyway. Some live in herds, some in families, some in societies, some alone. Horses and cats behave in completely different ways. Why should we compare ourselves with them?

226

'Nature is used against us in the most absurd way. It serves as a mythology to beat us over the head with. "We see that throughout nature, the mafele has only a secondary importance to the process of life," they say. Blah blah blah. What's that got to do with us? We're huwom beings too!

'And in huwom society, conception is *not* exclusively the manwom's responsibility.

'Wim use nature to prove whatever they want. If it suits wim to say nature is unjust, they say it. If it suits them to say nature is just, then that's what they say. It is unjust that menwim have muscular strength, but is it just that wim have the power of creating life. There is no consistency in this wim's ideology. But it is still brought out wherever we start talking about the position of menwim in society — and everywhere else too, for that matter.

'Wim come charging along with "the laws of nature" in their hands, shouting, "Menwim are superfluous! Why do we need menwim? It is only due to our great benevolence that they are even permitted to exist. For any idiot knows the huwom race can survive very well without menwim. We can preserve a few examples. We can deep-freeze your semen and put you to death, all of you. If we have boy-children we can put them to death too, keeping a few of them once in a while to replenish the sperm banks."

'Don't tell us we don't hear this. Such things are not said officially in Parliament, but we hear them everywhere, every day, whenever we dare to grumble. And often when we don't even grumble, but simply happen to be there.

'But I've been thinking about what it would have been like if we were living in a world where all this was the other way round — where menwim had the advantage over wim. Then perhaps such observations might be appropriate. Because when you hear these things, you'd think that's the way it was; you'd think it was wim who were oppressed by menwim.

'But it isn't like that in our society. In our society it is the menwim who are oppressed. In our society, therefore, it is menwim who are indispensable. You're the ones who couldn't manage without us. Because you exploit us and live on our backs.

'Yes, you exploit us. That's what everything rests on. You steal our labour-power and you steal our bodies. We don't receive the money we are entitled to for the work we do — whether in the workplace, the home or in bed. Our entire social system relies on the massive economic exploitation of menwim. And because not a single wom is capable of thinking of the word "manwom" without thinking "sex", menwim's entire rebellion is put down as a sexual rebellion.

'Jut think how many of you came here today in the hope of seeing a pornographic spectacle. What you're witnessing is not a sexual rebellion. It is a rebellion against monstrous economic injustice. And because we are poor and lacking in independence, we are forced to become your sexual servants. Sex is what our existence has been reduced to. That is why our rebellion started as a rebellion against the sexual oppression we experience.

'But that isn't the end of it. Manwom is alive! And this is a slave rebellion!

'It is characteristic of slave states that the slave-owner is dependent on her slaves, while the reverse is not true. The slaves are not dependent on the slave-owner, because the slaves work hard and the slave-owner doesn't. The slave-owner is the social parasite and, the slaves are the ones who actually keep society going.

'To prevent people from seeing this simple truth, the slave-owners have to create an ideology which makes it appear as though things are the exact reverse of the way they really are. They convince the slaves that it is their slave-owners who are indispensible and that the slaves are idle and worthless. As long as the slaves believe this, the slave-owners can sleep peacefully. Who would dare to rebel against someone who is indispensible to their existence?

'In the slave state of Egalia, therefore, the wim convince menwim that they are idle and worthless. "Menwim are unnecessary luxuries," say the wim. And as proof of this, they always roll out the beguiling and incontestable fact — that wim bear children.

'But why should you always use that against us? Why should you use that to take all power in society?

228

'What if we were to bellow, with the louder voices nature has given us, "AFTER ALL, WIM ARE THE ONES WHO BEAR CHILDREN SO THEY CAN DAMN WELL LOOK AFTER THEM AFTERWARDS TOO! YOU CAN'T HAVE YOUR CAKE AND EAT IT!"'?

'Utopia? A perverted dream of frustrated menwim?

'Perhaps. But if we're going to have dreams of a society that is different from this one, you're always going to call them perverse and frustrated. Because you pervert and frustrate us.

'We're no longer going to collaborate in this dehuwomization of menwim. And we're no longer going to put up with being regarded as breeding stock. We must strive for a society in which all are valued as huwom beings. That is why we are burning the principal symbol of menwim's subjection — the peho. The masculist cause is the huwom cause!' said Petronius.

The speech was quoted in several newspapers. The *Foghorn* picked up on it and made much out of the fact that a director's son should have stood up in this way on the platform, without a peho. Ruth Bram was hunted down, this time in person, by several journalists asking for her comments on what had happened and on the menwim's movement in general. Bram, however, refused to talk to them, whereupon, the *Foghorn* printed a giant headline on page two, saying, 'Ruth Bram hides her shame behind locked doors'.

It was also rumoured that Bram's youngest son, little Mirabello, has been seen on the masculist demonstration with a little placard saying, 'Where's Mum?' and many people thought it contemptible that small children had been taken along to be brainwashed and exposed to propaganda at such a young age.

After the speeches, the fifty menwim threw their pehoes onto a bonfire they had built in the middle of the square. Baldrian had fastened his and Petronius's to a spear and he went up onto the platform and hurled it. It arced through the air into the fire. It was at once an impressive and grotesque sight; frightening, many thought.

The menwim then marched off on a demonstration through the streets and up onto the Moonhill to the Narcisseum Club for Gentlewim. This was unexpected. Officially they had said they were going down to the North Bridge, where the marchers would disperse. Instead they went north. When they reached the club, they rang the door and before the watchwom knew what was happening, they were charging in across the thick, red carpets, and up the pillared staircase into the bars and saloons, where they sat down and ordered drinks and sandwiches as though they went there every day. Little Mirabello asked for a lemonade.

They were naturally refused service, but they remained seated until the forces of law and order arrived, armed with truncheons, and removed them.

The next day, the *Egalsund Times* printed a communiqué from the action committee explaining why they had invaded the club. 'There is nothing against mafele membership in the club rules. Nonetheless, it is a fact that only wim go there, while menwim sit at home minding the children. It is, moreover, a fact that the club is frequented only by wim with powerful positions. It is here that all their despicable decisions are taken. It is here that the management of Egalia is planned. It is here that wim glorify themselves in their own blinding fele chauvinism. The club on the Moonhill is actually Egalia's real, unelected Parliament. An assembly which the people have absolutely no control over. We demand that membership of this club be opened to everybody. And that, as anybody who thinks about it will realize, is exactly the same as saying we want the club closed down.'

Aha. So these fanatical wom-haters thought that people ought not even to be allowed to go for a quiet drink after a busy and wearisome day's work? Oh no. Now they were going too far. This sort of attack against personal freedom could not be tolerated.

The *Egalsund Times* dutifully printed the menwim's statement, but it also printed an editorial which made sure the readers were sickened by what had happened.

'Lawless attack on peace and privacy,' read the headline. 'Once again normality is no longer normal.'

Gro and Petronius — wom and manwom

'You're going to have a baby, Petronius.'

'How do you know it's mine?'

Gro gasped. 'Petronius! Can a father-to-be really care so little about a child he has himself conceived?'

'It isn't me that's going to have the child, for Jessica's sake! It's *you*. Or maybe the child isn't inside you? Lady God in heaven!'

They were sitting on a bare rocky promontory at the outermost point of the bay of Maybight. It was almost a dead calm. The sea was rippled by the lightest of airs, and gilded by the setting sun.

Once, Petronius would have been the world's happiest manwom at hearing these words from the mouth of his lover. 'You're going to have a baby, Petronius. You're going to have a baby.' Once he would have seen it as his only possibility of escape and he would have taken no precautions. He hadn't cared a damn how he was to obtain an education, as long as he had a baby by her. He hadn't cared a damn what his mother said about it, as long as he had a baby by her. Sometimes he had told her that. He had told her what he had felt over five years earlier, sitting in the Palace of Birth, waiting for Mirabello. Then he had thought of having a baby by Gro as the fulfilment of life itself — of existence.

He had stopped taking the pill some time ago, because it gave him headaches. He didn't know whether it was the pill that gave him headaches, but when he took the pill, his head ached, and when he stopped taking the pill, the headaches went. He had mentioned this to the doctor but she had merely said that it was a new brand he was taking,

231

and that research had proved that it had no side-effects whatsoever. So his headaches couldn't have anything to do with the pill. No doubt he was under stress and over-tired. Wasn't he rather actively involved with menwim's lib, by the way?

And here was the consequence. Which was worse — a headache or a baby?

'Do you know what one of the first things you ever said to me was, Gro?'

'No?'

'"You're mine," you said. "You're mine."'

'Aren't you, then?'

'No . . . No, I'm not.'

'But you'll have to take care of the child.'

'Yes.' He threw a stone out into the water. The Pill-registration office and the Fatherhood Office whirled round in his mind. He was an available sperm donor. There was no way out of it. 'Yes, I'll have to take care of the child,' he shouted; he could feel the rage rising within him, 'but I'm damn well not going to take care of you as well!'

Petronius felt a powerful, aching blow against the bridge of his nose. It came so suddenly and so violently, he couldn't believe what had happened. He gaped at her in astonishment. She hit him again in the same place. He felt his head vibrating as though a thousand electric pulses were shooting through his brain. He doubled up and covered his face with his hands. A crushing grip on his wrists tore his hands away and he felt a third blow strike him in the same place. Gro was white in the face. She seemed to be looking right through him. He saw her fist coming yet again and this time he ducked, and in doing so, he lost his balance and fell from the rocks. For a moment the pain vanished as he hit the cold water. He swam in towards a cleft in the rocks. She stood on the edge where he tried to pull himself ashore, kicking at his wrists and stamping on his fingers. He had to let go and swim back out into the water.

'Have you gone completely mad?' he yelled.

She made no reply. She was standing with her arms at her side, her elbows bent, her fists clenched, ready to jump at him if he tried again. Petronius was having trouble swimming on account of his clothes. He removed his shoes and threw them ashore. Gro picked them up, filled them with pebbles and flung them out towards him, aiming right at him. A hail of pebbles fell around him, but he was not hit. The shoes went to the bottom.

'So much for your favourite canoe-shoes!' she shouted.

'Your favourite — not mine!' He could scarcely shout. He tried to wriggle out of his jacket. It was difficult. He made an attempt to approach the cleft in the rocks in order to wedge it in there. She was waiting for him again.

'D'you want me to freeze to death here? It's cold!' He hurled his jacket up onto the rocks. She grabbed it and threw it several yards out to sea again. Petronius wanted to cry, but he couldn't. All that came were a few sobs. Now he was finding it difficult to say afloat. He swam towards the bank near the jetty. Gro kept pace with him along the shore. It would be more difficult to stop him coming ashore there. He had about thirty yards to go. She began throwing pebbles and shells at him. Some of them found their mark and hurt. He shouted at her to stop. She continued. Was she going to wade out and try to hold him down? Did she simply want to kill him? His teeth were chattering. He could feel the bottom under his feet now. He had an ache at the base of his nose. Gro was watching him from the shore. He waded in at an angle so as to avoid her. She moved over so as to meet him. He changed direction; so did she. Thus they continued. When he was within a few yards of the shore, she suddenly threw herself at him. He felt several punches hit the same place as before. Something warm was flowing. He clutched his face and saw that his hands were red. Yet another blow. He felt water surrounding him completely.

A giant peho is burning like a torch over the rocky islands. He sees that it is Baldrian who is holding it, and beside him is little Mirabello, trying to put on his canoe-shoes. 'Have you been born already, then?' asks Petronius. 'I thought that for the moment you were no more than an absent headache in my mind.' Mirabello smiles. 'Oh yes. I was born yesterday.' He is about five years old. The torch burns and Baldrian takes little Mirabello by the hand, saying, 'Now we're going to the Palace of Birth, because little Mirabello wasn't given a proper ceremony yesterday.' Petronius runs after them shouting that he wants to come too. But no matter how hard he runs he gets nowhere. There is so much water around his feet. Something is holding him back. Something behind him is holding him back. A grip. He watches the torch approaching, straight towards his face. He shields himself with his hands. 'Petronius.' It is Baldrian's voice. 'Petronius, I love you.' How can he love him if he is trying to walk away from him? They should be walking together. They have always been meant to go together. 'Petronius . . .' He can feel the torch burning and hurting his nose now. And at the same time he can feel Baldrian's gentle hand on his head.

'Petronius!'

Petronius was staring into Gro's face. He screamed.

Her hand continued to stroke his head. Gently. With infinite tenderness. She whispered his name again.

'Petronius. You were so restless. You were crying in your sleep. I had to wake you.'

He grasped her arm and stroked it for a while. Then he pulled her head down to him and sobbed. 'It hurts . . .'

'Yes. It hurts me too. It hurts just as much in my soul as it does in your body . . .'

He smiled wryly when she said that.

' . . . I was hoping . . .' she said. 'I mean . . . I think you've sort of drifted away from me.'

I certainly have now, anyway, he thought. I've drifted twice as far from you now. He was angry. He couldn't say what he was thinking. He felt confused. He remained silent.

'I was afraid of losing you. I was afraid that you and the other lads wouldn't come here any more . . .'

That was because you always had to be in charge of everything, Petronius thought. Even if you did teach us everything you could. It was fine as long as you were able to teach us. As long as you were superior. But even when

234

we knew as much as you, you wouldn't really let us go. Everything had to be done the way you wanted. You had to decide everything. On your home ground. We don't want leaders. You can't stand leaders yourself — the leaders that lead you and your class *down*. But you don't mind your own leadership. You think it's great, having all the boys here. What a shame they won't be coming any more. What a shame they prefer being at Spn Owlmoss's villa. What a shame you don't always have someone new to seduce. Who is the father of your baby? Is it Cyprian? Is it Fandango? Is it me? How can you know? What a shame you didn't manage to get a masculist centre here. Sparksism in theory and rape in practice. I'm frightened. Frightened and angry.

'I don't know why you don't want to come here any more. We had everything.' She rested her forehead against one hand. 'How could I do that to you, Petronius?'

I hate you, he thought. For doing that to me. You've crushed everything inside me. All feeling that I had for you has been crushed. 'Don't worry about it. It'll pass.'

'I feel so awful about it, Petronius. I don't know why . . .' She began to stroke him again, as though to console herself. 'Does it hurt terribly? Shall I get a cold compress?'

She got up and fetched a cold flannel and held it against his nose. Petronius turned slightly to the side and caught sight of a sea of white paper handkerchiefs, spattered with red, strewn over the floor.

'When I'm a bit better, I'll pick them up . . .' he said.

'I just don't understand . . . I felt so hurt and disappointed. I'd been hoping you'd come back to me . . . I'd been hoping it would bring us closer together again, because you always wanted a baby. And you wanted a baby by me. Didn't you, Petronius? And now you don't after all. Why don't you? Don't you? Really? What has changed between us? We love each other, don't we? We know that, don't we? We always have done. Have I changed? I've always been the same, haven't I? What is it that's suddenly wrong with me? Don't you want me any more?'

'It isn't just you . . .' He was terrified.

'You mean your mother?'

Petronius shook his head. Pain shot through his entire head at the movement. He felt his nose and noticed that it was swollen. It must have been at least twice its usual size.

'Can I have a mirror?'

'It doesn't matter what you look like . . .'

'I asked for a mirror . . .'

'Thinking of appearances first, as usual.' She fetched a little pocket mirror; cracked and grubby. Petronius beheld the transformation of his face. Big red bruises under his eyes and a swollen nose which seemed to have been repositioned at a peculiar angle.

'I certainly haven't made you any prettier, have I?' said Gro with a little smile.

I hate you, he thought. How can you smile? And how can you say it hurts you in your soul? D'you think it doesn't hurt in mine? D'you think just because I'm hurt physically, I'm not hurt psychically, too? D'you think it just hurts you? Does it hurt you? Does it really hurt? Are you really sorry for what you've done, or are you going to think of it as a comic incident? I suppose we're going to start laughing about it soon, are we? Are we soon going to start saying how funny it was with you standing there on the rocks, stamping on my fingers when I tried to get out of the icy water you forced me into? Are we soon going to see the hilarious side of your doing this to my face? Well? Oh — I'm scared. I daren't say anything to you. I'm frightened.

'No,' said Petronius. 'But it'll get better.'

'I thought perhaps your nose might be broken.' Gro began to feel it. He cried out. It was the same pain he had experienced when she punched him.

'But I don't think it is,' she said.

He held her hand. Suddenly she looked even more strong and beautiful than ever to him. More than anything, he just wanted to curl up with her, safe and warm against her strong body, her big breasts, and sleep for ever.

'Why don't you want me any more, Petronius? You love me, don't you?'

'Yes.'

'But you don't want me. You don't want me and you don't want your baby.'

I'm afraid, he thought. I daren't answer you. If I reply, you'll hit me again. I can't say anything to you, because you're sitting here, and I can't do anything. You can knock me senseless, if you want to. You can do worse. You can kill me, if you want to. What can I do? I can't tell you.

He put his arm around her head and drew it down towards him. He would think only of what he had once loved — but no more. A Gro who was once in his head. A Gro who had perhaps never been anywhere else. A dream of his love for a wom . . .

He felt the attraction that had drawn him so strongly to her. He felt that he could have gentle and tender feelings for her again. She was beautiful and strong.

'I love you,' he said. It simply came out of his mouth without his having thought about it. And he knew as soon as he said it that he could never live up to it. He couldn't live in that gentleness and softness he felt in her presence. Only at certain moments. But not in ordinary, everyday life. Not when they were doing things together — moving at the same time, but doing different things. Because all his movements were restricted in her presence. And his feelings of love for her deprived him of all will.

'But don't you want to be with me, then, if you love me? Don't you want to be here, together, you, me and the baby, and carry on with what we started?'

Yes, yes. He wanted that. He wanted to be with her. Everything was worthless without her, outside her presence. It was her presence that gave him life. Petronius nodded. He felt immeasurably tired.

'Say you want to, Petronius! Say yes!'

Gro was excited and happy now. She removed his hand from her head and lit a cigarette.

'D'you know what? There's some good news I haven't told you. Want to know what it is?'

Petronius nodded his head gingerly, and looked at her.

'There won't be any more problems out here. I can provide for us all. I've been given the job of leading the

Third Diving Division, as from this summer. It's disgustingly well paid. Bareskerry told me the other day. She recommended me. She came up and said we should forget our previous disagreements. Things could be so good for us — you and me. No more worries. Isn't that good news?'

'Yes.'

'Say it, Petronius. Say you want the baby and that we're going to live here together, all three of us and that we're going to love each other like we do now. Like we always have done. It's just you and me, and that's how it'll always be.'

'You . . . and I . . . and the baby,' he began. He closed his eyes and continued. 'You . . . and I and the baby are going to live here . . . here at Maybight. I'll receive your baby, and we'll love each other. We'll love one another, all four of us.'

'*Four*?'

Petronius was breathing evenly. She shook him. He opened his eyes slightly. 'What?'

'You said four!'

'Four?'

'Yes. Why did you say four?'

'Did I say four?'

'Yes. You said we'd love one another, all four of us. That's what you said. Why did you say that?'

'Oh. Did I say that? I must have meant three . . .'

'Yes, you meant three.'

'Gro?'

'Yes?'

'I love you.'

'I love you, too, Petronius.'

And her belly grew bigger and bigger. And no matter how he tried to get up, he bumped his head against her belly, so he couldn't stand, and he was pushed back under water again. It was always there, hanging over him, just above his head. Under water, he couldn't breathe.

Father and son

Christopher didn't believe his explanation. Petronius could see that clearly. This wasn't anything to do with falling out of a boat onto some rocks. He should have made up a better story.

Christopher took his sewing basket and sat on the edge of his bed. Petronius tried to stop thinking about it. It was so quiet and peaceful in the house. Christopher couldn't sew when Ruth was at home, because she said he got so involved in what he was doing, he didn't hear what she said to him.

Petronius looked at his father, wondering what he was thinking and what it was like, being him. He was almost completely bald now. The hair restorers he had once used expertly on elderly upper-class lords up on the Moonhill had all proved wholly ineffective. Christopher had always said that they helped. Petronius studied the smooth surface of his head. Was it really so ugly? Why should it be any more ugly than skin anywhere else? But he did look like an egg; that had to be admitted. The big end of an egg with a wreath around it.

When Ruth was at home, he always wore a wig. But she was seldom to be seen at home nowadays. As the years passed, Ruth became more and more involved with her work. Sometimes she was at it until late at night. Sometimes all night.

Petronius lay back on the pillow. It hurt. There were tears in his eyes; he made no attempt to hide them. Tears ran down his cheeks and he sobbed, thinking, if we don't talk about it now, we probably never will. We're so seldom together. There's so much I really should have talked to

239

him about. But he didn't know where to begin. He sighed deeply.

'Gro hit me.'

Christopher nodded. 'I thought as much as soon as I saw you this morning.' Christopher stood up. He was shocked. Petronius noticed that he was trembling slightly. He had known. And now he'd said it, he was still shocked. 'I think I'll get some wine,' he said and went out. He returned a moment later with a bottle and two glasses.

'Wouldn't you like some too?'

Petronius never drank with his parents. He didn't like the atmosphere that was created when his mother drank.

'Yes, please,' he said, and out came the whole story.

'You mustn't get fatherhood-protection with her, Petronius! You *mustn't*!' Christopher was almost shouting. He was still trembling. Petronius shook his head. He was surprised at his father's vehemence. 'It's drudgery and toil, from beginning to end, twenty four hours a day for thirty years, or however long you can stand it.'

He emptied the glass and refilled it.

'And if we don't do this round-the-clock job to her satisfaction down to the last detail, all we get is abuse. Good Lady, Petronius! If I were you, today . . . If I was in your place, I'd do what I wanted to do. I'd say to hell with all dreams of home and babies, and concentrate on myself.'

He got up and went out for a while. Petronius noticed how nicely he had prepared the room for him. There were all his things. The seawom, his shell-bracelet and everything. Exactly as they had been during all those years. Christopher returned with a pile of heavy envelopes. He opened them carefully, one after another. Petronius's eyes widened. They contained drawings, each one better than the last. Christopher spread them out on the bedcover in front of him. There were suspension bridges and cantilever bridges and footbridges and drawbridges and silver bridges and gold bridges and rust-red bridges. Detailed construction drawings for various bridges. Bird's-eye and fish-eye views of bridges. Distant perspectives of bridges against landscape backgrounds, seen across the sea and seen from a hilltop.

The Lux Bridge and the North Bridge, as they looked when they were just being started, when they were a quarter finished, half-finished and complete. There were bridges of every possible size and shape. Bridges in every imaginable colour. Discreet bridges in black and white, as sober as on an engineer's drawing. Big colourful fantasy bridges which could never possibly be constructed.

'Did . . . did you draw all these?' Petronius was red-faced. Carefully, as though they might disintegrate if he handled them too roughly, he picked up each drawing in turn and gazed at it. He looked up at his father in amazement, and back at the drawings again.

'No one knows about them,' said Christopher quietly. 'You're the first person I've ever shown them to.'

They sat there for a long time, looking at the drawings, and Christopher told him when he had done each one, what he had been thinking, how each one was constructed, and why some of them were mere flights of fancy, and how he had once, as a boy, spent his spare time talking to engineers and reading everything he could about bridges. How he had been hoping to take it up again and then Ruth had told him he was going to have Mirabello. And he told his son how degraded he felt at growing old, and how he had simply acquiesced resignedly when Ruth demanded that he be castrated, how he didn't feel he was any good for anything any more and how much this hurt him — because he no longer felt he could be a proper father to little Mirabello, as he felt he had nothing left to give, and he felt guilty about this. And in one way or another he had drawn all these things into his bridges.

'I've also been hit, Petronius. Several times.'

Petronius looked up. 'By Mum?'

Christopher nodded. 'And I always had to make up some lie to conceal the fact. And she hit me for the most pathetic reasons. Usually because she thought I'd been with another wom.'

Petronius sighed deeply. He had thought as much. He had known it. But he had never dared ask. He stroked his father's arm.

241

'Once she thought I'd been to bed with Liz Bareskerry!' Christopher smiled wryly.

'Liz Bareskerry is gay.'

'What?'

'Liz Bareskerry is homosexual.'

'What? I mean . . . ho . . . ho . . . did you say homosexual?'

'Yes. Met her in a gay bar. Went there with Baldrian.'

He tried to make it sound casual. He didn't know why he suddenly felt awkward. Father and son peered intently into each other's eyes. Then they each took two big gulps of wine.

'She had a multi-layered wig,' said Petronius in order to make it sound more plausible. But he realized immediately that this bit of information might only have the opposite effect.

'No, Petronius. Now I think you're letting your imagination get the better of you.' Christopher laughed. Petronius was relieved.

'It's true!'

'Well . . . no doubt it's more common that we think . . .'

'Common? Sometimes I don't think I see anything else. Sometimes I think the whole of our society is just one giant playground for homosexual wim, where they can frolic and play and fight with one another, admire one another, cultivate one another, while keeping menwim in their homes, sending them out to do the nastiest jobs, sending them to Palluria, while they pursue and cling to their sacred sisterhood in beautiful yachts and wim's clubs and firms and sports grounds. And it makes no difference whether they're homosexuals in a physical or merely a spiritual way, because it seems to me that they're homosexual to the extent that they love one another, and disdain us. They love and cultivate their own bodies and celebrate the triumph of their own sex's honour and virtue, but as soon as the menwim show the slightest sign of being the tiniest bit pallurian, they immediately turn on us and call us perverts, when all we're trying to do is to enjoy a tiny little fraction of all those joys they take for granted — the freedom to go where we want and to love one another. But as soon as we show the slightest sign of affection for one another, and spend any time at all together, they immediately jump on us as though our enjoying ourselves ruins their game, as though for them to enjoy themselves in their gigantic fele homosexuality, *we* are required to remain one hundred per cent heterosexual, in the sense that we mustn't have anything to do with one another, but must be split up into our thousands of cosy little homes, where we stand cooking potatoes, happy at the thought that they might, possibly, come home sooner or later, and scared stiff at the thought that they might not come home, and before we even get to that cosy little home where we cook the potatoes, we're terrified that we might never *get there* to cook those potatoes, but if in the end we are so fortunate as to get that far, we then have to look after and protect the thousand little alibis they use to pretend they're not homosexual. Once in a while, we're allowed to go out with them, to share in their triumphs in the Palaces of Birth or the Menstruation Games and the sports grounds. It makes me sick. That's why society treats homosexual wim with such contempt and disgust. Because they reveal that all wim are homosexual.'

Christopher looked at his son. He was an extraordinary sight, sitting upright in bed, with his mangled face, fiery eyes, gesticulating wildly with his hands. Ruth was an intelligent wom. No doubt Petronius had inherited some of her intelligence. Perhaps he had also inherited some of his own capacity for understanding things . . .?

He took his hand and squeezed it gently. 'I wish I were you,' he said.

Petronius looked at him questioningly.

Consciousness-raising in the 'Fighting Cock' menwim's group

The thirteenth month of the year had finally arrived and the Grand Menstruation Games were about to be held. Every wom in Egalia looked forward to being able to go out to play and have a few drinks with her comrades. And every manwom dreaded having to get all the clothes ready for the wim and children and having to drag the kids around the park to see all the festivities. Every child in Egalia was told that they ought to be happy because the Menstruation Games were the year's most exciting event.

Baldrian, Fandango, Petronius and Lisello (they always called Spn Owlmoss Lisello now) were sitting and chatting at the masculist centre up on the Moonhill. It was a warm and sunny autumn day and the fruit trees bore an unusually good crop this year. They were sitting out on the little veranda on the first floor, soaking up the afternoon sun and a particularly good vintage of old Principal Owlmoss's apple wine. They had discussed jokingly whether it wasn't really rather anti-masculist to be drinking wine made by a wom, but they had soon stopped worrying about that, since they might then just as well stop eating. For the moment, at any rate. They had heard about some menwim's groups in Pax which ran their own farming communities, to which wim were not admitted. But as far as they knew, they were the only menwim in Egalia who grew their own produce.

The four of them had started a consciousness-raising group which they called 'Fighting Cock'. They had chosen the name in order to strengthen themselves and to overcome some of their own prejudices. The cock was regarded as the stupidest animal there was, and it was therefore frequently used as a derogatory term for menwim — when anyone wanted to be really abusive. The cock's way of expressing itself was also regarded as the most idiotic. However you look at it, there was something utterly ridiculous and, at the same time, slightly obscene about these birds, which, for some mysterious reason, led to their being compared constantly with menwim.

Spn Owlmoss had initially been reluctant to join a group. He had seen himself as a sort of necessary background figure. A privileged, upper-class manwom who happened to have a house and an estate he could put at the young menwim's disposal. He took all the rumours which circulated in the town — the rumour that he was a pallurian had been given new impetus — in his stride with a devastating calm. He was so used to them that he took them for granted, almost as part of the natural order. But he was not quite certain whether he was himself part of the menwim's movement. He thought he would be a burden for the young menwim, and considered himself too old to change in the ways that the masculists wanted menwim to — by thinking about how people functioned and trying to behave differently.

Fandango, however, had pressed him to join them. They needed his knowledge and his experience, he said, adding that he thought the entire menwim's movement would be stillborn if they didn't manage to involve older menwim. They were usually the ones with most experience. And since the menwim's movement was based on menwim's own experiences, it would be foolish not to try to bring in older menwim. Spn Owlmoss hesitated, nonetheless, until they proposed that 'Fighting Cocks' should be a patriarchy group.

It was a cosy little group and they enjoyed themselves greatly. At the end of the first meeting, they felt they had already made considerable progress, and they decided to keep the group at its current size. If others wanted to discuss the patriarchy of the future, they could form new groups of their own.

'Fighting Cocks' decided that the first topic of discussion would be the coming events in Chlorophyll Park, so they would take their own experiences in relation to menstruation as their starting point.

Fandango told them how Ba used to drag him into the bushes on their way to school. He had never told anybody before and he had been feeling more and more guilty about it. He had always thought he was about to witness a great miracle. 'I think I really thought that one fine day she would be sitting there, wrapped in pink clouds, telling me that she loved me, caressing my back gently and tenderly, or something like that.' But it had never happened. Instead, she would show him her breasts and nipples and tell him how big and fine they were going to be. And the day she had her first period, she had opened the flap on her trousers, lain on her back and let him look at the blood from her vagina, explaining that this meant that now she was really and truly in harmony with the forces of nature. He, on the other hand, would never reach any equivalent maturity, but would be condemned to eternal immaturity. As he was now. Fandango recounted that he had always felt ashamed that he didn't menstruate, and as he grew bigger, he had felt more and more ashamed of his own, flat-chested body and the way it was developing. Or rather: not developing at all.

Petronius would never forget Ba's first period. She had gone charging through the house early one morning, shouting, 'Daaaaaaad! I've started, I've staaaaaaaaaarted!!! Yippeeeeeee!' And everybody had got up immediately to congratulate her. Afterwards, she had gone off to the Health Office, where she had been issued with huge boxes of blood towels, which she had unpacked on the dining room table, pulling them out and waving them in front of Petronius's face. She had put one of them on, and then gone up to Petronius and punched him playfully in the chest, beside herself with excitement. At about the same time, his father had taken him quietly into the kitchen and said that he thought it was about time he started wearing a peho. Petronius had also noticed that it was during his mother's blood periods that she would take him aside and tell him what was right and wrong in the world. She always saw things so clearly when she menstruated.

246

Baldrian could not say that he thought his mother had ever made a big issue of menstruation. She had hardly ever mentioned it, had she, Fandango? No, Fandango couldn't remember Liz Bareskerry ever mentioning her periods as anything special, either. They had almost been passed over in silence. But sometimes his father had said that when her catch of spearbiters was particularly big, it was nearly always during her period. Baldrian described a game he and Wolfram had played regularly when they were small. They pretended they were two grown wim who always had their periods at the same time. They each lived on their own farm, inland, and they each had twenty mares which they took it in turns to ride out to inspect the crops in the fields. But he had actually never felt any real desire to menstruate himself. He had always been told that he was a fantastically good-looking manwom, and he had believed this, and been glad. Eva had always insisted on having sex with him during her periods, and recently, it was true, he had begun to dread this somewhat. She got so carried away, gripping him twice as tightly as at other times. No doubt it was such a powerful experience for her, it was impossible for her to control herself.

Spn Owlmoss said that when he was small, he thought that only wim had blood inside them. And he had believed, therefore, that a manwom living with a wom would die when she died. If menwim bled it was only because they had blood just under the skin, he had imagined, having none inside their bodies, like wim. Old Principal Owlmoss had told him that everyone started menstruation when they were half-grown, and little Lisello had been delighted. He had waited many years for his menstruation to start. If his mother said it happened to everyone, it must be true. Then he happened to hear from some girls in the street that menwim never menstruated. He went home to his mother, perplexed, and said she had told him everyone started menstruating when they were half-grown. His mother roared with laughter. Shortly afterwards, he began to have wet dreams, which embarrassed him terribly, as he had never heard anything about this phenomenon, and thought it was a type of mafele menstruation — only it looked so peculiar. As a result he became convinced that there was something terribly wrong with his body, because he thought that such emissions ought to occur only once a month, like menstruation. But he had them much more frequently, and for a long time he had thought he was seriously ill. Spn Owlmoss recalled that in his childhood only wim were permitted to take part in the Menstruation Games. He had imagined that it was a great festival for wim which enabled them to have children afterwards, as though they created some sort of sexual milieu amongst themselves which made it possible for them to impregnate themselves. That was when he was very young. Later he had become more and more unhappy, as he was growing so fast, becoming taller and taller and broader and broader across the shoulders, while having such narrow hips. And it only got worse.

The menwim recognized so many common experiences among the things they were telling one another. The shame of having a manwom's body. The shame of having a penis and a shamebag. Why should it be called a shamebag? Oughtn't they to find a new word? The shame of lacking breasts and hips and proper thighs and buttocks. The shame of not menstruating. The shame of having hair and the shame of not having hair. The shame of feeling one's beard beginning to grow. The shame of having a hairy chest. The shame of going bald. The shame of hearing one's voice break into a peculiar, deep sound at adolescence, and losing the pleasant, normal sounding huwom voice they had had as children. The shame of nocturnal emissions. The shame of lacking the ability to bear children. Shame, shame, shame.

Why was menwim's chest hair shameful, when wim's pubic hair was not? Why could wim be proud of their hair, no matter where it was, when menwim could not be proud of theirs? What could they do about it? They drew up a plan of action, laughing in a liberating defiance.

The Grand Menstruation Games

At last the thirteenth month of the year had come. The Grand Menstruation Games had begun. The Egalians all turned out for the occasion. The park teemed with people of all ages. Egalia's wim drank and played games with their comrades. Egalia's menwim came out, after having prepared all the wim's and children's clothes, and Egalia's children were dragged around by Egalia's menwim, and told that they ought to be enjoying themselves. Three big tents had been set up, along with numerous small tents, pavilions, stalls, booths and temporary toilets ('There are three wim's toilets, and only one for menwim,' Petronius observed). A big fifty-wom orchestra was playing in the pavilion, and all sorts of shows and activities were in progress in the tents. The Grand Crowing Contest was to start at one o'clock, followed by the popular boar races. Spn Owlmoss had put his bet on the smallest, tattiest and drabbest of the cocks. In the smaller tents, Egalsund's shopkeepers were selling their wares at what they claimed was half-price. The masculists had noticed, in particular, the little porno-tent. It was packed with wim who had managed to get away from the old ram and the kids, for once, and who had been out drinking and carousing with their cronies during the morning. Inside, they were selling big colourful magazines full of photos of young boys with tiny penises and fine fat bellies, and big wim, with enormous breasts and clitorises, fondling their tiny penises, and experimenting with them in every position you could imagine, so the little boys with tiny penises and fat bellies had to assume all the positions of a contortionist in order to keep up with the sexual aerobatics. And they were all equally wanton, no matter what position they were in or what treatment they were being subjected to. All seemed equally eager to get these huge wim's huge nipples and clitorises into their mouths. There was also an assortment of artificial breasts in the tent — some in wax, some in foam-rubber. They came in all colours and sizes and sat there in a line with their nipples conspicuously erect. On the shelf above were candles in the form of artificial clitorises. Donna only knew who bought such items, but there must certainly be a market for them, since they were always being produced in new and elegant shapes, and they were constantly being advertised.

The loudspeaker boomed, 'Little Gerd, aged five, in a red, checked shirt, is crying and asking for her father. She can be picked up at the platform in the south pavilion.' Children were crying everywhere, holding daddy's hand in one hand and a big toffee-apple in the other. Everyone said how important it was to make children enjoy themselves on Menstruation Day, which nowadays had become a real outdoor occasion for the whole family.

Another loudspeaker announced that now was the last chance to place bets on the cocks in the Grand Crowing Contest. Spn Owlmoss, Petronius, Baldrian and Fandango hurried towards the grandstand. They ran into the big brass band which had just begun its first circuit. At the front were two big, dark red banners, symbolizing menstrual blood, then came the musicians — a band composed of twenty pregnant wim playing a victory march, followed by a troop of fifteen more wim waving blood towels of various colours, throwing them up into the air and catching them, juggling with them — at least five at once — in time with the music. At the tail end came the menwim, with children in their arms or holding them by the hand. When the pregnant brass-players had finished their march, the menwim began singing the 'Hymn to the Life-force', which was about the pregnant daughters of the motherland.

The four menwim from the Masculine League made their way through the crowd to the North Grandstand. Fifteen cocks stood in a line, each on its own tall box, and next to them sat a jury which was to judge their 'cockadoodledoos' and award points for pitch, precision and execution. Those who had bet on the cock the jury favoured were rewarded with fine, multi-coloured cock feathers 'which you can take home to the housebound'. And above the stage, in big letters, a notice asked, 'Doesn't your old manwom like to dress up?' and 'When did you last give your housebound a feather?'

The wom announcer gave the signal for the contest to begin and the cocks immediately began to crow, each in turn, each cockadoodledoo higher than the last, while the jurywim listened with serious and thoughtful expressions on their faces, making notes. The four masculists had concealed themselves behind some bushes just next to the stage. Several hundred excited spectators were watching the crowing and the awarding of points, and some of the jury's decisions were greeted by wim who thought them unfair with such loud shouts of protest anyone would have thought their lives were in danger.

At first, nobody understood what was happening, but suddenly the birds began to flutter down from their boxes. Four figures dressed in enormous feathered costumes climbed up where they had been. Everything happened so quickly that no one had time to interfere before the figures threw off their feather costumes, revealing four menwim, stripped to the waist. There they stood, in all their flat-chested indecency — and two of them even had hairy chests! Worst of all, one of them was clearly a manwom of advanced age. They began throwing their feathered finery into the audience. One of these four masculist fanatics somehow got hold of the microphone, and he began shouting, 'Away with all menwim's finery and decoration! Why should we be forced to hide our bodies? Wim are free to bare their breasts and their bellies, pregnant or unpregnant; they can show their naked bodies. Why should we have to cover ours? And rig ourselves up in ridiculous and impractical garments, just to please wim? We demand the right to be as we are.' At this moment a gasp of astonishment ran through the crowd. The older manwom tore off his wig and flung it up into the air. The crown of his head was

251

completely bald.

It was the most horrific and obscene sight the hundreds of spectators had ever seen. Of course, most of them had probably seen bald heads in the privacy of their own bedrooms. But here, in public! A bald head in the open air! The crowd was seething with anger and a torrent of abuse was directed towards the four perverted exhibitionists.

'We demand . . .'

The microphone was torn away from the speaker, so no one, thank Jessica, had to listen to any more of his demands. Menwim's voices, in any case, were more than anyone could stand listening to when they thundered out of the loudspeakers in their deafening way. It was happening far too often these days. They ought to save their vocal chords for their coffee-mornings. That was what most people thought.

If action had not been taken at an earlier stage to spare the public this indecent spectacle, it was because the contest organizer had momentarily misunderstood the situation. At first she thought it was a troupe of lords from the pornotent who had come over at the wrong time. The north stage was to be used later for a titillating little entertainment with menwim wearing feathers.

By now the police had arrived and they grabbed the four exhibitionist wom-haters and forced them down from their pedestals, so the crowing contest might continue. The chance to take a feather home to your housebound had not been spoilt in any way. 'Yes, the opportunity is still there; you still have a chance,' announced the wom's voice temptingly, once the microphone had been recaptured. 'Don't let this . . . er . . . rather sordid little episode spoil our fun. It's now the turn of cock number *thirteen*. Lucky number, there, lordies and gentlewim! Who's betting on number thirteen?'

But in fact the chance of taking a feather home to your housebound had indeed been spoilt, because the cocks had been thoroughly disconcerted, and by the time they were finally recovered from the bushes they had taken refuge in, they refused to crow any more. And cock number thirteen had disappeared without a trace.

The four were taken to the police station, where they were fined for causing public offence through exhibitionism and indecent exposure. This time, however, the Masculine League had allied themselves with the press. They had got a manwom journalist to cover the action with reports and photographs — and he described conscientiously what it had signified, adding, for his own part, that the fines the masculists had been given for outraging public decency were the clearest possible proof that this was a matriarchal society, where judgements and penalties reflected wim's thinking. And wim's thinking always assumed that everything menwim ever did was connected with sex. They were therefore obliged to brand menwim's resistance as a manifestation of some sexual perversion — in this case, exhibitionism.

'Fighting Cock' had previously discussed at great length whether this sort of action was correct or effective — since they were afraid it might be used against them.

'But everything, absolutely everything, can be used against us,' said Spn Owlmoss. 'We mustn't let that handicap us.'

'But don't wim and menwim actually have to wear different sorts of clothes?' asked Petronius. 'My mother always says the reason menwim can't wear trousers is because there isn't enough room in them for their penises and shamebags.'

'That's only ideology,' said Baldrian. 'It's just a question of how loose the trousers are. There's no reason we have to wander round in anything so impractical as a skirt.'

'No, obviously. Sometimes it drives me up the wall.'

The Menstruation Games continued, otherwise undisturbed by the little irregularity at the north stage. In the pavilion, the wim from the troupes of jugglers got up, one after another, and gave long speeches about important things.

Finally, the Lady Chancellor of the Parliamentary Palace made her annual speech praising Egalia. And, as every year, her praises of Egalsund's bio-system came first. Every year, she began her speech with the same words, so well-known and so dear to the Egalians, 'Earth, air, and water are our elements — and in the most profound sense, our dwelling.' She paused, looking out over the festively turned-out crowd. 'Without them, Egalia would not exist.' She explained how Egalia's bio-system was arranged so as to preserve the natural cycles of life, and of course it was connected organically with the rest of Egalia and, thanks to a permanent arrangement with Pax, with the Paxian system, since, as everyone knew, air and water never took any notice of national frontiers or declarations of sovereignty. They took care that no more oxygen was used, and no more nitrogen released, than was compatible with preserving the balance. The big areas of parkland were intended to preserve the balance in the assimilation of carbon dioxide.

The Lady Chancellor recited some figures, which were greeted with applause, and went on to quote statistics for the fisheries, where the same principles applied. The state of the fish stocks was given and it was confirmed that the size of catches was fully compatible with the preservation of stocks. She confirmed, with even more satisfaction, that there had been very little need to enforce the regulations since it was of course obvious to any idiot that it would be absurd to catch more fish than were being spawned.

She gave a reminder, nonetheless, for the sake of safety or tradition, of the severe penalties which applied if the regulations were contravened. She did this every year, and some of her audience would head for home while she was still speaking. In the general interests of prevention, she considered herself obliged to remind her audience that anyone breaking the fishery laws would be locked in a room with instructions as to how to set up an aquarium, and not released until she had redressed the imbalance in the aquarium. If any species died, she had to find the reason, and if she couldn't identify her mistake, she was sent for education. She received no salary during this entire period.

Next, the Lady Chancellor reminded her audience that the Effluent Treatment Plant was still one of the most expensive items on Egalsund's budget, and she gave details of the strict regulations governing its operation. Again she emphasized the stringent penalties for allowing pollutants to escape into the water or the air. The offender would be locked in a badly ventilated room. She would be well fed but there would be nowhere for her to relieve herself; she would therefore have to do this on the floor. Eventually, she would be wading around in a squalid slurry of her own excrement, hardly able to breathe. Then she would be taken out into the fresh air for a few days and reminded that if everybody followed her example in releasing effluent and poisonous pollutants, there would eventually be no fresh air left to breathe, and the whole of Egalia, indeed the whole earth, would be reduced to the state of her cell.

Once again, the Lady Chancellor was pleased to announce that this penalty had not had to be imposed during the previous year, since none of the industrial proprietors had committed any offence. 'This shows a healthy and matriotic good sense among our leading industrialists, and in particular, our trading companies,' she said. 'And what would be the purpose of these annual Menstruation Games, in honour of the life-force and the cycle of nature, if it were not so that we can celebrate the profound interrelationship that exists between huwom life and nature — if we could not celebrate the most profound meaning of civilization, which is the preservation of nature for huwom beings and their offspring? This is the highest form of culture.'

The Lady Chancellor was rewarded with moderate applause, because most of the audience had gone home during the course of her speech. The menwim, who would have liked to stay out of respect, had had to go home because their children were getting so tired and fretful. And those who remained had heard her say the same things Donna knows how many times before. The pregnant brass-players began to play the popular 'Healthy Children in Strong Bellies' and everyone joined in, their voices soaring up towards the clear, blue Egalian sky.

Walking around the egalitarian city

Petronius was standing at the crossroads by the big gentle-wim's outfitters, waiting for the little red wom in the traffic light to turn green. On a billboard across the street was a huge, fluorescent advertisement for Chestosilk chesthair-remover. One picture showed a wom pulling the top of a manwom's blouse and wrinkling her nose as she peers inside. The next picture showed the two of them in the same position, except that the wom was beaming with delight at the beautification that had taken place under the manwom's blouse in the meantime.

Petronius had let his own hair grow for the menstruation day action. He hadn't felt like removing it again. Whatever depilatory he used, it made his skin sore. In any case, that was how he *was*. He had finally come to terms with that. He *had* a hairy chest. That was all there was to it.

The little green walking wom appeared on the traffic light. Some girls on bicycles punched him as they sped past on the pedestrian crossing, shouting at one another. It was impossible to distinguish a single word. They were simply bellowing. No doubt they understood one another.

It was a warm autumn day. Many wim were walking about shirtless. Breasts of all shapes bounced all around him. Round and buoyant, long and flabby, small ones — almost as small as menwim's, great big nipples pointing upwards or outwards, nipples that were long and cylindrical from being sucked. They all came bouncing towards him. He thought how he would once have thought these torsos were beautiful. Was he not, in fact, rather envious, even now? He was sweating under his blouse.

The traffic was heavy. Many families were heading out into the country for the holiday. Petronius watched the cars gliding past with wim behind the wheel and their housebounds beside them and the kids in the back seat. He stopped by a bank on the corner. One of the bank's brochures was displayed in the window. In bright blue letters on shiny white paper, it said, 'A secure future for you and your family'. A wom sat thumbing thoughtfully through some bank papers, while a manwom stood looking over her shoulder, smiling happily and confidently. 'You can insure your housebound, your children and yourself with our government guaranteed loan,' said the brochure. The next picture showed the secure house you could secure yourself with the secure loan, and in the next, you and your family were inside your secure home. You were sitting in a chair, your housebound was standing, and your children were playing securely on the floor.

Petronius walked through the streets of Egalsund, writing and rewriting a letter to Gro in his head. He missed her. But as soon as he began to think what it was actually like being with her, he no longer missed her. Then he thought how attractive she was to him and he missed her again. But what was that attraction? What did it consist of? Was he fascinated by the fact that she dominated him? He could continue like that for a long time. Yes, no, yes, no.

But in his mind he had decided. He would write a letter to her, telling her that he would come to the Palace of Birth when she went there to give birth. He would go there, and be present during the ceremony, and he would receive the child; but he didn't want fatherhood-protection.

That went against all custom and tradition. There was, admittedly, no rule saying that fathers had to be protected when they came to the Palace of Birth. It was merely an unwritten law. But in fact he wanted the child. And because Gro knew he wanted it, she had threatened him with an abortion several times. That was just to perplex him and to make him beg her to go through with the pregnancy. He had said that to her on the telephone.

'But I want you to decide,' she had said.

'I'm not going to make a decision now that will give you the power of making all decisions for me for the rest of my life,' he had replied.

He felt tough. He had not given way and he felt tough. He wanted a life of his own — and he felt guilty for wanting it. That was how it was.

'Having to have children by us is just a weapon they use against us,' said Baldrian. 'You mustn't give in.' Baldrian, who had always dreamt of being a principal's daughter's housebound, and in due course the principal's housebound, had also decided never to get fatherhood-protected. 'I've no intention of doing three times as much work,' Baldrian would say. It was so simple and so liberating.

Petronius went into a library. He had plenty of time; the meeting he had to go to was not until the evening. He could write his letter inside. It was always so quiet and peaceful there. But once inside the library, he found he couldn't concentrate there either. He scanned the shelves, somewhat restlessly. Perhaps he ought to pull himself together and tackle some of these books on farming. He and Baldrian had looked for jobs in the agricultural districts inland. They had been on the waiting list for two months and had heard nothing. 'It's hard to get those jobs, if you're a manwom,' said the manwom in the office. 'It's easier if you're hitched up with some of the wim there.' They had heard there was a shortage of labour.

'It's impossible to get a good job unless you're equipped with tits,' said Baldrian. 'As though one did the job with one's tits!'

He scanned the shelves.

'Can I help you in any way?' It was the librarian.

'Yes. D'you have any books about pallurian menwim?'

The librarian blushed. 'No,' he said. 'But there is one. *The Depths of Dreariness*, by Clifford Laing. It was published in 508 under a pseudonym. D'you want me to get it from the central library?'

'Yes, would you?'

Petronius went out quickly and sat on a bench in the little library garden. What a strange whim to strike him so suddenly. And now he didn't dare go back in and ask for books on farming.

An old wom in ragged clothes stood under a tree. Her hat lay on the ground in front of her, and she was playing a harmonica, painfully badly. She kept missing the notes. Menwim hurried past with big heavy bags full of groceries. Many of them were big and fat, waddling laboriously on swollen legs, sweating in their blouses so that big dark patches appeared under the armpits. The older ones sweated under their wigs. Why should menwim who toiled so hard always have such bad, fat legs, and walk with such difficulty? Petronius wondered. It was just as though the only purpose ageing and fading menwim could find in life was in hauling around hundreds of bags and boxes of all sizes, full of treats and things to eat.

He pulled out the newspaper he had bought. He didn't really feel like reading it, so he turned to the cartoons. Usually there would be a string of cartoons portraying huge great menwim scolding scruffy little wim. Gord lady! thought Petronius. The menwim in these cartoons were so big and strong it was hard to imagine how they could get into the houses they were shown standing outside.

One of the cartoons showed a huge manwom and a skinny little wom who had ended up together on a desert island with a single palm tree on it. In the distance the bow of the sinking ship pointed up into the sky. The enormous manwom was bellowing furiously to the skinny little wom, 'But we never go swimming on Mondays, Edna!'

'Ha ha,' said Petronius aloud to himself. The wom with the harmonica stopped playing. She tittered toothlessly, with a gleam of amusement in her eye.

A small boy came over to him and curtsyed nicely. 'D'you want to buy a flower?' he asked.

'What does the money go to, then?'

'It goes to . . . well, it's for peace, and the family and all that . . .' said the boy, looking embarrassed.

Petronius bought two flowers. The boy smiled and thanked him and went on his way. Petronius knew well enough what it was for. As a result of all the talk about the subjection of menwim, the National Co-operative Directorate had decided to make a gesture towards menwim, and had therefore declared the first holiday after Donna Jessica's Demise, and the following seven days, would be National Menwim's Week. Pretty blue plastic flowers were made specially for the occasion and schoolchildren in Egalia were all given a half day off to go out and sell Menwim's Week flowers in aid of greater peace and understanding between the sexes. Officially, it was called 'Equality', but all the propaganda was concerned with greater peace and understanding.

Some of the newspapers, too, began to make occasional concessions to the idea of sexual equality. It was not unusual to find such sentences as, 'When an ordinary citizen walks through the streets, she/he will notice many examples of downright sexist thinking.'

Petronius watched the people going past and thought that the whole world, no matter where one went, was proof of the fact that menwim got a bad deal. He couldn't understand why he hadn't always seen this, or why it wasn't obvious to everybody. All you had to do was open your eyes. But wim wanted to reduce the whole manwom question to details. And the Sparksists only talked about class antagonisms, and the exploitation of cheap labour power. That was a central concept in their analysis. If Egalia's millions of fathers working at home, and low-paid working unprotected fathers, were not the victims of economic oppression, then what were they? Just because the masculists dumped their pehoes, the whole thing was reduced to a purely personal or sexual issue.

Petronius got up. He stole a dollable from the harmonica-players cap and ran. He had to get home now and write to Gro. And then he would go and meet Baldrian and build a new world. *A new world.* Just like that.

'The Sons of Democracy'

'After all it is women who bear children,' said Berg, throwing his daughter a reproving glance over the top of the *Echo*. It was evident that he was finding it difficult to control his temper. 'Anyway, I'm reading the paper.'

'But I want to be a sailor! I'll just take the baby with me,' said Petra ingeniously.

'And what do you think the child's father would say? Oh no. There are some things in life you have to put up with. In time you'll learn to appreciate them. Even in a democratic society like ours, everyone can't be completely equal. Besides, it would be tremendously boring. Dreary and depressing.'

'It's more dreary and depressing not being able to be what one wants!'

'Who said you can't be what you want? All I'm saying is, you must be realistic. You can't have your cake and eat it. If you have children, you have children. Listen, Petra, when I was a lad I had a lot of grandiose dreams, too, about what I was going to be. The romance of the sea, that's what you're suffering from. You'll have to stop reading all those adventure stories about the exploits of men at sea, and stick to books for girls instead. Then your dreams will be more realistic. No real women want to go to sea.'

'But most of the seamen I know of have children!'

'That's another matter altogether. A father can never be like a mother to a child, Petra.'

Her brother laughed derisively. He was a year and a half younger and he teased her constantly. 'Ha ha! And a woman can't be a seaman either. A female sea*man*! Ho ho! Or perhaps you're going to be a cabin-*girl* or a sea*woman*.

I'll die laughing, I will. The only women who go to sea are either whores or lesbians.'

'Lesbians?'

'Exactly. Lesbians. And in every harbour the whores stand in line waiting for the sailors.' He tugged her hair.

'Mum! Bill's pulling my hair!'

'God almighty! Is there never any peace and quiet in this house?' Mrs Berg, the director's wife, came rushing out of the bathroom with her hair full of curlers. 'Calm down, you kids! Bill, remember Petra has soft hair.'

'Soft hair and soft all over. "Remember Petra has soft hair! Remember Petra belongs to the frail sex!"' That always annoyed her. He continued maliciously, 'Mum? Oughtn't Petra to start wearing a bra soon?'

Petra turned a deep red.

'Be quiet!' the director growled. 'I'm reading.'

'More coffee, Ralph?' his wife asked placatingly.

'Mmmm,' he replied absently. 'That was much too strong by the way . . .'

Petronius read through the first page of his manuscript. Good lady! This book was going to be completely crazy!

The reader's final farewell to Ruth Bram, her son Petronius and the others

Most of the reviewers of Petronius's book, *The Sons of Democracy*, were wim. Mostly, they used the opportunity to say what *they* thought of menwim's liberation, which was currently making considerable headway. The more liberal papers were relatively kind, having only minor reservations, such as, 'Ultimately it must be said that the wim in Petronius Bram's novel are, on the whole, content — even though the principal characters are most untypical, rebellious wim. So the fictional society is in fact a harmonious society, though this is presumably not the author's intention.' Liberals were all for complete equality between the sexes and were thus in agreement with a certain critique of the status quo, but they thought the book went too far. One reviewer ended by saying, 'All this is well and good, and it is enthralling to read about this fictional patriarchy (Is it the author's idea of a utopia, one wonders?); but can Petronius Bram imagine a society in which menwim are *not* the ones who engender children?'

The Sparksist paper, *Smash*, printed a long review covering two pages in which the book was branded as individualistic masculist-separatist propaganda. It was indeed a striking illustration of the Masculine League's total inability to co-operate with wim. They therefore had no will, or ability, to produce a fruitful analysis. The fact that the principal character ultimately states, or thinks, that the oppression of wim in this utopia(?) has an economic character, is and remains a superficial postulate, tacked on the end, which is given no foundation whatsoever in the book. The *Smash* reviewer wrote that the lack of economic analysis was not surprising, considering how thoroughly it was

263

obscured and suppressed in the feminists' bourgeois background. This circumstance, and the analysis that went with it, would, in the opinion of the Sparksist reviewer, change the moment the Masculine Leaguers began to co-operate with wim. By 'wim', *Smash* meant, Sparksist wim ('whose background is just as bourgeois' Baldrian remarked).

Smash's reviewer had noticed that the 'women's movement' in *The Sons of Democracy* used Egalsund's traffic sign meaning 'Police Station' as its emblem — a red circle with a fist within it and a cross below — a sign which symbolized order, not struggle. 'Yet another sign of the author's incorrect analysis — here in symbolic form,' wrote the reviewer. For Spn Bram this was evidently meant to symbolize the abuse of power by wim over menwim in our society. But in fact this sign stood for order and civilization in society. Indeed the reviewer thought that the whole idea of using the traffic sign as a symbol of 'women's' struggle was farfetched and 'artistically unsuccessful', not to say crude.

'If there is ever a society in which wim are oppressed, they would never choose such a peaceful symbol as a symbol of their struggle. They would more likely choose something more frightening and powerful, such as a red triangle containing two huge, bulging breasts on a white background,' wrote the reviewer.

Police Station

A more plausible feminist symbol

The reviewer added that the word 'woman' was, incidentally, quite funny, but wasn't it rather unlikely, or at least awkward. And how did the author imagine it should be pronounced?

The *Egalsund Times* did not review the book. There were some sorts of literature that were not literature at all.

Most of this newspaper's journalists read books of this type under the bedclothes at home. *The Sons of Democracy* was in this category. Even the opening sentence, 'After all, it is women who bear children', which was repeated endlessly throughout the book, indicated a sexual hang-up — as though there were something wrong with giving birth to children. Or as though such a sentence could conceivably form part of an argument!

Because of this newspaper's traditional role as the serious and objective voice of the motherland, it made no mention of the book.

Donna Jessica's Message considered trying to get the book banned, since they regarded it as pornographic. Was it really necessary to print the work 'cock'? Reading it was enough to make you lose your appetite completely, wrote the reviewer in *Message*, without using the word herself. ('Who says you have to eat while reading the book?' Petronius asked Baldrian.)

In fact the word 'cunt' occurred much more frequently, and that was evidently rather less shocking. But wasn't there altogether too much talk of cunts and private parts which 'women' were supposed to be ashamed of in this patriarchy? That surely couldn't be the only thing 'men' ever thought about?

Apart from the language, the scenes of sexual intercourse were clearly perverse. Any society which abandoned itself to such bestial behaviour would disintegrate completely. Petronius Bram had described the wom lying on her back. On her *back*! Even in the state of nature, mafele animals never force such brutal indignities upon the feles. A blatant manoeuvre for forcing her into submission — on her back, with her legs apart and the manwom on top of her, thrusting wildly as though his member were some sort of tool of conquest, for the manwom's own pleasure! It was nothing other than a lady-slave relationship, where the manwom was the lady. That was where Donna Jessica's Message drew the line, as far as decency in literature was concerned.

Although none of the reviewers wrote as much, many of them were hardened in their view that the masculists really were pallurians. Implicit in this conclusion was the sense that there was no need to pay any particular attention to what they said.

Some people disliked the book and stopped reading half way through. There was nothing particularly funny about portraying 'men' as muscle-bound supermen, always carrying on and shouting and ordering people about, while 'women' went round smiling and behaving like servile dolls in pretty dresses. It was grotesque. No culture which managed to distort the natural characteristics of the two sexes to such a degree could be regarded as a real culture.

Ba had taken the opportunity of reading the book while it was still in manuscript. She told Ann she thought the whole book had been written out of frustration and envy of herself. When girls wave their blood towels around, boys go green with jealousy. And then they became neurotic and started getting involved with menwim's lib. It was all very well for them to revolt, but would they ever be able to menstruate? Unfortunately, there was nothing the State could do about that. Alas. It would of course be nice if menwim could be as valuable as wim, but that, unfortunately, was impossible.

Bosomby, the school principal, read the book in secret, and did not think that the character called 'Principal Brumblebrow' bore the slightest resemblance to herself. She was also quite convinced that the ideas behind this rather extreme masculist novel had certainly not been fostered at her school. But it was imaginative. And in her heart Principal Bosomby was proud that one of her school's former pupils could write a book.

Opinions were divided in the menwim's movement. Some thought that if things could go the way of Petronius's patriarchy, then there was no alternative to complete separation of the sexes. And that, surely couldn't be their intention. What they were fighting for was integration and equality. 'Menwim's struggle is class struggle! Class struggle is menwim's struggle!' That was a maxim they had to stand firm by.

Others thought the book undermined the whole menwim's movement. Weren't menwim naturally more peaceful and considerate than wim, and wasn't it on this basis the menwim's movement should create the new society? Surely the idea wasn't simply to take over wim's ways of doing things.

Spn Owlmoss enjoyed the book and read it several times. 'That schoolteacher, Miss Oggleson, that's me, isn't it?' he asked Petronius quietly. He did however have certain purely historical reservations. He was for example doubtful as to whether it was realistic to have mothers staying at home with their children, as Petronius had portrayed them, while fathers went off. After all, inheritance had to pass through the mother. He didn't see how that could be changed. And how would the menwim live? 'There is no evidence, written or otherwise, that such a society has ever existed,' said Spn Owlmoss.

Little chubby Fandango was wildly enthusiastic about the book and decided at once to immerse himself in menwim's history.

Baldrian liked the book and said it had made him think about many things he had never considered before. He had never thought, for example, that it was possible to tell wim they could damn well make their own arrangements for getting their babies to their own breasts while they were nursing. And he was horrified on many occasions to read about the awful lives the 'women' lived — not being given a single penny for getting pregnant, but being penalized for it instead. To that extent, he actually thought the whole book was more tragic than comic.

Christopher thought the book was delightful.

'Why don't you write something that appeals to people,' asked Ruth Bram bad-temperedly. But Christopher went on laughing until he fell over, while Ruth yelled at him to stop his constant guffaws.

'It really can't be *that* funny, reading about wim being ridiculed!'

But Christopher carried on regardless, laughing his way through the whole book. He felt invigorated by it. Finally, he marched in and slammed his fist on the table where

Ruth was sitting and said, 'Right! I'm going to start that engineering course whether you like it or not, and that's all there is to it!'

That was when Ruth Bram, who had just started her period, decided to have a final serious word with her son.

'Patriarchy!' she exploded, next time she saw him. She still hadn't found time to read the book. 'It's all very well, you writing, Petronius. And I'm told that you write with great humour and fluency. But couldn't you have chosen something else to write about? Patriarchy! I suppose that's some sort of society where menwim rule and control everything, is it?'

'Yes! Spn Owlmoss says that . . .'

'Unthinkable!' interrupted his mother.

'"Unthinkable". That's your word for anything that isn't exactly as it is now!'

'I'm sorry, Petronius, but it *is* unthinkable! You may well be right that I'm conservative, and I want to keep power relations the way they are today . . . because . . . because . . . well, because I'm in a position of power myself, for goodness' sake! But then I hold that position with the complete conviction that I'm making the right decisions.'

She stopped for a moment. Petronius said nothing; he was dumbfounded by this admission on the part of his mother.

'And I think it's perfectly in order for you to make yourself a spokeswom for menwim's liberation, Petronius. But a society where menwim rule! Where menwim plan and govern society! Unthinkable!'

'It *isn't* unthinkable. Such societies have *existed*! Only we never hear anything about them, because we live in this awful matriarchy!'

'*Have* existed! Precisely. They *have* existed. And what do you think happened to them, Petronius?'

Petronius remained silent.

'What d'you think happened to those patriarchies you say used to exist, which we never hear anything about?'

She paused. He still said nothing.

'Why do you think there is no single piece of evidence that they ever did exist? Why do you think we don't have one single clear proof of their existence? Well?'

Petronius didn't know what to say. He felt bewildered.

'No, Petronius. You see . . . menwim are never really in touch with life. They have no physical contact with their offspring. So they're not capable of considering what will happen to the people of the world when they themselves are dead. In a society where menwim were allowed to rule, all terrestrial life would die out. If menwim weren't kept down, if they weren't restrained, if they weren't civilized, if they weren't *kept in their place*, life would perish . . .'

And as always, Ruth Bram had the final word.

GERD BRANTENBERG was born in 1941 in Oslo, Norway, and spent her childhood and youth in Fredrikstad. After obtaining her arts degree in English, History and Social Science at the University of Oslo in 1970, she became a high school teacher in 1971, teaching in Copenhagen and Oslo until 1982.

She has been active in the feminist movement since the early 1970s, working in particular with the Women's House in Oslo and the Refuge for Battered Wives and helping to form an Inter-Library Women's Forum. She has been a board member of the Norwegian Writers' Union and currently holds a State Scholarship for Artists and Writers.

Her published works include: *Opp alle jordens homofile* (1973), translated into Danish, Swedish and German; *Egalias døtre* (1977), translated into Swedish, German, Dutch, English, and adapted for theatre in Sweden and Norway; *Ja vi slutter* (1978), translated into Swedish and Danish; *Sangen om St. Croix* (1979), translated into Swedish and German; *Ved fergestedet*, due to be published in 1985.

women in translation

Cora Sandel: Selected Short Stories
translated by Barbara Wilson
Long considered one of Norway's classic writers, Cora Sandel (1880-1974) brings a feminist sensibility and a poignant humor to her tales of women on the edge of society. This collection contains Sandel's most important stories from the 1920s through the 1940s.
Paper, $8.95 (ISBN: 0-931188-30-x)
Cloth, $16.95 (ISBN: 0-931188-31-8)

Early Spring
by Tove Ditlevsen
translated by Tiina Nunnally
The memoirs of one of Denmark's best-loved writers.
"…a poet's book, written with immediacy and radiance."
— Tillie Olsen
"…an imagination so literary that it is almost feverish."
— Publishers Weekly
Paper, $8.95 (ISBN: 0-931188-28-8)
Cloth, $14.95 (ISBN: 0-931188-29-6)

An Everyday Story: Norwegian Women's Fiction
edited by Katherine Hanson
Norway's tradition of storytelling comes alive in this important anthology of women's prose fiction, the first to appear in English translation. Twenty-four authors are represented, including Camilla Collett, Sigrid Undset, Ebba Haslund and Cecilie Løveid.
"…An excellent opportunity to sample an interesting, often memorable variety of styles and voices."
— The Los Angeles Times
Paper, $8.95 (ISBN: 0-931188-22-9)
Cloth, $16.95 (ISBN: 0-931188-21-0)

(All prices subject to change without notice.)

Please write to The Seal Press for the most recent list of other women's titles of interest: P.O. Box 13, Seattle, WA 98111.